Let's Play
BRIDGE

*A Guide
to Learning
and Understanding
Contract Bridge*

RICHARD V. SMITH

A FIRESIDE BOOK
Published by Simon & Schuster, Inc.
NEW YORK

A Fireside Book

Published by Simon & Schuster, Inc.
Simon & Schuster Building
Rockefeller Center
1230 Avenue of the Americas
New York, New York 10020

FIRESIDE and colophon are registered trademarks of Simon & Schuster, Inc.

Designed by Stanley S. Drate/Folio Graphics Co. Inc.

Manufactured in the United States of America

10 9 8 7 6 5 4 3 2 1

Library of Congress Cataloging in Publication Data

Smith, Richard V.
   Let's play bridge.

   "A Fireside book."
   1. Contract bridge. I. Title.
GV12823.S5945   1987   795.41'5   86–29686
ISBN: 0-671-63382-1

CONTENTS

APPENDIX

INTRODUCTION

Welcome to the world of contract bridge. Whether you are just learning bridge or have already played for some time and want to understand the game better, this is the book for you.

If you are a beginner, the first part of this book will show you how to get started. From then on you will be playing bridge like the rest of us and will see why we have become so fond of the game. The remainder of the book will give you the understanding needed to improve your level of play.

Bridge is a game of skill which is equally challenging for the beginner as it is for the expert. You simply never outgrow the game. As you play, you will see you need more knowledge and understanding of the game. As you read, you will become more eager to play.

Bridge can be a social game, played mostly for fun, or it can be a serious game, played as a competition. Either way, you will be playing with a variety of friends or possible future friends. Each deal represents a short problem, with time between deals for conversation or discussion.

Bridge is also a partnership game that requires a great deal of cooperation and teamwork. Systematic ways of cooperating have been built up over the years. You will learn these ways as you go through this book.

Now let's take a look at why bridge has become the intriguing game it is today.

Bridge Yesterday

To the best of our knowledge, playing cards were invented by the Chinese at least as far back as the 10th century A.D. and were brought from there to Europe, possibly by Marco Polo in the 13th century. Cards became associated with fortune-telling and gambling, and became known as "the devil's picture book."

A lot of games were built around a pack of cards, but the most persistent was whist. Some form of whist was played in England back in the 16th century, and even today there are a few whist players left.

In whist, the entire pack of 52 cards is dealt to four players, those on opposite sides of the table being partners. A trump suit is determined by revealing the last card dealt. The four players then play their cards to take tricks, much as is done in bridge. The skill required to be a good player is remarkable for a game with such simple rules. Undoubtedly whist would still be popular today if it had not developed in some new and exciting ways.

It is not known for sure where whist originated, but Russia or Turkey seems to be the most likely. By the 19th century, upper-class travelers had spread whist in various forms throughout Europe, the British Empire and the Middle East. In one variation, the hand belonging to the dealer's partner was exposed and its owner became a "dummy" while the hand was played by the dealer. In another, the dealer or his partner was allowed to decide on what the trump suit would be, or even to decide to play without any trump suit at all.

The word *bridge* was first applied to the game in the late 19th century, and historians are still debating where the word came from. Some think that if the dealer did not wish to name the trump suit he "bridged" the decision across the table to his partner. Others say that it came from the obsolete Russian *biritch,* because that word was found in an English pamphlet about the game published in 1886.

Soon after the turn of this century, the various ideas about how to play the game were brought together under the name of *Auction Bridge,* its rules were formalized by two English clubs. In Auction Bridge, the players bid for the privilege of naming the trump suit or of deciding to play with no trump suit. The auction was won by the player offering to take the most tricks with his proposed trump or notrump selection.

I was taught Auction Bridge by my parents, but already the world was buzzing with news of a new form of bridge. While on a cruise in 1925, Harold S. Vanderbilt had worked out a game he called *Contract Bridge*. The principal new feature was the scoring, based on the novel concept of "vulnerability." Vanderbilt produced such a fine balance of bonuses and penalties that only one minor change has been introduced since he worked out his game. He also included the idea of a contract, a feature borrowed from a French variation on bridge called *Plafond*. The final bid in the auction became a contract to take that number of tricks. Now a bonus was to be offered for bidding up to the higher levels and then fulfilling the elevated contract. Additional bonuses were given for bidding and making a slam, which required taking all or all but one of the tricks.

Vanderbilt gave out a few copies of notes on how to play and tried out his game with friends who were cruising with him. He paid little further attention to his efforts, but the rest of the world was intrigued. Members of High Society were eager to do anything that Vanderbilt did, and they organized parties to play Contract Bridge. News of the game traveled fast. Everyone wanted to follow Society's lead and the craze was on.

THE CULBERTSON ERA

Soon an unknown named Ely Culbertson came on the scene. His father, an American, had married a Russian woman and was working abroad when Ely was born. Young Culbertson was given the citizenship of his father but attended school in Russia. When the Russian Revolution wiped out his father's fortune, Ely went first to Paris and then to New York, overcoming his poverty with his skill at cards. In New York he met and soon married his wife, Josephine. She was an outstanding bridge teacher and the two made a brilliant pair at the card table.

Soon after Contract Bridge was invented, the Culbertsons took up the game and immediately became noted for their successes. Ely Culbertson was not only a superb player but also a fine theorist. He worked out his own methods and was convinced that they were superior to any others known. His conviction turned out to be justified.

In 1931 Culbertson issued his famous challenge to Sidney Lenz for an extended match. Not only was Lenz considered by many to be the best player of his day, but his writings on bridge had established him as the leading authority on the game. He had become wealthy at a very early age through skillful business dealings and was much in demand for society bridge parties.

Although Culbertson did not have the social and financial advantages that Lenz had, he was a promoter and a showman without peer. He made his challenge with a fanfare that excited the newspapers by offering to bet $5,000 to Lenz's $1,000 on the outcome, the amount to go to charity, whoever the winner might be. Lenz could hardly refuse.

The match began in December 1931 and lasted into January. Over 800 hands were dealt. Radio programs announced the results daily. Movie theaters offered shorts on the event. Newspapers were hard pressed to find suitable writers to analyze the deals. Like many others, I too was caught up in the hoopla and the excitement of learning the game.

Culbertson's partner usually was his wife, while Lenz played mostly with Oswald Jacoby, a brilliant and fearless player. Later Jacoby's name would be associated with a number of bidding methods of his own devising. He would eventually earn more masterpoints than Charles Goren. His many successes at the bridge table were to continue until just before his death in 1984 when, as an ailing octogenarian, he would play on the winning team for the Reisinger Memorial Trophy. But in the Culbertson-Lenz match, the Culbertsons were to be the winners by a significant margin.

Culbertson lost no time in capitalizing on his success. He so thoroughly promoted himself and his system that most bridge players thought there was no other expert, no other authority, no other system. Culbertson boasted that 98 percent of all bridge players played the Culbertson system. He was probably right, but the other 2 percent contained many experts who were lost behind the smokescreen. One of them was named Charles Goren.

THE GOREN ERA

Goren started out as a lawyer, but soon found that his talent for bridge was even greater. He sprang into public prominence when he replaced Culbertson as the syndicated bridge columnist for the Chicago *Tribune* and the New York *Daily News*. Out of his intimate knowledge of the game Goren developed some definite ideas on how to improve on Culbertson's methods. When Goren published his system, Culbertson was infuriated and derided Goren's efforts, while halfheartedly adopting the same point-count system which Goren had espoused. But Culbertson had given little attention to bridge for some time and his death in 1955 meant the death of his system too.

Like Culbertson, Goren promoted himself and his system as though no other player or method had comparable merit. He was without doubt a magnificent player, winning just about every major tournament in North America. A lifelong bachelor, bridge was his sole occupation and preoccupation until he retired from active play in 1966. Shortly afterwards, the American Contract Bridge League honored him with the title of "Mr. Bridge." It was truly the end of an era. The brilliant glow which surrounded him blinded the eye to the next development that was already in the making.

THE ITALIAN ERA

The Bermuda Bowl is to bridge what the Superbowl is to football. Teams from the United States had won the first four Bowls, and after a loss to England and another loss to France, they had dug in for another win. In 1957, however, the winner was Italy. Moreover, the winner for ten successive years was Italy. The great Italian team broke up for several years and then returned to win three more times. The Italian team also won three times in the World Team Olympiad, a quadrennial event which parallels the Olympics in the sports world. Many of the top International Grand Masters today are from that team: Giorgio Belladonna, Benito Garozzo and others. Something was obviously wrong with the American style of play.

The bidding system used by the Italians was quite different from that used by the Americans, although the Italians had built on an idea that had been proposed by Harold Vanderbilt some years before. Some American experts thought that a radical change in methods was necessary. The Chinese-American C. C. Wei developed a system along the Italian lines which he called Precision. He became the nonplaying captain of a team from Taiwan which used Precision to catapult itself into the finals of the 1969 Bermuda Bowl, almost winning the event. His wife, Kathy Wei, went from nonplayer to expert Precision player in a phenomenally short time, and a number of top American players turned to his system. Even some members of the Italian team adopted Precision for their later successes, gracing it with embellishments of their own.

Good though Precision is, it has not taken over the bridge world. A lot of thinking by a lot of experts has brought them to the conclusion that the more familiar style of American bridge can be made just as effective if the appropriate adjustments are made.

Bridge Today

Italy's triumphs in the Bermuda Bowl came to an end in 1976 when a team from the United States, representing all of North America, defeated the Italian team which included both Garozzo and Belladonna. Since that time the Bermuda Bowl has been dominated by teams from the United States. But in the World Team Olympiad, the story has been different. Men from the United States, playing in open competition, lost to France in 1980 and to Poland in 1984. However, the United States' women's team starred, winning the women's competition in both 1980 and 1984.

Since Goren's withdrawal from public play, many notable experts have emerged but none has dominated the bridge world. Perhaps the one unique person would be Barry Crane, who accumulated some 10,000 masterpoints more than any other person ever—he held 35,084 masterpoints at the time of his sudden death in 1985. Crane was a television producer and director who was too busy to publish his methods. But he was known for his extreme boldness in bidding, backed up by an ability to make good on most of his contracts.

A Few Words to You

The methods promoted by Goren had come to be considered standard for the majority of the non-expert players. But the Italians convinced us that slightly more aggressive bidding is a must, with greater emphasis on the major suits (spades and hearts) and on notrump. They also taught us that we need to fight harder when both sides are bidding. So the standard methods of today have moved in that direction.

The most widely accepted of today's methods are presented in this book. Learn to play well with the modern straightforward system given here and you will do better than those who stumble while trying expert methods they do not fully grasp.

Do not get hung up by trying to remember too much. It is unnecessary. As you play the game, more and more things will become important to you. And as you see that something is important, you will find yourself noticing and remembering it automatically. Intermix reading and playing. When you encounter a problem at the bridge table, go back and read about it.

Throughout the book you will find short boxed guidelines in boldface print. These summarize the basic principles that will steer you into the best line of action at any point in the game. When you want a quick review, the boxes will make it easy for you to pick out the key information. At the bridge table, however, you will employ whatever you have learned so far and let your best judgment take care of the rest.

Also, many sample hands are provided in this book. Usually a question is asked before the sample hand is illustrated. Try to answer it before looking at the comment(s) beside the hand. This in effect will give you the same kind of practice you would get at the table.

The English language has posed a problem in regard to the use of pronouns. For the sake of simplicity, I have settled on using the masculine pronoun to apply to both genders. I beg your tolerance as well as that of my regular partners, two of whom are women.

Now, shall we begin?

Let's Play
BRIDGE

Chapter 1 //

STARTING OFF

A
Pre-Bridge

The Basic Idea

Bridge is played by four players. Those sitting opposite each other are PARTNERS. The game is played with the familiar pack of 52 cards. One player DEALS out all the cards, 13 to each player. Each player in turn plays a card. The four cards form a TRICK. The highest card wins the trick. The number of tricks won by each partnership determines which partnership gets a score for that deal.

The Pack

The four SUITS in a pack of cards are:

♠ spades   ♡ hearts   ◇ diamonds   ♣ clubs

Within each suit the 13 cards rank from high to low as follows:

the HONORS:
     A (ace)   K (king)   Q (queen)   J (jack)   10 (ten)

the SMALL CARDS:
     9 (nine)   and so on down to . . . 2 (two)

Your 13 cards form your HAND. You sort your cards by putting all the cards of one suit together. Within each suit you sort the cards from highest to lowest. Most people put the highest on the left, but you can put the highest on the right if you prefer. It is also usual to alternate red suits and black suits to avoid confusion.

The best way to learn to play bridge is to play some simpler games first. You should play at least four hands of each of the three games which follow. As you play each game, you will be learning the skills and gaining the understanding to begin playing bridge properly. By Game 3 you will have moved close to the game of bridge itself.

Game 1

Four players sit at a table. The players sitting opposite each other are partners. The two sides thus formed compete with each other to see which side can take the most tricks after each deal of the cards.

The players decide who will be the first dealer. After shuffling the pack the dealer lays it on the table next to his right-hand opponent, who CUTS the pack. The cut is made by lifting off the top half of the pack (more or less) and placing it on the table nearer the dealer than the bottom half. The dealer then picks up the bottom half of the pack and places it on the top half. While the dealer is dealing the cards, his partner is shuffling a second pack which will be used for the next deal.

The dealer deals out all the cards, one at a time, facedown. He begins with the player on his left and proceeds around the table clockwise. If the pack is dealt correctly, the last card will go to the dealer, and each player will have 13 cards. Each player then picks up his cards and sorts his hand.

The player to the left of the dealer LEADS any card he wishes; he removes the card from his hand and places it faceup on the table near the center. Each other player, in turn, clockwise, PLAYS any card he wishes from the *same* suit as was led. But if he cannot FOLLOW SUIT, because he has no card of the suit led, he may play any card at all. He too places his chosen card faceup near the center of the table. The four cards make up a trick. The trick is won by the highest card of the *same* suit as was led.

One player in each partnership keeps all the tricks which he and his partner have won. As a matter of courtesy, if your partner is the first to win a trick for your side, you should be the one to keep the tricks. You gather up the four cards in a neat little packet and place them in front of you. Keep each of your tricks in the order it was won.

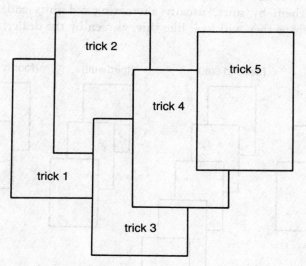

The player who wins a trick leads (plays the first card) for the next trick. Play continues until all 13 tricks have been played and won. The side with the most tricks wins. If you wish to keep score, the winning side gets one point for each trick over six which it has won. (The first six tricks won by any one side do not count.)

Now you are ready for a new deal with a new dealer. The new dealer is the player to the left of the previous dealer. Four deals make a ROUND. Players may change partners at the end of a round, but this is optional.

HINTS: Do not fight with your partner to take (win) a trick. Every trick he takes counts for you too. If your partner plays a king and you have the ace of the same suit, do not play it on his king. Let the king win this trick. Use your ace to take a second trick later on.

Game 2

Game 2 is similar to Game 1 except that immediately after the lead to the first trick, before any other player has played any card, the partner of the dealer puts his cards on the table, faceup. He arranges them by suits, usually alternating red suits and black suits. Perhaps they will look like this, as seen by the dealer:

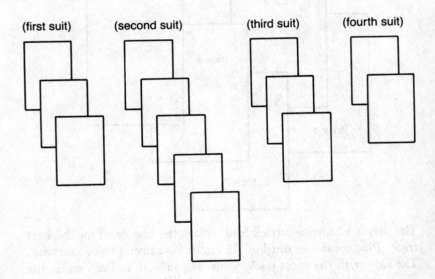

(first suit)   (second suit)   (third suit)   (fourth suit)

The player who lays down his cards becomes the DUMMY. He does not participate any further in this hand (this deal). His cards become the DUMMY HAND. The partner of the dummy becomes known as the DECLARER. The declarer decides which cards will be played from both hands for his side. The other two players are known as the DEFENDERS.

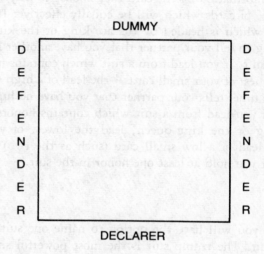

When it is the dummy's turn to play, the declarer selects a card from the dummy hand and places it near the center of the table. When it is his own turn to play, he selects a card from his own hand and plays it. If a trick is won with a card from the dummy hand, the lead (first card) for the next trick must come from the dummy. But if a trick is won with a card from the declarer's hand, the lead for the next trick must come from the declarer.

SUGGESTIONS

The declarer should look carefully at what cards he and the dummy hold in each suit. In this way he can get an idea of what resources he has to win tricks with. The defenders also should pay good attention to the dummy to plan their play to the best advantage.

Generally think in terms of using the highest or the lowest card in a suit. Use a middle card only when it will win the trick in place of a higher card.

The defenders cannot see each other's hands, but they can give each other information by the card they choose to play when they have a choice of cards which will be equally effective. If you lead from a suit which is headed by the ace-king or the king-queen, lead the king to tell your partner that you have another important card in the suit. If you lead from a suit which contains no honors, lead the highest of your small cards—the lead of a high small card (such as the nine) tells your partner that you have no high card in that suit. If you lead from a suit which contains honors, but not the ace-king or the king-queen, lead the lowest of your small cards—the lead of a low small card (such as the two) tells your partner that you hold at least one honor in the suit.

Game 3

In Game 3 you will have the option to name one suit to be the TRUMP suit. The trump suit is the most powerful suit for this reason: If you cannot follow suit (cannot play a card of the same suit as was led), then you may, if you wish, play a trump card. A trump card, however low, wins over any other card, however high. If more than one player plays a trump, the highest trump played wins the trick.

Playing a trump card when you cannot follow suit is called TRUMPING or RUFFING. Be careful to follow suit whenever you are able to—the rules of the game require it. But if you cannot follow suit, you may play a trump or any other card, whichever is to your best advantage. When you cannot or do not wish to ruff, you will want to DISCARD (play some useless card).

In Game 3 the trump suit is decided by the dealer and his partner cooperatively in a process known as BIDDING. To introduce the idea we will start with *simplex bidding,* which is in certain important ways similar to true bridge bidding.

Bidding starts after the cards are dealt and before any card is played. If you are the dealer, you make the OPENING BID (first bid). After looking at your hand, suggest what suit might make a good trump suit by naming that suit. Or if you think your partnership would benefit by not having any trump suit, you say NOTRUMP. Thus you must select one of five bids, corresponding to the five available DENOMINATIONS:

NOTRUMP   SPADES   HEARTS   DIAMONDS   CLUBS

Let us suppose you say HEARTS. Now your partner bids. If your partner agrees with the suggestion that hearts be trump, he also says HEARTS, which ends the bidding and makes hearts the trump suit. Or your partner may make a counter-suggestion— perhaps DIAMONDS or NOTRUMP. The bidding continues between the two players alternately until one repeats a bid that was made previously by the other. This fixes what the trump suit will be, if any.

After the bidding ends, the declarer is the player who *first* bid the trump suit or who was the *first* to bid notrump, if that is the final agreement. The player to the left of the declarer makes the OPENING LEAD (the first lead of the deal). The declarer's partner, who will be the dummy, now lays down his hand on the table. If there is a trump suit, he always places it to his own right (to the left as seen by his partner).

SUGGESTIONS

It is advantageous to have a lot of trump cards. Imagine if you named a trump suit and then found out your opponents had more trumps than your side did. Actually your side should have eight or more trumps, otherwise you will probably do better with notrump. So you bid your longest suit first. Go for quantity, not for high cards. High cards usually take tricks whether they are trumps or not. If you have an extra long suit (six cards or more) bid it twice if necessary. If your partner bids a suit, agree with that suit by also bidding it if you have a few cards to go with his. Three cards in his suit will do, or two cards is enough if he has bid it twice. Otherwise make another suggestion by bidding another suit or by bidding notrump.

Playing in notrump is usually satisfactory only if you hold no SINGLETON (only one card in your hand from some suit) and no VOID (no cards in your hand from some suit).

NOTE: The only difference between Game 3 and the game of bridge is that in the latter the rules which govern bidding and scoring are different. Continue playing Game 3 until you are comfortable with it. You can begin reading Chapter 2, "Elementary Play of the Cards," at this time. When you are ready to go from Game 3 to contract bridge, go on to the next section.

B

Contract Bridge

The Forms of Contract Bridge

Because contract bridge is the only form of bridge played today, we refer to the game simply as bridge. There are several types of contract bridge which are popular. The simplest is PRO-GRESSIVE BRIDGE. In progressive bridge, four deals make a round, after which players may change partners or opponents or both. The name came from the idea that players may progress from one partner to another, and if there is more than one table in play, they may progress from one table to another.

There are two forms of progressive bridge. We will start with GAME-IN-HAND progressive bridge because each deal is bid and scored independently of each other deal, eliminating certain complexities that we do not want to face yet. (The other, more complicated, form of progressive bridge is CHICAGO bridge.)

The other forms of bridge are not played in four-deal rounds. If you are in a bridge class, you may be taught to play DUPLICATE bridge. The name comes from the fact that the exact same hand is played by more than one partnership. At this stage you will not find duplicate bridge to be very much different from game-in-hand except for some mechanics in preserving the hands so that they can be played again.

In RUBBER bridge, a variable number of hands make a "rubber," which is the equivalent of a round. Rubber bridge has essentially the same complications as Chicago bridge, so we will set aside this form of bridge for the present. Descriptions of rubber bridge and Chicago bridge are found in the appendix.

Playing Bridge

BIDDING

In bridge, as in Game 3, each bid you make must name one of the five denominations: notrump, spades, hearts, diamonds or clubs. But in bridge your bid must also promise to take a specific number of tricks. The first six tricks you take do not count. All tricks you win after the first six are called ODD TRICKS. If you bid 1 HEART, you are offering to take one odd trick (or seven tricks in all) with hearts as trumps. With a bid of 7 NOTRUMP you are offering to take seven odd tricks (all thirteen tricks) with no trump suit.

Both sides may enter the bidding, and the highest bid becomes a CONTRACT. If your side makes the highest bid, you must win at least the number of odd tricks which you have contracted for in order to receive a score. If you succeed, you have MADE your contract. If you fail, you have been SET (you have GONE DOWN). In that case, as a penalty, it is your opponents who receive a score.

The dealer begins the bidding, which proceeds in rotation to the left. Any player may bid at his turn, if he wishes. Otherwise he must say PASS, but that does not prevent him from bidding at a later turn. Each bid (not a pass) must be higher than the preceding bid. Either it must offer to take a larger number of odd tricks than the preceding bid, or it must offer to take the same number of odd tricks in a higher ranking denomination. The five denominations in order of rank, from highest to lowest, are:

NOTRUMP   SPADES   HEARTS   DIAMONDS   CLUBS

Thus if one player bids 1 CLUB, another may then bid 1 HEART, which is higher. After that, a bid of 1 NOTRUMP or 2 CLUBS would be permissible.

If all four players decide not to bid, but say PASS instead, the hand (the deal) is over and a new hand is dealt. In progressive bridge, the same dealer deals again when a hand is PASSED OUT (all four players do nothing but pass).

If any player makes a bid, the bidding continues until three players in succession pass. Then the side which made the high bid has won the contract in whatever denomination was named by the high bid. If the high bid was 3 HEARTS, the player on that side who *first* bid hearts becomes the declarer (he plays the cards for the partnership) and his partner becomes the dummy. The opponent to the left of the declarer makes the opening lead, after which the dummy lays down his hand. Play now continues as in Game 3.

SCORING
The following simplified scoring will do for now.

If you make your contract, you receive:	
• In a NOTRUMP contract	
—for the first ODD trick:	40 points
—for additional ODD tricks:	30 points each
• In a SPADE or HEART contract	
—for all ODD tricks:	30 points each
• In a DIAMOND or CLUB contract	
—for all ODD tricks:	20 points each
• And, in addition, a bonus:	50 points

If you are set, your opponents receive:

- For tricks short of your contract
  (UNDERTRICKS):   50 points each

Note that if you make more tricks than you contracted for, these OVERTRICKS also count for you.

HAND EVALUATION

In bridge you cannot bid without offering to contract for at least one odd trick. But perhaps your hand plus your partner's hand will not take even that many tricks. If one of you does start bidding, it may take several bids by you and your partner to find the best denomination in which to play. This can result in an even higher contract. So you need some way of at least estimating how many tricks your side can take.

The strength of your hand depends on the HIGH CARDS (aces, kings, queens and jacks) you hold. It also depends on how the cards in your hand are distributed among the four suits. You can evaluate your own hand by using POINT COUNT as follows:

For each occurrence in your hand:

- An ACE counts 4 points.
- A KING counts 3 points.
- A QUEEN counts 2 points.
- A JACK counts 1 point.

- A 5-card or 6-card suit counts 1 point.
- A SINGLETON (1-card suit) counts 1 point.

- A 7-card or 8-card suit counts 2 points.
- A VOID (suit with NO cards) counts 2 points.

Once you have evaluted your hand, use the following as temporary guidelines until we are able to be more precise:

- Do not be the first in your partnership to bid unless you have at least 13 points.
- If your partner is the first in your partnership to bid, do not continue the bidding unless you have at least 6 points.
- In either case, do not carry the bidding above 2 SPADES unless you have at least 4 extra points over the minimum given above.

FORMALITIES

Players draw cards to determine who will be the first dealer. If partnerships have not already been agreed upon, the players drawing the two highest cards become partners. In any case, the player drawing the highest card becomes the first dealer. (If two players draw cards of the same rank, two aces for example, the denomination breaks the tie in the order listed above.)

The player to the left of the dealer shuffles the cards and puts them on the table to his right. The dealer moves the cards over to the player on his right, who cuts the cards. The dealer then deals the cards. No one may pick up his cards until the deal is completed.

Two packs of cards are used, one at a time. While the dealer is dealing, his partner shuffles the other pack (to be used for the next deal) and then places it on the table to his right.

The dummy should not look at anyone else's hand. This is forbidden in duplicate bridge and is considered rather amateurish in other forms of bridge. The dummy must not make any comments about the game until the play of the hand is over. However, assuming that the dummy has not looked at any other hand, he may say where the lead is so as to prevent his partner from leading from the wrong hand. Also, if anyone fails to follow suit, he may call attention to it, just in case it was an error.

PRACTICE

Now play some hands. Wait until you feel at home with the above information before you go on to the next section. While you are playing at this level, continue reading in Chapter 2.

Games and Slams

To make the game of bridge more interesting and to encourage higher bidding, bonuses are offered for certain higher contracts which are bid and made. Your partnership has made a GAME and you receive a game bonus if you *bid* and *make* a contract of any one of the following:

> 3 NOTRUMP
> 4 SPADES
> 4 HEARTS
> 5 DIAMONDS
> 5 CLUBS

Spades and hearts are called the MAJOR suits (or simply "the majors"). Obviously it is easier for you to make a game in notrump or in the majors because of the lower requirements. However, it turns out to be about as difficult for you to make 3 NOTRUMP as it is for you to make four in one of the major suits because of the absence of a trump suit. It is the most difficult to make a game in the MINOR suits—diamonds and clubs—because you must take five odd tricks. For this reason you must shun the minors in favor of notrump or the majors if your hand together with your partner's hand give you any logical choice.

For still higher contracts, still higher bonuses are given to you. Your partnership has achieved a SMALL SLAM if you bid and make a contract for six odd tricks in any of the five denominations. Your partnership gets the top bonus when you successfully bring off any contract for seven odd tricks, a GRAND SLAM. However, if you are only able to bid part way to a game, you will still receive the small PARTSCORE bonus if you make your contract.

For the present, use the following scoring:

Partscore bonus	50	
Game bonus	300	(instead of partscore bonus)
Small slam bonus	500	(in addition to game bonus)
Grand slam bonus	1000	(in addition to game bonus)

HINTS: When your partnership holds 26 points between the two hands, the chances are good for making a game in 3 NOTRUMP or 4 SPADES or 4 HEARTS. With 25 points your chances are only fair, and with less than that your chances are so poor that a game should not be bid.

> Indications that your partnership has enough strength to bid a game in notrump or a major are:
>
> - your partner starts the bidding for your side, showing at least 13 points, and you also have 13 points,
>
> or
>
> - your partner pushes the bidding above 2 SPADES, showing that he has at least 4 extra points, and you have at least 2 extra points yourself.

Unless the bidding suggests that you and your partner have at least eight hearts between you for a game in hearts, or eight spades for a game in spades, you may be best off in notrump. However, notrump is usually not a good contract if you or your partner hold a singleton or void. You can try for a game at 5 CLUBS or 5 DIAMONDS with enough cards in one of those suits, but you will need about 3 additional points (29 in all) to be able to make so high a contract. Slams are generally beyond the ability of beginners and don't occur that often even for more advanced players. A small slam usually requires 33 points within the partnership, and a grand slam usually requires 37 points.

Vulnerability and Doubling

This section rounds out the description of game-in-hand bridge. You can ignore the details in this section for now if you want to keep things simple. Or you may read the section for information but not apply it to your games for the time being.

VULNERABILITY

It is part of the game of bridge to vary the penalties applied for not making a contract. This is done by declaring one or both part-nerships to be VULNERABLE at certain times. *Vulnerable* comes from the Latin word meaning woundable. When a side is vulnera-ble, the penalties for going set are increased, but so also are the bonuses for making a game or a slam. The partscore bonus remains the same in either case.

The bonus for game and slam contracts bid and made is:

	Not vulnerable	Vulnerable
Partscore bonus	50	50
Game bonus	300	500
Small slam bonus	500	750
Grand slam bonus	1000	1500

The penalty for contracts which are set is:

For each undertrick	50	100

Note that the score for odd tricks is unchanged by vulnerability. The suggested scoring in the previous sections was based on having both sides not vulnerable at all times. This is perfectly adequate while learning. However the regulation way to play is:

In a 4-deal round:

- On the first deal neither side is vulnerable.
- On the next two deals only the side which deals is vulnerable.
- On the last deal both sides are vulnerable.

DOUBLING

During the bidding there is one other action which the bidders may take besides passing or bidding in one of the five denominations. When it is your turn to bid, and the last bid (not counting passes) was made by the opponents, you may say DOUBLE if you feel that they cannot make their contract. If the hand is then played at that contract, the penalty is increased if they fail to make their contract. The penalty takes the form of a score for your side, so you will get more points if you set an opponent's contract which you have doubled.

On the other hand, if the opponents are allowed to play in the doubled contract, and if they make their contract, they will receive additional points because of your double. Furthermore, if you have doubled and their confidence in making their contract is unshaken, either of them at his turn to bid may say REDOUBLE. This further increase the points awarded to the successful side. In your early learning stages you will not be doubling or redoubling, so this need not concern you. However, if someone does venture a double, perhaps followed by a redouble, use the table in the appendix where the complete scoring is given.

After you double, any further bid by anyone (except for a pass or a redouble) cancels your double. In the same way, after you redouble, any further bid cancels your redouble. But if you have a further opportunity to double or redouble, you may do so.

There is another aspect of doubling and redoubling which you should understand. Suppose the bidding goes:

OPPONENT	YOUR PARTNER	OTHER OPPONENT	YOU
1 HEART	PASS	2 HEARTS	DOUBLE
PASS	PASS	PASS	

The contract is now 2 HEARTS DOUBLED. If the contract is made, the two tricks which were contracted for are counted double toward game—that is, as if 4 HEARTS had been bid and made. Since 4 HEARTS bid and made is a game, the opponents are credited with having made a game and they get a game bonus. (But they cannot get a slam bonus that way—they must actually bid six or seven and make their contract to be credited with a slam.)

If the opponents played a contract of 1 HEART DOUBLED and actually made two hearts, they would not have a game. Only the one trick which they contracted for would count (double) toward game. However, if they had redoubled, the contract is now 1 HEART REDOUBLED. If the contract is made, each trick contracted for counts quadruple toward game. So making 1 HEART REDOUBLED counts as if 4 HEARTS had been bid and made and the opponents would be credited with a game. For all of these cases, see the appendix for the exact scoring.

Chapter 2 /////////////////////////////////////

ELEMENTARY PLAY OF THE CARDS

/////////////////////////////////////

A
Taking Tricks With High Cards

For every hand of bridge there are two periods, each requiring its own kind of skill. First is the AUCTION period, during which you are bidding. Then comes the PLAY period, during which you are playing the cards, either as the declarer or as a defender. It is hard to say which requires the most skill. You will find both of them challenging. Right now we are going to look at some ideas for playing the cards.

Taking Tricks with Top Cards

The easiest way to take tricks is with top cards. Perhaps, in spades:

YOU HOLD

♠ A K Q

When you have the lead, you can play the ace, the king and the queen, taking three tricks (if nobody can play a trump).

Sometimes you are missing the top card.

YOU HOLD

♠ K Q J

Lead the king, which will lose to the ace. But now your queen and jack have been PROMOTED to be the top spades. When you get the lead again, you can then lead them for two tricks. Sometimes we say that the king will FORCE the ace, because an opponent is forced to play the ace if he wishes to take the trick.

Sometimes the top cards are divided between you and your partner. When you are the declarer, you can see and play your partner's hand (the dummy).

YOU (DECLARER)	DUMMY
♠ A Q 3	♠ K 6

Notice that between the two hands you hold the ace, king and queen. They are all top cards, so for your purposes they are all EQUAL to each other. If you have the lead in your own hand, you could lead the ace and play the six from the dummy, then lead the three and play the king from the dummy. The lead is now in the dummy, but you have no spades left to lead. A better plan is first to lead the three and play the king from the dummy. Now the lead is in the dummy, so lead the six and put the ace on it. Now the lead is in your hand—lead the ace and DISCARD (play a worthless card) on it from the dummy.

Now let's state a guideline for the situation you've just encountered. Guidelines are not applicable to every possible case, but they do state what is generally true.

First, notice that your hand has the longer holding in spades, and the dummy hand has the shorter holding. The guideline is:

> **Among equal high cards, play those in the short holding first.**

Now try these situations.

You are the declarer. The lead is in your hand. How do you play the following?

YOU (DECLARER)	DUMMY	
♠ A K	♠ 7 2	Lead the ace, then the king.

♡ K Q J 10	♡ 9 8 3 2	Lead the king, which will force the opponents to play the ace (or otherwise they will lose the trick). When you get the chance again, use the remaining hearts to take tricks. If the opponents should refuse to put their ace on your king, you win the trick and can continue by leading your queen.

◇ Q J 10 9	◇ 5 3	Lead the queen to force out the ace or the king. Later use the jack to force out whichever high diamond remains in the opponents' hands. Then your ten and nine will be good for tricks—they have been promoted to be the top cards.

♣ A 10	♣ K 4	Lead the ace and put the four on it, then lead the ten and put the king on it. Or you can do vice versa. In the first

		case, the *next* (third) lead will be from the dummy; in the second case it will be from your own hand.
♠ A K 4	♠ Q 9	Lead the four and play the queen, then lead the nine and play the ace, then lead the king. Do you see why you should not take the first trick with the ace or the king?
♡ A	♡ K Q 3	You have no choice here. Lead the ace and play the three. Now you must find some other trick to take in the dummy in order to get the lead there. Then you can lead the king and the queen.
◇ K J 8	◇ Q 4	Start by leading the eight to the queen. This uses the high card from the short holding and forces out the opponents' ace. Your king and jack are then promoted to be the top cards.
♣ Q 9 4 2	♣ J 10 5 3	Do you see that you have the queen, jack, ten, and nine? You can do this one yourself, playing the lowest card from one hand and the highest card from the other hand.
♠ A Q	♠ K J 10	This time it is your hand which has the short holding. Play the ace first and put the ten on it. Now be careful!

Play the queen and put the king on it so that the lead will be in the dummy. Now you can play the jack which has become the top card. How unfortunate to be able to take only three tricks with five top cards.

Establishing Tricks

The top card in a suit can always be led to take a trick. However, if there is any possibility of playing your top card on some high card belonging to an opponent, you should hold on to the card until you can do so.

YOU (DECLARER)	DUMMY
♠ K Q J	♠ 4 3 2
♡ A 5 2	♡ 6 3

At first it may seem that you should lead your ace of hearts and take an immediate trick. But you would rather put the ace on the king or queen of hearts, which the opponents hold. Besides that, you can't take tricks with your high spades until the opponents play their ace. And one more thing: The opponents can't take tricks with their high hearts until you play your ace.

Do you see how effective it is to hold on to your ace and start by playing your spades? You play your king of spades to force the opponents to put their ace on it (unless they want to lose the trick). This ESTABLISHES (sets up) your queen and jack as tricks because they have been promoted to be top cards. Now the opponents may play a heart but you are ready with your ace to put on it. This gets the lead back for you. Perhaps you could not have ever gotten the lead again if you had played off your ace of hearts earlier. And now you can take your tricks with your two established spades.

> • First work on tricks that need establishing, even though you lose the lead in doing so.
> • Hold your top cards to put on the opponents' high cards and to get the lead back.

Taking Tricks By Finessing

FINESSE originally meant a sly play. Here's how it works.

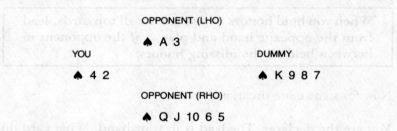

OPPONENT (LHO)

♠ A 3

YOU   DUMMY

♠ 4 2   ♠ K 9 8 7

OPPONENT (RHO)

♠ Q J 10 6 5

The lead is in the dummy. If you lead the king, it will simply lose to the ace and do you no good. Instead, find a trick you can take in your hand so that you can lead from your hand. Then lead the two of spades. If your left-hand opponent (LHO) plays his ace, you play the seven from the dummy—your king is now the top card for a later trick. But if your left-hand opponent plays his three, you play your king from the dummy, which now wins. You don't *know* that your left-hand opponent has the ace until he actually plays it, but you *hope* he does. If your right-hand opponent (RHO) is the one with the ace, he will put it on your king. Too bad! You win some, you lose some. But if you don't finesse you don't win any.

Sometimes you will hold two high cards in one suit which are not TOUCHING (are not in sequence with each other), for example an ace and a queen. Such a combination is called a TENACE (pronounced "ten-ACE," with the accent on the second syllable, or TEN-nis, if you prefer).

YOU (DECLARER)   DUMMY

♠ 8 4   ♠ A Q 5

Start from your own hand, leading the four of hearts. Your left-hand opponent is the second to play to this trick, so he is called the SECOND HAND. If the second hand plays the king, put the dummy's ace on it. If the second hand plays low, you hope he has the king and you play your queen. You have a 50-50 chance that the queen will win the trick, assuming that your left-hand opponent has the king half of the time and your right-hand opponent has the king the other half of the time.

When you hold honors which are not all top cards, lead from the opposite hand and play *as if* the opponent in between held all the missing honors.

Now for some more situations.

You are the declarer. The lead is in your hand. What card do you lead? If the second player plays a low card, what card do you play from the dummy?

YOU	DUMMY	
♠ 6 4 2	♠ K 9	Lead the two. If the second player plays low, play the king just as if you knew that the second player held the ace. Half the time you will be right and you will win; half the time you will be wrong and you will lose.
♡ 7	♡ A Q 3	You have only the seven to lead. If the second hand plays low, you must play as if he held the king. If he does, the queen will win so that is the card you play. If it wins, you can now play the ace. If not,

you must get to the dummy hand later with some other trick. Then you can use the ace.

| ◇ 8 3 2 | ◇ K Q 5 | With only two high cards, missing the ace, you must finesse for best results. Lead the two. If the second hand plays low, play the king. If it wins, remember that the ace is still in the opponents' hands. So get back to your hand with some other trick and then finesse again by leading low toward the queen. If the ace is on your left, as you hope, you will make both the king and the queen good (will take tricks with them). |

| ♣ 6 5 4 | ♣ A Q J | Lead the four toward the ten-ace in the dummy. If the second hand plays low, play the queen. If the queen wins, you can repeat the finesse against the opponents' king. Get to your hand and lead the five toward the ace-jack, which still remain in the dummy. Play the jack if the second hand still plays low. The ace will take a third trick. |

| ♠ 8 3 2 | ♠ K J 4 | Lead the two. If the second hand really has the ace and |

queen as you hope, and if the second hand plays low, your jack will take the trick. So the general rule for finessing is: If the second hand plays low, play your lowest honor from the third hand (your jack in this case); if the second hand plays high, COVER his high card with the smallest honor which will beat it (cover the queen with the king, but the ace can't be covered, so discard the four).

An opponent is the declarer. You are a defender making the opening (first) lead for this hand, so you cannot see any of the other hands. You have two suits which you might lead. Which one do you choose?

YOU	PARTNER
♠ 9 4 2	???
♡ K Q J 3	???

Lead the king of hearts in order to establish the queen and jack as tricks. Your side will make tricks in spades only if your partner has some high spades. Go for the sure thing—start the hearts. It is conventional for a defender to start with the king when he holds the king-queen or the ace-king.

♠ A Q 4	???
♢ 4 3 2	???

You do not want to lead away from a tenace such as the ace-queen—you want your partner to lead the spades to you so you can finesse. On the other hand, your partner could just be waiting for you to lead diamonds so that he can take a finesse. So give diamonds a try. Even if that doesn't help, you will probably get your finesse later. It is conventional for a defender to lead the highest card when he has a worthless holding, so lead the four of diamonds.

♠ K 3	???
◊ 8 4 3	???

Here again you have a combination in spades where you will lose if you lead away from it but may win if your partner leads toward it. So you lead the eight of diamonds and keep your spades for a later finesse.

B
Defender Play

Conventional Leads

A CONVENTION is an artificial way of playing or bidding in order to convey a message to your partner. The declarer sees and plays both hands, so he has no need to send a message to his partner. But with defenders it is quite the opposite case. Here are some of the ways that you can legally SIGNAL to your partner when you are leading a suit for the first time.

YOU HOLD:	HOW TO SIGNAL:
♠ A K 3 2	Whenever you hold an ace-king sequence, you must lead the king. When your partner sees the king win, he will know that you also have the ace.
♠ Q J 10 3	Whenever you lead from other sequences headed by an honor, lead the top honor in the sequence. When your partner sees you lead the queen, he will know that you also have the jack (but not the king or you would have led it).
♠ 8 5 2	Whenever you lead from a suit which contains no honors, lead the highest of your small cards. This is called leading the "top of nothing." When your partner sees you lead the eight, which is rather large for a small card, he will suspect that you have no tricks in this suit.
♠ Q 8 5 2	Whenever you lead from an honor which is not in a sequence, lead your lowest card. When your partner sees you lead one of the lower small cards, he will suspect that you hold an honor in that suit.

These signals will help your partner to decide what to do if he gets the lead later on. If he can see that you have a high card or two in the suit which you led, he will probably lead that suit again. But if you have led the top of nothing, he will probably decide that your side cannot profit from leading that particular suit and will look for some other suit to lead. Cooperation between defenders is essential if you are going to make as many tricks as possible.

Which card would you lead when first playing the spade suit?

♠ A K Q 3	Lead the king from any ace-king combination.
♠ K Q	Lead the king from king-queen. If your partner has the ace, or if the king loses to the opponents' ace, your partner will know that you have the queen.
♠ J 10 7	Lead the top of a sequence—the jack.
♠ 10 9 8 3	Remember that the ten is an honor. Since it heads a sequence, lead the ten.
♠ J 8 2	Lead the two—low from an honor not in a sequence.
♠ 10 3 2	Lead the two again—low from an honor (the ten) not in a sequence.
♠ 9 3	Lead the nine—top of nothing.
♠ 4 3 2	Lead the four—top of nothing. The four isn't very big, so your partner may not be able to read your signal this time.
♠ K J 7 2	Lead the two. This is not a good honor combination to lead from. You would rather have your partner lead this suit so you can finesse.

Your partner is the first to lead the heart suit. He has led the card shown. What does he probably hold in hearts?

PARTNER'S LEAD

♡ J	Your partner must have started with a jack-ten combination at the head of his heart suit.
♡ K	Your partner may have started with an ace-king or a king-queen. Usually you can tell the difference. Perhaps he even has all of

	these cards—an ace-king-queen combination.
♡ 2	This lowest of all small cards probably signals that your partner is leading from an honor. But no signal is absolutely trustworthy. He may have had only one heart to begin with—the two.
♡ 9	The nine is virtually always a top-of-nothing lead.
♡ 5	Fives and sixes are difficult to read because they are neither high nor low among the small cards. Look at your own hand and the dummy. If you can see the four, three and two, your partner has led the smallest card he had and probably holds an honor. Figuring out whether your partner led his smallest or whether he led top of nothing is sometimes a tough problem. You can see that good defensive play involves good detective work.

More About Conventional Leads

When you lead from a suit where you have an honor but no sequence of honors, you have learned to lead your lowest card. However, there is an exception which may seem like a quirk until later when we are able to explain its value. When convention calls for a low lead, you do not initially lead lower than your fourth-highest card, counting from the top.

♠ Q 8 5 <u>3</u> 2	Lead the three, your fourth-highest, not the two.
♠ Q 8 5 <u>3</u>	Lead the three.
♠ Q 8 <u>5</u>	Lead the five.

When you have a sequence of honors, you have learned to lead the king from an ace-king combination and the highest honor from any other sequence. However, when a hand is being played at notrump, it is better to hold back a *2-card* sequence if you can lead a fourth-highest card instead. If you have four or more cards in a suit headed by a 2-card sequence, lead your fourth-highest card at notrump.

♠ A K 6 5	At a trump contract, lead the king. At a notrump contract, hold back your 2-card ace-king sequence by starting with a lead of your five.
♠ K Q 8 7 4 2	At a trump contract, lead the king. At notrump, you want to hold back your king-queen, so start with the seven, your fourth-highest card.
♠ K Q 8	At any contract, lead the king first. At notrump you would make a fourth-highest lead if you had more cards in this suit, but in this case you don't.
♠ K Q J 6 4	At any contract, lead the king. A lead from a *3-card* sequence is always a strong lead and is usually your first choice.

At notrump, your best lead is usually from a long suit of five or more cards whenever you have such a suit. If you and your partner keep leading this suit, you may be able to run the opponents out. Then your remaining cards in the suit will be established as good tricks. This will not work at a trump contract, because as soon as the declarer or the dummy is out of your suit, he can play a trump when you lead your suit.

Third Hand Tactics

As a defender you not only want to take tricks yourself, but you also want to help your partner take tricks. Suppose your partner is the first to lead the spade suit:

DECLARER
♠ 3 (his play)

PARTNER
♠ 2 (his lead)

YOU
♠ K 9 5

DUMMY
♠ A 10 6

Your partner probably has some high card, perhaps the queen. You must play your king to force the declarer to play the ace from the dummy. This situation arises when your partner leads, making you the third hand to play to the trick. Generally the third hand plays high whenever it is necessary to take the trick or to force a high card from the fourth hand.

As third hand, which card do you play?

DUMMY
♡ 4 3 2

PARTNER
♡ 5 (led)

YOU
♡ Q 10 6

You must play your queen to force out a high card from the declarer, who is the fourth hand to play on this trick. You hope that your partner has the king or jack. Your play of the queen may help your partner make a trick later.

DUMMY
♡ 4 3 2

PARTNER
♡ Q (led)

YOU
♡ K 9 5

This is no point in your playing high in this case—your partner's queen is equal to (as good as) your king. So discard your nine. A high discard shows that you like the suit. Here, you like hearts because you have the king.

DUMMY
♡ Q 3 2
(plays the 2)

PARTNER
♡ 4 (led)

YOU
♡ K J 5

Do you see that your jack will do the same job that your king will? If the dummy had played the queen, you would have covered it (played higher) with your king.

But since the two has been played from the dummy, you will save your king and play your jack instead.

	DECLARER	
	♡ 4 (played)	
PARTNER		YOU
♡ 7 (led)		♡ K J 8 2
	DUMMY	
	♡ A 10 3	

In this case your jack is high enough to force the dummy to play his ace. Your partner could have the queen, but his lead of the seven suggests that he has led the top of nothing.

	DUMMY	
	♡ A 10 3	
	(ace played)	
PARTNER		YOU
♡ 7 (led)		♡ K J 8 2

You can't beat the dummy's ace so you will discard. You will pick the eight rather than the two in order to tell your partner that you have high cards in this suit. That will encourage him to lead hearts when he gets a chance.

Second Hand Tactics

Whenever possible, you want to use your high cards to capture a lesser high card belonging to the opponents. This takes some cooperation with your partner when you are defending. Suppose you could see all four hands:

	DUMMY	
	◇ J 4 2	
YOU		PARTNER
◇ A 10 3		◇ Q 9 5
	DECLARER	
	◇ K 8 7 6	

You can see that when the declarer plays his king, you are sitting right behind him ready to put your ace on it. When the declarer plays the jack, your partner is ready with his queen to put on it. But your side will manage all this only if you both are careful.

Let's say the declarer starts in this suit by leading the six of diamonds. If this is real play, you can see only your own hand and the dummy. Still you should know that you must not play your ace at this time. You would like to use your ace to cover a high card held by your right-hand opponent, not the miserable six which the declarer has just led. Besides that, you can see that possibly your partner can take this trick if he has the king or the queen. So play your three. Even if your partner cannot take the trick, you have made the best play.

The idea is to use your high cards to top a lesser high card held by your *right-hand* opponent. When you are the second hand to play to a trick, if the first hand leads a small card, you should play low. But if the first hand leads an honor, you should cover it with a higher honor if you can, even if your card won't win the trick.

The opponents start the club suit. As second hand, which card do you play?

DUMMY
♣ 9 3 2

YOU
♣ K 10 5

PARTNER
♣ ???

DECLARER
♣ 4 (led)

You could win the trick with the ten or the king. But you are the second hand and you know it is better if you play low, letting your partner win the trick if he can—and he probably can in this case. Perhaps the declarer has the queen or the jack which you can capture later with your king.

DUMMY
♣ A Q 10

YOU
♣ K 6 5

PARTNER
♣ ???

DECLARER
♣ 2 (led)

You can see that the declarer is about to finesse against your king and is going to succeed. Calmly play second hand low (play the five). Sometimes the declarer has good reason not to finesse, unless he sees that you are agitated and thus knows that his finesse will succeed.

DUMMY
♣ A 4 2

YOU   PARTNER
♣ K 10 3   ♣ ???

DECLARER
♣ Q (led)

This time you have a chance to cover an honor which has been led. Put your king on the declarer's queen. He will have to put the dummy's ace on his own queen in order to take the trick. The next club trick will be taken by whoever has the jack (probably the declarer), making your ten the top card for the third trick. Covering an honor with an honor has paid off for your side.

DECLARER
♣ ???

YOU   PARTNER
♣ Q 9 3   ♣ ???

DUMMY
♣ J 4 2
(2 is led)

Don't fret about it. Play second hand low and see what happens next. If the dummy had led the jack, you would cover it with your queen.

C

Taking Tricks With Small Cards

The opportunity to take tricks with small cards is not so evident as it is with high cards. The following opportunities abound, but you must look for them.

Taking Tricks by Ruffing

When you hold no cards in a suit which is led by someone else, you may play a trump if you wish. This is called TRUMPING, or

RUFFING. The trump which you play will take the trick unless someone else also is able to ruff and plays a trump which is higher than yours. Ruffing is a good source of tricks for the dummy and the two defenders. But the declarer should not ruff from his own hand unnecessarily—his trumps are often needed for other purposes.

```
YOU (DECLARER)      DUMMY

♠ A K Q J 10        ♠ 5 4 2        ←SPADES are trump
♡ 6 3               ♡ —
```

The dummy has no hearts. You can lead a heart from your own hand and ruff it in the dummy with a small trump, say the two. Now you can get the lead back into your own hand by leading the four of spades and taking the trick with the ace. And now you can lead your other small heart and ruff again in the dummy.

```
YOU (DECLARER)      DUMMY

♠ A K 9 8 3         ♠ Q J 2        ←SPADES are trump
♣ 5 4               ♣ 8
```

You could ruff if the dummy had no clubs. Lead a club from either hand, following suit from the other hand. You lose the trick, but look! Now the dummy has no clubs! At your next opportunity lead a club from the declarer's hand and ruff with the two of spades. This is another example of how you can work to establish a trick.

```
YOU (DEFENDER)      PARTNER

♡ A 3 2             ???            ←HEARTS are trump
♢ 4                 ???
```

If you lead a diamond, you will then have no more of them. If anyone leads diamonds while you still have some trumps left, you may ruff. Your partner may suspect this and lead a diamond when he gets a chance. Of course you will not ruff if your partner is going to take the trick anyway.

How can you make ruffs with the following holdings?

YOU (DECLARER)	DUMMY
♠ K J 4 3 2	♠ A Q 5
◇ A 5	◇ 3

←SPADES are trump

Lead the ace of diamonds. Now the dummy is out of diamonds. Lead the five of diamonds and ruff with the five of spades.

♠ K Q 8 4 2	♠ J 9 6 3
◇ A 4 2	◇ 6 3

←SPADES are trump

To eliminate the dummy's diamonds, lead the ace of diamonds, then on the next trick lead the two of diamonds (which will lose). Later you can lead the four of diamonds for a ruff.

♡ K 8 6 5 4 3	♡ Q 7 2
♣ A K	♣ —

←HEARTS are trump

Of course you could lead the ace of clubs and ruff it, but would you? When you lead the ace of clubs, throw (discard) a useless diamond or spade on it from the dummy.

♡ A Q J 8 7	♡ 10 9 3
◇ A 8	◇ 4 3
♣ A K 8 4	♣ 7 2

←HEARTS are trump

You could eliminate the dummy's diamonds by leading first the ace of diamonds and then the eight of diamonds. But you would have no diamond left in your hand to lead for a ruff. You need a suit where you have more cards in the declarer's hand than you have in the dummy's hand for a ruff in the dummy. Clubs is such a suit. On the third and fourth round of clubs, ruff.

With the declarer on your right, can you win by ruffing in the following situations?

YOU (DEFENDER)

♠ 6 4 3 2
♡ —
◇ A K Q
♣ 10 9 7 4 3 2

←SPADES are trump

Your partner leads the ♡2.
Your RHO plays the ♡A.

This is your chance to ruff. Play a small trump and take the trick.

SAME HAND, but:
Your partner leads ♡A.
Your RHO trumps with ♠ 5.

Your partner leads the ace of hearts and your right-hand opponent trumps it with the five of spades. Your opponent's trump will win over your partner's ace. But you can OVER-RUFF. Play the six of spades which beats the opponent's five of spades. If he had ruffed with the higher spade, you would not have been able to overruff. Instead you would have discarded (played) a small club, saving your trumps for the future.

SAME HAND, but:
Your partner leads ♡A.
Your RHO plays the ♡3.

Your partner is going to take this trick with his ace of hearts. It would be a crime to trump your partner's good card. So discard a small club.

Establishing the 8-card Fit

Small cards in a long suit can often take tricks:

YOU (DECLARER)   DUMMY

♠ A K Q 3 2   ♠ 6 5 4   ←SPADES are trump

Between you and the dummy you hold a combined spade suit of eight cards. We call this an 8-CARD FIT. A simple subtraction tells you that the opponents hold five spades between them. Usually (about two-thirds of the time) one opponent will hold three of them and the other will hold two (a 3-2 SPLIT). Pretending we could look into their hands, we might see:

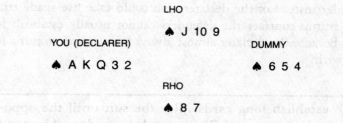

One of your maneuvers as declarer is to DRAW the trumps away from the opponents. When you play the ace of spades, you take two of the opponents' spades away from them. The king takes two more, the queen takes the last one. Since spades are trump in this example, the opponents now have no trumps. They cannot ruff any card which you play. Now only you hold any spades. Your two small remaining spades are called LONG cards because they are left when no one else has any more. They have been established as good tricks. Since in this case your long cards are trumps, you will not use them until time in need. They will be useful in trumping when the opponents have the lead. In that way you can get the lead back for yourself.

Now suppose that hearts are trump and the spade holdings are the same as before. If you start right off playing spades, by the time you get to play the queen your right-hand opponent has no more spades. He will trump your queen. You want none of that. Instead you must draw the opponents' trumps (hearts) first. Now you can play spades without having your tricks trumped. After you take tricks with the ace, king and queen, the opponents will have no more spades, but you will still have two small long spades left. These two cards are good for tricks because no one has any other spades to top them with and the opponents have no trumps to trump them with. Since they are not trump, you may take these tricks right away.

Now suppose that you are playing in notrump and the spade holdings are the same. You can go right to the spade suit for five tricks, because there is no possibility of a ruff. Even if you were a defender instead of the declarer, you could take five spade tricks. At a trump contract the defenders cannot usually establish long cards because the declarer almost always has a trump to ruff a long card with.

> To establish long cards, play the suit until the opponents have no more. Then your long cards will be good unless they can be trumped.

The lead is in your hand. How can you establish some long cards?

YOU (DECLARER)	DUMMY	
♠ A K 7 4 2	♠ 8 5 3	(NOTRUMP)

The four hands are:

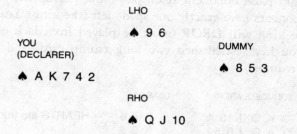

Lead the ace, then the king, then the two. You will pick up two of the opponents' trumps on each of the first two leads. Your two of spades will lose to the opponents' queen. When you get the lead again, you can take two more tricks with your two established long spades.

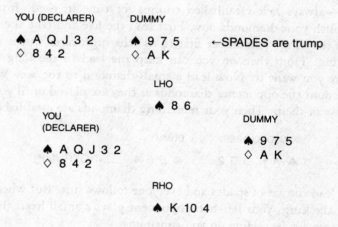

Did you see the finesse in spades?

Lead the two of diamonds to the dummy's ace to get the lead in the dummy. Lead the five of spades to which your right-hand opponent should play low (the second hand to play to a trick usually plays low). PUT UP (play) the queen, which takes the trick. Lead another diamond to the king. Now you can lead the seven of spades for a second finesse against the same king. When your right-hand opponent again plays low, put up the jack. Now the opponents have exactly one spade left (the king). Lead the ace and the king will DROP (must be played from lack of choice). Now you have established two long trump cards and you have drawn trumps.

YOU (DECLARER)	DUMMY	
♡ K Q J 10 4	♡ 8 7 6	← HEARTS are trump
◇ A Q J 8 5	◇ K 3 2	

If you start first to establish diamonds, one of the opponents will soon run out of them and will trump one of your good diamonds. So lead the king of hearts which will lose to the ace. As soon as you win a trick from the opponents, continue playing hearts until the opponents are all out of them. Don't play your established hearts now—always save established trumps for time in need. Instead, establish your diamonds now. First lead the five and take the trick with the king. Remember first to use the high cards in the short holding. From then on you can keep the lead in the long hand where you want it. Now lead a small diamond to the ace. Watch and count the opponents' diamonds as they are played until you see all five of them. Then your remaining diamonds are established.

YOU (DECLARER)	DUMMY	
♠ A K Q 3 2	♠ 6 5 4	(NOTRUMP)

You lead the ace of spades and everyone follows suit. But when you play the king, your left-hand opponent plays a small heart (he has no more spades). How do you continue?

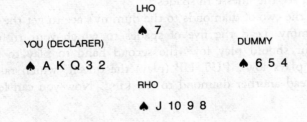

LHO
♠ 7

YOU (DECLARER)   DUMMY
♠ A K Q 3 2   ♠ 6 5 4

RHO
♠ J 10 9 8

You lead the ace of spades and everyone follows suit. But when you play the king, your left-hand opponent plays a small heart so you know that he started with one spade and your right-hand opponent started with four. The simplest continuation is to lead the queen and then the three to eliminate your right-hand opponents' spades. Later you can take a trick with your long two of spades.

YOU (DECLARER)	DUMMY	
◇ A K Q 8 4	◇ 9 7 2	← DIAMONDS are trump
♣ A 3 2	♣ 5	

You might think first about drawing trumps, but you cannot take your ruffs in clubs if you draw trumps first. Always look for ruffs in the dummy before deciding to draw trumps. Play the ace of clubs and then lead a small club for a ruff. Now get the lead back in your hand, perhaps by leading a small diamond to your ace. Now ruff another club. Get the lead back to your own hand any way you can and you will be able to draw trumps.

Establishing the 7-card Fit

When you and your partner combined hold only seven cards in a suit, you are considerably worse off than with eight cards.

YOU	DUMMY
♠ A K Q 3 2	♠ 6 5

The opponents now have six spades between them. It is a strange but true fact that the six cards will usually split 4–2 (not 3–3) between the two opponents. In the usual case you will have to play spades four times to run the opponents out of spades. (With *eight* cards in the combined hands you would usually only need three rounds of spades to exhaust the opponents' holdings.) Still, with the holding above, you probably can establish one small spade after playing spades four times.

Here is another 7-card fit:

YOU	DUMMY
♠ A K Q 2	♠ 6 5 4

If it takes four rounds to exhaust the opponents' spades, how many will you have left? None! Usually you cannot establish any long cards with this holding. But when lucky (about one-third of the time) the opponents' spades will split 3–3 and you can establish one long spade trick.

When it comes to establishing long cards:

- We like an 8-card fit—longer fits are even better.
- We have trouble with a 7-card fit—shorter fits are even worse.

A 4–3 fit is the worst of the 7-card fits. A 5–2 fit is better and a 6–1 fit is almost as good as an 8-card fit.

How many long cards would you *usually* be able to establish in the following cases when playing in notrump?

YOU	DUMMY	
♡ K Q 5 4 2	♡ A 7 6	(NOTRUMP)

You plus the dummy have eight hearts. The opponents have five hearts, usually split 3–2. After three rounds of hearts, the opponents should be out of hearts and you will have established two long cards. (Remember to take the ace first before the king and queen.)

♡ K Q 5 4　　♡ A 7 6 3　　(NOTRUMP)

You hold eight hearts. Usually the opponents will be out of hearts after three rounds. You will have established one long card—actually you will have one card left in each hand, but only one will win a trick.

♡ K Q 5 4 2　　♡ A 7　　(NOTRUMP)

Now you hold seven hearts. The opponents have six hearts, usually split 4–2. After four rounds to take out the opponents' hearts you should have established one long heart.

♡ K Q 5 4　　♡ A 7 6　　(NOTRUMP)

Again you hold seven hearts. After four rounds to exhaust the opponents' hearts you will have none left yourself. Usually you will not be able to establish any long cards. You could be lucky and find that the hearts split 3–3, or you could be unlucky and find that they split 5–1! A 6–0 split would be quite unusual—voids don't occur very often.

You want to establish your most profitable suit first. Which suit do you choose to begin with?

YOU	DUMMY	
◇ 6 5 4	◇ A K 10 9 2	(NOTRUMP)
♣ K Q 4 3	♣ A 7 6	With eight diamonds and only seven clubs, tackle the diamonds first. The clubs offer little hope for a long card anyway.

♠ K 5 3	♠ Q J 6 4 2	(NOTRUMP)
♡ K 9 4 3 2	♡ A Q	The eight spades promise a possible pair of long cards while the seven hearts will probably yield only one.

◇ A K Q J	◇ 8 4 2	← DIAMONDS are trump
♣ A K Q J 3	♣ 6 5 4	If you start with clubs, the opponents will soon be ruffing you. You will have to draw trumps first. Too bad you picked the 7-card fit to be trumps instead of picking the 8-card fit.

D
Declarer Play

Assessing the Situation

When you are the declarer, you will play the hand for the partnership. First you will see the opening lead and then the dummy. *Stop!* You must assess the situation before doing anything at all.

First look at your trump suit, mentally putting together the dummy's cards with your own. How long is the trump fit? What high cards do you have? Will it be easy or difficult to draw trumps?

Next look at each of the other suits. Is there a possibility for a ruff in the dummy in that suit? Is the fit long enough that you may be able to establish some long card in that suit? What high cards do you have?

When you come to the suit that was led, look at the specific card which was led. Does it tell you anything about what the left-hand opponent holds or how he is going to try to defeat you? He has tried to lead a suit that will be favorable to him, not to you.

Later you will learn to plan the entire hand before you play the first card. But for now, look over your assets carefully before you make your first play.

Arranging the Order of Business

The order of business for a declarer at a trump contract usually breaks down into:

• Actions which must be taken before trumps are drawn
• Drawing trumps
• Actions which can be taken after trumps are drawn

Before drawing trumps, take *only* those actions which require the presence of your trump cards.

BEFORE DRAWING TRUMPS

Before you think about drawing trumps, think about taking ruffs. You must take your ruffs in the hand which has the shortest holding in trumps. That hand is called the SHORT HAND and it is almost always the dummy hand.

Sometimes your own hand is the short hand. And sometimes both hands have the same number of trumps—in that case you should pick the most favorable hand to be the "short hand" and take all the ruffs in that hand. You will not take ruffs in the LONG HAND unnecessarily because those trumps will probably be needed later.

The reason that you usually must take your short-hand ruffs before drawing trumps is simply that you usually won't have any trumps left in the short hand once you have drawn trumps, or you may not have enough of them left to make all the ruffs you want. Besides, you must get to your ruffs immediately. Once the opponents see that you intend to ruff, they will probably lead trumps whenever they can so as to reduce the ability of the short hand to ruff.

When the hand offers an opportunity to ruff, do that first unless you are sure you can wait until you have drawn trumps. You have already learned that you may have to lose a trick or two while setting up your ruff. Go to it!

As you gain experience, you will see other actions which will succeed only if they are taken before drawing trumps. But unless you specifically recognize such an action, the very next thing to do is to draw trumps.

YOU	DUMMY	
♠ A K Q J 10	♠ 9 8 7	← SPADES are trump
♡ A K 3	♡ —	

If you play your spades first, you will make five spade tricks and two heart tricks. The three of hearts is of no use and will lose to the opponents' queen. But if you ruff your small heart first and then play your spades, your spades will take six tricks. Your small heart will not lose because it has been ruffed. But you cannot make this ruff unless you do it before all the dummy trumps are gone.

DRAWING TRUMPS

Once you have taken your ruffs, you will normally draw trumps next. You don't want the opponents to get any ruffs if you can help it, especially since they would be ruffing your good cards.

If you have at least an 8-card trump fit, and if the trumps split nicely, you probably won't have any trouble drawing trumps. You may lose some tricks in the process of drawing trumps because you may not hold all the high cards in the suit. Possibly you won't hold any! Nevertheless, you will usually be best off by drawing trumps even though you lose some tricks on the way. Obviously you must count the opponents' trumps as they fall so you will know when they have no more. Do not continue playing trumps after the opponents are out of them if you can help it. You need those trumps.

The most likely way for the outstanding cards to split is slightly unevenly. When an even split is possible, it is not the most likely.

THE OPPONENTS HOLD:	THE MOST LIKELY SPLIT IS:
6	4–2
5	3–2
4	3–1
3	2–1

There is no guarantee that the outstanding trumps will split the most likely way. What if the trumps split badly? Perhaps one opponent will have more trumps than you do. Or even if he only has as many as you do, you may find that catastrophe will strike if you use all of your own trumps in the process of drawing your opponents' trumps. One strategy is to play trumps until one opponent is out. Then let the other opponent ruff when he is able. At least you will have a trump or two left to ruff with and thus get the lead back.

```
                         DUMMY
                       ♠ 4 3 2
       LHO                             RHO
     ♠ A K Q                         ♠ J 10
                          YOU
                       ♠ 9 8 7 6 5
```

With spades as trumps, your holding plus the dummy's holding looks terrible. But if the spades split in the most likely way, the opponents can only make three spade tricks *unless* your right-hand opponent (the opponents' short hand) can make a ruff. Then they will make four tricks with their spades instead of three. If you draw trumps, or at least lead them twice, before they can make such a ruff, you can prevent them from making the extra trick.

AFTER DRAWING TRUMPS

Once you have drawn trumps you must look around to see what other tricks you can take. You may have an impulse to play your top cards right away because they will yield immediate tricks. Unless you see that you can fulfill your contract with these immediate tricks, using up your top cards or your remaining trump cards is invariably wrong. To make your contract you will normally have to give up the lead to the opponents one or more times. When they have the lead, they are going to play suits which are favorable to them. The way you get the lead back is through your top cards and your trumps. Then you can return to playing suits which are favorable to you.

Some of the best sources of additional tricks are long cards. If you have a fit which will yield long cards, you should go about setting them up. You may not be able to take all the early tricks in that suit, but never mind. You will keep leading the suit every time you have the lead, and you will count the opponents' cards in the suit as they fall. Just as with the trump suit, you need to know when the opponents have no more. Then you have established your long tricks which you play off. You have to make up your mind early, when you first assess the situation, that you are going to try for long tricks in a certain suit—otherwise you may find yourself discarding some of the cards from the very suit which you later need to establish.

Finesses are another source of tricks. You must think ahead about which hand you must lead from to take a finesse. A finesse may or may not yield a trick depending on whether or not it succeeds. But you have to take your chances unless you have some other way of taking tricks and making your contract. If a finesse loses, you also lose the lead. The top cards and trumps which you have been saving up will help you get the lead back again.

When You Play at Notrump

The best sources of tricks at notrump are long cards, but of course the availability of long cards depends on your having a good fit in some suit. As declarer, you must do two things: establish your own long cards if you have any, and thwart the opponents' attempt at establishing any long cards they may have.

You already know how to establish your own long cards. Start in just as soon as you get the lead. An 8-card fit (or longer) is your best chance, the longer the better. But any 5-card holding in your hand or the dummy hand is a possible source of long cards.

The defenders will try to find their long fit and play it until your side has no more. This is the principal way they have of defeating you at notrump. The opening lead will very frequently be from a 5-card holding. If both you and the dummy are short in this suit (two or three cards each), this is probably their long suit. The best countermeasure, if you have the ace of their suit, is to HOLD UP the use of your ace as long as you can. Simply play a small card and let them take the trick until you have no more small cards. Sometimes you can hold up the playing of other high cards in their suit, but not when that would result in your never getting a trick with those high cards.

Besides any long fits which may yield tricks, you have all the usual possibilities of taking tricks with high cards, some of which may require finessing. Hold on to your top cards and work first on establishing other high cards or taking finesses. Once you have enough tricks set up to make your contract, you can play them off.

E
Summary

Declarer Highlights

At trump contracts:

- Ruff in the short hand.
- Draw trumps.
- Establish enough other tricks to make your contract.

At notrump contracts:

- Attack a long suit (if you have one) to establish long cards.
- Establish enough other tricks to make your contract.

Establish means to work on the tricks which need setting up and which may involve losing the lead in order to do so. This includes taking any necessary finesse, which will lose the lead if it fails.

Establish First:

- Hold on to your top cards and any long trumps to use for the purpose of getting the lead back again.
- When you have enough tricks established to make your contract, then you may take in all your tricks.

Defender Highlights

Follow the standard conventions when you are the first to lead a suit. When your partner is the first to lead a suit, read the card he leads as a signal to you.

The standard leads given so far are:

- King from ace-king or king-queen
- Highest honor from other sequences
- Top of nothing
- Low from an honor not in sequence

LOW means your lowest card, but not lower than your fourth highest. At notrump contracts only, hold back a two-card sequence if you can make a fourth-highest lead from that suit.

Use the following tactics unless you can see that you will do better following some other line of play.

- Play third hand high.
- Play second hand low.
- Cover an honor with an honor.

At notrump, whoever has the opening lead must start immediately playing a long suit if he has one. The other partner must cooperate when he gets the lead by also leading the same suit. Long cards are the very best source of tricks at notrump.

At a trump contract, long cards will usually be trumped, so long cards are not normally a source of tricks for the defense. The defense must depend on tricks from high cards and possibly from a ruff or two.

Chapter 3 ////////////////////////////////////

THE FIRST BID

//

A
First Bidding Notions

Bidding Goals

Fit. When you are bidding, you are working with your partner to discover how well your two hands fit together.

- Are the two hands suitable for play in notrump?
- Are the two hands suitable for play in a trump suit? If so, which suit?

Strength. You are also trying to discover how strong the two hands together are, in order to know whether they are good enough to try for a game bonus or perhaps even a slam bonus.

A GAME bonus is awarded for bidding and making one of the following:

- 3 NOTRUMP
- 4 SPADES or 4 HEARTS (the major suits)
- 5 DIAMONDS or 5 CLUBS (the minor suits)

Because we have to bid so high for a game in a minor suit, we give priority to the major suits and to notrump.

A SLAM bonus is awarded for bidding and making one of the following:

- 6 NOTRUMP or 6 in any SUIT (a small slam)
- 7 NOTRUMP or 7 in any SUIT (a grand slam)

The decisions you have to make while bidding require information about your partner's hand, and his decisions must be based on information about your hand. Bidding becomes a stab in the dark when it is based on knowledge about one hand alone.

Standard American. Since bidding is such a highly cooperative undertaking between partners, your bids and those of your partner must have a meaning you both understand. *You must agree with your partner on some bidding system.* Only then can each of you take intelligent action. The most widely used bidding system is Standard American, known to all players even if they sometimes use other systems. We will stick to Standard American, but you should be aware that there are a few common variations. (Advanced players use many additions to Standard American, but partners must agree with each other *in advance* if they plan to use any such embellishments, and they must let their opponents know also.)

Classifying Distribution

DISTRIBUTION refers to how the cards are distributed between the four suits. A 5-4-3-1 distribution means that a hand has five cards in one suit, four in another, three in another and one in another.

Balance. A hand is called BALANCED if it has no singleton or void. It may have a doubleton, but only one of them. Only three distributions qualify as balanced:

4-3-3-3
4-4-3-2
5-3-3-2

What is your distribution when you hold each of the following hands? Is your hand balanced?

YOU

♠ 8 2
♡ A K 4 3
♦ 10 8 3
♣ A 5 4 3

Your distribution is 4-4-3-2 and is balanced. Your shortest suit is the doubleton in spades, and it is the only doubleton in your hand.

♠ 8 2
♡ 9
♦ Q J 10 9 8 7 4
♣ 6 5 4

Your distribution is 7-3-2-1 and is unbalanced because of your singleton heart.

♠ A K 4 2
♡ A K 10
♦ K Q 10
♣ 8 3 2

Your distribution is 4-3-3-3 and your hand is balanced. We often call this distribution *square* or *perfectly balanced* because the cards are distributed as evenly as possible among the four suits. However, it is a rather unfavorable distribution.

♠ A K Q 8 7 6
♡ K Q J 7 4 2
♦ —
♣ A

Your distribution is 6-6-1-0 and is unbalanced because of your void in diamonds and your singleton club.

♠ K 8
♡ A 10 8 3 2
♦ K 4 3 2
♣ 5 4

Your distribution is 5-4-2-2. And your hand is unbalanced because it contains two doubletons. Some people like to call a hand *semibalanced* if it contains more than one doubleton but no singleton or void. However, it is really only necessary for us to distinguish between balanced and unbalanced.

Judging Fit

Notrump Fit. The two hands in a partnership form a normal NOTRUMP FIT if *both* hands are balanced. With a notrump fit, notrump may be a suitable denomination in which to play the hand.

Trump Fit. The two hands in a partnership have a normal TRUMP FIT in any suit where the two hands have a *combined* holding of eight or more cards in that suit. With a normal trump fit in some suit, it may be right to play the hand with that suit as trump.

Do the following pairs of hands form a normal notrump fit? In which suits (if any) do they have a normal trump fit?

YOU	PARTNER	
♠ A K 3	♠ Q 10 4 2	Both hands are balanced, so they do form a normal notrump fit. There is no normal trump fit in any of the suits.
♡ K Q 2	♡ J 10 8 4	
◇ A Q 3 2	◇ 8 7	
♣ J 10 4	♣ Q 9 8	
♠ K Q 7 8 3	♠ A 10 9	Your hand is unbalanced so there is no normal notrump fit. There is a normal trump fit in spades (an 8-card fit) and in hearts (a 9-card fit).
♡ J 10 9 4 2	♡ K Q 8 3	
◇ A 3	◇ K 8 7 6	
♣ A	♣ 3 2	
♠ J 10 9 7	♠ Q 8 3	Both hands are balanced, so there is a normal notrump fit. There is also an 8-card normal trump fit in hearts.
♡ Q J 4 2	♡ A 9 8 3	
◇ K 8 2	◇ A J 10 9	
♣ A 10	♣ K Q	
♠ A K 4 3 2	♠ 9	Both hands are unbalanced, so there is no normal notrump fit. Neither is there any normal trump fit. This is
♡ 4 3	♡ A Q J 10 6	
◇ A K Q 10 8	◇ 4	
♣ 10	♣ A K J 8 3 2	

always a sad situation. The
best we have is a 7-card fit in
hearts and also in clubs.

Measuring Strength

The strength of your hand is determined by a system of points. The strength of your partnership can then be estimated by adding together your points and those of your partner, as best you can determine them.

High-Card Points (HCP). Count each occurrence in your hand of each of the following:

> Ace: 4 points
> King: 3 points
> Queen: 2 points
> Jack: 1 point

Distribution Points. Count each occurrence in your hand of each of the following:

> 5-card or 6-card suit: 1 point
> singleton: 1 point
>
> 7-card or 8-card suit: 2 points
> void: 2 points

Exception. Do not count any distribution points for a

> singleton KING
> singleton QUEEN
> singleton JACK

but do count the high-card value involved. (Count a singleton *ace* for both distribution and high-card points.)

Add the high-card points and the distribution points to get your total points. Your total points are a measure of the strength of your hand.

NOTE: If you are already used to a different method of evaluating distribution, see the appendix for a discussion of this subject.

For each of the following hands which you might hold, count up the HCP (high-card points) and the distribution points. Add them together to get your total points.

♠ A K 4 3 ♡ Q 10 9 8 ◇ Q J 3 ♣ 10 2	You have 7 HCP in spades, 2 in hearts, 3 in diamonds and none in clubs, making 12 HCP in all. You have no distribution points. Your total points are therefore 12.
♠ 10 9 8 7 6 ♡ 8 3 2 ◇ 10 7 6 5 ♣ 4	You have no HCP, which is most unusual. In distribution you have 1 point for the five spades and 1 point for the singleton club, making 2 points in all. Your total points are therefore 2.
♠ A Q 10 9 6 5 ♡ — ◇ Q 4 ♣ K Q J 4 2	You have 14 HCP. You also have 4 distribution points—1 for the 6-card spade suit, 2 for the void in hearts, and 1 for the 5-card club suit. Your 14 HCP plus your 4 distribution points give you 18 total points.
♠ A K Q J ♡ A K Q ◇ A K Q ♣ A K Q	You have 37 of the 40 HCP in the pack. I should be so lucky! Are you concerned that you have no distribution points?
♠ K ♡ A K Q J 8 7 6 ◇ J 8 ♣ 5 3 2	You have 14 HCP. The spade king counts for 3 HCP but does not count for distribution. Thus you have 2 distribution points for your heart suit, making 16 total points. When a jack occurs in a doubleton, we are not too happy about it, but we count it anyway.

B

Opening the Bidding

The first person at the table to bid (not pass) on any one deal is called the OPENER. The opener bids for the purpose of:

- Suggesting a denomination (notrump or a suit) in which the hand might be played
- Indicating that his hand contains some strength

The side that opens the bidding is called the OFFENSE.

Deciding Whether to Open

When you are considering whether to open the bidding, use this guideline:

> Always open the bidding when you hold at least 13 total points.

If your hand is balanced, you would like to indicate your interest in notrump. It has been found best to limit each notrump bid to a small point range. The guideline is:

> Open with 1 NOTRUMP whenever you hold:
> - A balanced hand
> - 16, 17, or 18 points (no more, no less)

When your hand does not fit the guideline for opening 1 NOTRUMP, but is strong enough for an opening bid, you must open by bidding a suit. This will announce that you have some strength and it can suggest a possible trump suit. Any interest you may have in notrump must be shown at a later time.

Open with 1 in a SUIT whenever you hold:

- **An unbalanced hand, or a balanced hand not qualifying for 1 NOTRUMP**
- **13 or more points**

For some hands, over 20 points, there are special guidelines which we will come to later.

Would you open the bidding with these hands? If so, would you open with a notrump bid or a suit bid?

♠ A K Q 7 6 4 ♡ K 10 6 ◇ J 10 8 3 ♣ —	This is an unbalanced hand containing 13 HCP and 3 distribution points. You should open in a suit (spades).
♠ Q J 4 3 ♡ Q 8 5 ◇ 2 ♣ Q 9 8 7 4	7 HCP and 2 distribution points are not enough to open the bidding. You must PASS.
♠ K Q 8 ♡ J 9 3 ◇ A J 10 ♣ A 10 9 8	You have 15 points, all in high cards. Your hand is balanced but is not quite in the 1-notrump range. You must open the bidding in a suit (clubs).
♠ 8 2 ♡ K J 10 ◇ A K 9 8 7 ♣ A 8 4	Here you have 15 HCP and 1 distribution point for the long diamonds. The hand is balanced, and 16 points is within the right range to bid 1 NOTRUMP. You should not consider any other bid.

NOTE: Formerly, experts objected to bidding 1 NOTRUMP on the above hand for two reasons: it contains a small doubleton, and one of the 16 points comes from distribution. Today we know that notrump is the best bid for this hand because it describes the hand so precisely.

Choosing a Suit to Open With

In bidding a suit, you are normally suggesting that your partnership may have a fit in that suit, and you are asking your partner if he agrees. For your partner to judge, he must have as good an idea as possible as to how many cards you have in that suit.

When you are opening the bidding in a suit:

- A major suit must contain at least 5 cards
- A minor suit must contain at least 3 cards

In picking a trump suit, you are looking to have a lot of trumps between you and your partner. You do not consider the strength of the trump suit. Of course you want to have strength somewhere in the two hands, but it does not have to be in the trump suit. When you are stuck with bidding a 3-card minor suit, you are not seriously suggesting it as a trump suit, but at least your bid shows your strength. Later in the bidding your partnership will select a trump suit or will select notrump.

Here are some general guidelines which we will use all the time in deciding which suit to bid first:

- When you have several suits of proper length, bid the *longest* suit first.
- In case of a tie between two 5-card suits or two 6-card suits, bid the *higher-ranking* suit first.
- In case of a tie between several 3-card suits or several 4-card suits, bid the *cheapest* suit first.

By "cheapest suit" we mean the one that can be named with the lowest bid on the scale that runs from 1 CLUB to 7 NOTRUMP. For example, on the opening bid the choice will occasionally be between two 3-card minor suits. Clubs is the cheapest bid in this instance.

In the case of several short suits, your partner is just as likely to bid one of them as you are, so you make the cheapest bid to give your partner as much room as possible to bid one of them himself. If the case of long suits, you expect to have to bid one, and if that does not find a fit in your partner's hand, you yourself will have to bid the other. For example, with five hearts and five diamonds, you start with the higher ranking suit:

YOU	PARTNER
1 HEART	1 SPADE
2 DIAMONDS	

Your partner can, if he wishes, pass at 2 DIAMONDS or bid 2 HEARTS. But if you were to bid them in the reverse order, your second bid would be 2 HEARTS. Then if your partner prefers to play in diamonds, he would have to bid 3 DIAMONDS. To avoid getting so high unnecessarily, the guidelines call for starting with the higher ranking of two long suits of equal length.

On the following hands, would you PASS? Or bid 1 SPADE? Or bid 1 HEART? Or 1 DIAMOND? Or 1 CLUB?

♠ K Q 8 7 3 2 You only have 9 points. You must PASS.
♡ 8 4 3
◇ 9 4
♣ K 2

♠ A Q 8 4 3 With 15 points, you can certainly open. This
♡ K 10 is an unbalanced hand, so choose your long-
◇ K Q 5 3 est suit. Bid 1 SPADE.
♣ 8 5

♠ A 4 2
♡ A
◇ 8 7 6 4 2
♣ A K Q 9

You have 19 points. Your clubs are certainly strong, but they are not as long as your diamonds. So bid 1 DIAMOND. The high cards in clubs will be good at any contract.

♠ Q 10 8 5 4
♡ K Q 10 3 2
◇ A K
♣ 9

Now you have 17 points and two 5-card suits to choose from. Choose spades, because they are the higher-ranking. Bid 1 SPADE.

♠ K
♡ K Q J 8 7
◇ 8
♣ A 9 8 4 3 2

This is a rather unusual distribution. You have 13 HCP and 3 distribution points, each one in hearts, diamonds and clubs. The longest suit is clubs so they are bid first: 1 CLUB.

♠ A K 8 3
♡ K 3
◇ 8 7 6 4
♣ Q J 3

Here you have a balanced hand and 13 points—not enough to bid notrump. You have no 5-card suit, and since we don't open in 4-card majors, you must choose 1 DIAMOND, the longer minor.

♠ Q J 6
♡ A 8 5 2
◇ Q J 5
♣ A 9 8

You don't want to pass with 14 points, so you have to face a choice between two 3-card minors. Follow the guidelines—bid 1 CLUB. It's the cheapest bid you can make.

When you are opening the bidding and have to choose between two 4-card minor suits, you will find that the guidelines given above do not always work out to best advantage. This is because after opening with one minor you may need to bid the other later. Therefore it is better to start with the diamonds, the higher-ranking suit, so that you can bid the clubs comfortably later on. This is a special case that applies only to the opening bid—you can ignore it for now if you wish, and make the cheaper club bid.

♠ 5
♡ A Q 4 2
◇ A 5 4 3
♣ A 8 3 2

With 15 points and a choice of minors of equal 4-card length, the diamonds are the better choice. The hearts cannot be picked for the opening bid because they are a major and only 4 cards long.

NOTE: Some people play a variation of Standard American which permits opening with a 4-card major if it contains at least 3 HCP. When no longer suit is available, the highest-ranking eligible 4-card suit is chosen, except that priority is given to any which rank below the shortest suit in the hand. Those who follow this variation are said to play "4-card majors." But "5-card majors," as given in the first guideline in this section, is the choice of almost all experts today. Have an understanding with your partner as to which variation you will use, but we will assume it will be 5-card majors.

C
Overcalling

When the opponents open the bidding, your side is the DEFENSE. That does not bar your side from entering the bidding. But certain precautions are necessary because one opponent is known to be strong, and that leaves fewer points which your partner could hold to help the partnership out.

Overcalling in a Suit

Any bid you make after the opponents have opened the bidding is called an OVERCALL. An overcall in a suit is very unwise unless you have a *good* suit. This is quite different from an opening bid, where you are concerned with length alone. A good suit must contain two of the following:

A   K   Q   J–10

That means that you must hold one of the following combinations of honors (or better) to make a good suit:

A K	A Q	K Q
A J 10	K J 10	Q J 10

If you have a good suit, you are in a position to fight back against the opponents' opening bid. If you can overcall at the 1-level, you can get along with fewer points than you would need for opening. But if you can make your overcall only by bidding at the 2-level, you need slightly better than the minimum for an opening hand.

When you can overcall by bidding *1* in your SUIT, you need:

- A good 5-card suit (or longer)
- 11 points

When you can overcall only by bidding *2* in your SUIT, you need:

- A good 5-card suit (or longer)
- 14 points

Point count is not the most important factor in making an overcall, but we are not ready yet to discuss the other factors. The count given above is the NOMINAL count (the number of points which your partner will assume you have). You may actually have less than the nominal count when there are compensating features in your hand. A good 6-card suit, for example, will compensate for the lack of a point.

Overcalling at the 2-level is particularly dangerous. You are not only more likely to get set, but you are also more likely to be doubled by the opponents. This increases the penalty which you pay, in terms of points awarded to the opponents, if they are able to set you. You will be safer if you hold a good 6-card suit, even if you only hold 13 points. Should the opponents open in notrump, you must absolutely hold a good 6-card suit to overcall because of the extra strength revealed by the opening bid.

Overcalling in Notrump

After the opponents have opened the bidding, you may overcall in notrump with the same kind of hand you could have opened with in notrump. However, you must have a STOPPER (a high card) in the opponents' suit so that you can prevent them from taking all the tricks in that suit. A stopper is usually an ace, a king or a queen-jack combination.

When you want to overcall with a bid of 1 NOTRUMP, you need:

- A balanced hand
- 16, 17 or 18 points
- A stopper in the opponents' suit

Passing

When your hand does not fit the given guidelines, simply pass—even if your hand is quite strong and would have allowed you to open the bidding. In this case you can use your strength to try and set the opponents rather than make some dangerous bid of your own. This also applies when the opponents have bid your best suit. You can pass and know you can give them plenty of trouble.

Your right-hand opponent opened the bidding with 1 DIAMOND. Would you overcall with the following hands? What would you bid?

♠ Q 9 8 6 4
♡ Q J 9
◇ K 7 6
♣ K J

Your RHO has opened the bidding with 1 DIAMOND, so it would be possible for you to overcall 1 SPADE. Should you? No! Although you have 13 points, your suit is not a good one. Simply PASS.

♠ A K 10 8 4
♡ 8 7
◇ 8 4 3 2
♣ K 7

Now you only have 11 points, but you have a good spade suit. Get in there and fight! Bid 1 SPADE.

♠ A 8 4 2
♡ Q 7 4
◇ K J 10 8 2
♣ 9

You have 12 points and a decent diamond suit. If your right-hand opponent had bid 1 CLUB you could overcall with 1 DIA-MOND. But over his opening 1 DIAMOND you will simply PASS.

♠ K Q 8 4 3
♡ A J 10 9 5
◇ K 7
♣ 8

Now you have two good suits to choose from, plus 16 points. You always start with the longer suit, or in case of a tie, start with the higher-ranking one. Overcall 1 SPADE.

♠ A Q 9
♡ K Q 10
◇ A 7 6 4
♣ J 10 8

You were expecting to open with 1 NOTRUMP when your RHO beat you to the opening bid with his 1 DIAMOND. Since you have his diamond suit stopped, your 16 points still call for an overcall of 1 NOTRUMP.

♠ Q 8
♡ Q J 6 3
◇ 4 3
♣ K Q 10 5 4

To make an overcall in clubs, the lowest you can bid is 2 CLUBS. An overcall at the 2-level calls for slightly better than an opening hand. With only 11 points, you must PASS.

♠ A 4 3
♡ K J 7 4
◇ 7
♣ K Q J 7 5

There is no problem overcalling with 2 CLUBS with this hand. You have 16 points and a good club suit.

♠ K Q 10
♡ 10 4
◇ 8 5
♣ A Q J 10 5 4

This hand only adds up to 13 points, but the very good 6-card club suit makes it safe enough for an overcall of 2 CLUBS.

D
Preview of Future Bidding

Here is some typical bidding when you, as opener, have not much more than an opening bid. Let's assume that your partner likewise has minimum values. Both of you will seek a fit and then stop bidding while you are still *below* 2 NOTRUMP.

YOU

♠ K 3 2
♡ Q 8 4
◇ A Q J 4
♣ A J 10

You open with 1 NOTRUMP. If your partner agrees with notrump, he will PASS. (We're assuming he has a minimum hand.) If he disagrees, because his hand is unbalanced, he may respond in his own long suit, say by bidding 2 HEARTS, and you will PASS.

♠ 4 3
♡ A 10 9 6
◇ K Q 8 4
♣ A 3 2

You open with 1 DIAMOND. If your partner responds 1 HEART, you will express agreement by bidding 2 HEARTS and your partner will PASS. But if instead of responding 1 HEART, your partner should respond 1 SPADE, you will bid 1 NOTRUMP with your balanced hand. Now if your partner sees a notrump fit, he will PASS. But if not, he might suggest another suit, say by bidding 2 CLUBS, and you will PASS.

♠ A K 4 3 2
♡ K 10 9 4 3
◇ J 4
♣ 6

You open 1 SPADE. If your partner responds 2 SPADES you are quite happy and will PASS. But if he responds 1 NOTRUMP you will bid 2 HEARTS, asking your partner to choose between spades and hearts. He may PASS if he thinks the partnership has more hearts than spades, or in the opposite case he may bid 2 SPADES and you will PASS.

♠ 9 4
♡ A 8 7 6
◇ A Q J 9 5 2
♣ 9

You open 1 DIAMOND. If your partner responds 1 HEART you are glad to bid 2 HEARTS. But if your partner responds 1 SPADE or 1 NOTRUMP you will rebid your long diamond suit, 2 DIAMONDS, showing your six diamonds. Your partner, being minimum, will PASS even if he is short in diamonds.

From Across the Table

Sometimes it is your partner who opens the bidding. The various bids we have been discussing take on a different perspective when they are made from the other side of the table. Here is a summary of how those bids look when they are made by your partner.

OPENING BID	POINTS PROMISED	SUIT LENGTH PROMISED
Your partner opens 1 CLUB or 1 DIAMOND	13 up	3 cards or more
Your partner opens 1 HEART or 1 SPADE	13 up	5 cards or more
Your partner opens 1 NOTRUMP	16,17,18	no suit less than 2 cards (balanced hand)
OVERCALL		
Your partner overcalls 1 in any SUIT	11 up	5 cards or more
Your partner overcalls 2 in any SUIT	14 up	5 cards or more
Your partner overcalls 1 NOTRUMP	16,17,18	no suit less than 2 cards (balanced hand)

Chapter 4

THE FIRST RESPONSE

A

Additional Bidding Notions

Recognizing a Fit

Your first goal in bidding is to try to find a fit between the two hands in the partnership. A fit gives you a place where the hands may be played comfortably. You must keep the bidding low while searching for a fit.

Remember that a normal notrump fit occurs when both hands in the partnership are balanced. And a normal trump fit occurs when the two hands combined hold eight or more cards in some suit. An 8-card fit could be divided:

x x x x	x x x x	(4 − 4)
x x x x x	x x x	(5 − 3)
x x x x x x	x x	(6 − 2)

or even

x x x x x x x	x	(7 – 1)
x x x x x x x x	—	(8 – 0)

We are more anxious to find certain fits than others. Since we can get to game in a major or in notrump at a lower level than in a minor, we prefer these two. However, a major contract will frequently yield a few more points than a notrump contract, and besides, a trump contract is generally a little more resistant to being set than a notrump contract.

The ideal fits in order of priority are:

1. In a major suit with an 8-card normal trump fit (or better)
2. In notrump with a normal notrump fit (both hands balanced)

When neither of these possibilities exist, we compromise on the next best alternative.

As a compromise, a hand may be played:

- In a minor suit with an 8-card normal trump fit (or better)
- In any suit with a 7-card subnormal trump fit
- In notrump without a normal notrump fit

Your partner has opened 1 NOTRUMP. Does your partnership have a normal fit in notrump when you hold each of the following hands?

♠ 10 8 2
♡ 9 5 4 3
◇ J 8 3
♣ 9 7 6

Your partner has promised a balanced hand and your hand is also balanced. You may not like your hand very well, but you do have a normal notrump fit.

♠ 4
♡ K 8 5 4 3 2
◇ 9 7 5
♣ 10 9 3

This hand is no beauty either. It is unbalanced, so you do not have a notrump fit. Since your partner has shown a balanced hand, he must have at least two hearts. So you know your partnership has a normal fit in hearts (eight cards or more).

♠ K 4
♡ 9 8 5
◇ 10 6 3
♣ A K Q 4 2

This hand is balanced, so you do have a normal fit in notrump. You are more interested in notrump than in any possible fit in clubs, which is a minor.

Your partner has opened 1 HEART, promising at least five hearts. Does your partnership have a normal trump fit in hearts when you hold each of the following hands?

♠ A 10
♡ 4 3 2
◇ A 9 8 3
♣ 10 9 7 5

Your three hearts plus your partner's promised five give your partnership a normal 8-card heart fit. This is true even though your hearts are all small ones.

♠ A 10 9 4 3
♡ J 3
◇ Q 7 3 2
♣ 10 8

Now you can only be sure of seven hearts. Of course your partner could have six hearts, but if so he will normally bid hearts a second time, signaling a 6-card suit. Then you could see a normal heart fit, but for now you cannot. Perhaps your partner will have three spades to go with your five.

♠ J 8 7	Here you have at least a 9-card fit—even
♡ A K 4 2	better than a minimum normal fit.
◇ 9 7 6 5	
♣ 10 8	

Your partner has opened the bidding with 1 DIAMOND. Do you and your partner have a normal fit with the following? (Remember that 1 DIAMOND only promises three cards in the diamond suit.)

♠ 8 3	Your five diamonds with your partner's prom-
♡ K 2	ised three surely give your side a normal
◇ Q 8 7 6 4	diamond fit. If your partner has more than
♣ J 10 4 3	three diamonds, your fit is even better. For
	now, assume an 8-card fit.

♠ J 10 9 7 6 3	If your partner has three diamonds and you
♡ 4	have three, that only makes six. The oppo-
◇ A K 2	nents would have more diamonds than your
♣ 8 6 5	side would. That is no fit at all. Perhaps you
	can find a fit in spades.

♠ 4 2	If your partner has three diamonds, you have
♡ 8 7 6	a 7-card fit—a subnormal fit, but at least
◇ A K 6 5	some kind of fit. Of course your partner may
♣ 10 9 8 3	have additional diamonds, but you can't tell
	at this time.

The Value of Strength

Experience has shown that it is as difficult to succeed at a three notrump contract as it is at a 4-level contract in a suit. Also, two notrump is as difficult as a 3-level suit contract and so on. So we consider that:

- 1 NOTRUMP is at the 2-level
- 2 NOTRUMP is at the 3-level
- 3 NOTRUMP is at the 4-level

Up to the game level we can visualize the bidding space as follows:

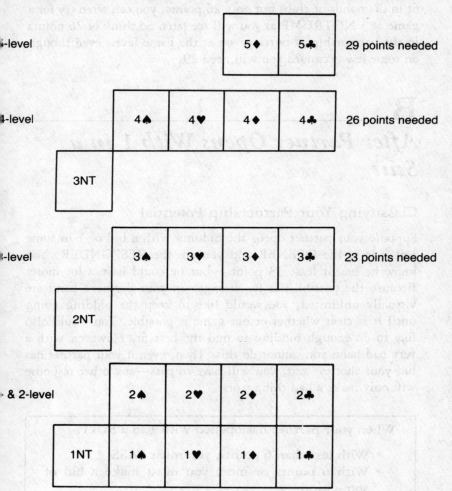

Experience has shown that 26 points in the two hands within your partnership will usually permit a 4-level contract to be made. With 26 points you will try to reach a game contract of 3 NOTRUMP or 4 SPADES or 4 HEARTS. With 29 points you may bid 5 DIAMONDS or 5 CLUBS, but your partnership won't get that many points very often. When you are frustrated, with a good fit in diamonds or clubs but only 26 points, you can often try for a game at 3 NOTRUMP as you will see later. So think of 26 points in the partnership as putting you at the game level, even though on some few occasions you will need 29.

B

After Partner Opens With 1 in a Suit

Classifying Your Partnership Potential

Suppose your partner opens the bidding with a bid of 1 in some suit. He is the OPENER and you are the RESPONDER. You know he has at least 13 points—but he could have a lot more. Because the possibilities for strength in your partner's hand are virtually unlimited, you would like to keep the bidding going until it is clear whether or not game is possible. You would also like to do enough bidding to find the best fit. However, with a very bad hand you cannot do this. Then, even if your partner has bid your shortest suit, you will have to pass—any other response will only make a bad thing worse.

When your partner has opened with 1 in a SUIT:

- With less than 6 points, you must PASS.
- With 6 points or more you must make a bid of some kind.

Whenever you have at least 6 points, and therefore plan to respond with a bid, you add your points to the 13 points promised by your partner to get the PARTNERSHIP POINTS known to you. You use this total to make a tentative classification of the partnership potential. You base this classification on the fact that it takes 26 points for a good chance at making a 4-level contract and 23 points for a good chance at making a 3-level contract.

For suit bidding, when your partnership points are:

- At least 26, your partnership is at the game level
- At least 23, your partnership is at the near-game level
- Below 23, your partnership is at the minimum level

Your partner has opened the bidding with 1 HEART. As you see it at this time, is your partnership at the game level? The near-game level? Or the minimum level?

YOU

♠ K Q 3 2
♡ Q 5 4
◇ A 10 9 3
♣ K 9

Your 14 points plus the 13 promised by your partner bring the partnership points to 27. Your partnership is at the game level.

♠ A 9 8
♡ A 10 5
◇ 9 7 4 3
♣ Q 10 8

You have 10 points. That brings the partnership just up to 23 points. You are at the near-game level as you see it now. Perhaps your partner will actually have enough extra points to bring you to the game level, but you must act on the assumption that you are at the near-game level until you find out otherwise.

♠ 8 7
♡ Q 3 2
◇ A 9 7 6
♣ 5 4 3 2

You can scrape up just 6 points. If you had any less you would not even be able to bid. It is hardly necessary to compute the partnership total of 19 points to know that your partnership is at a minimum level as it appears to you now.

For now we are going to give the most attention to the minimum level. When *both* partners have minimum hands, you both will cooperate in the search for a fit. You both will keep the bidding below 2 NOTRUMP. You both will stop bidding as soon as any kind of fit is found, even a poor one. The bidding space available for this FIT AND QUIT strategy is:

1- & 2-level	2♠	2♥	2♦	2♣
1NT	1♠	1♥	1♦	1♣

As responder you will consider your hand MINIMUM but biddable whenever you hold 6, 7, 8, 9 points. With less you could not bid at all, with 10 points you would count 23 partnership points, which is better than minimum. With a minimum biddable hand for responding to your partner's opening bid, you will make one of the following conservative bids:

- If you can find some kind of fit for your partner's suit, you may RAISE it (make another bid in your partner's suit).

- You may bid another suit if you can do so at the *1-level*.

- You may bid 1 NOTRUMP.

Let's explore these possibilities.

Raising

RESPONDING WITH A SINGLE RAISE
When you see a fit in your partner's suit, you should consider making a SINGLE RAISE. For example, a single raise of your partner's 1 HEART bid means bidding hearts at the next level:

PARTNER   YOU

1 HEART   2 HEARTS

When your partner opens the bidding with 1 HEART, you should take a look immediately at your holding in hearts. Your partner is suggesting hearts as the trump suit. The cards you hold in hearts are your SUPPORT for his suit. The number of cards you hold in his suit is the most important thing, not the size of them, because you would like to have lots of trumps.

A single raise declares that you have a fit, and that your strength is limited to that of a minimum hand. You must see less than 23 partnership points to make this bid. With more, you must take some other action. When your partner hears you make a single raise, and your partner also counts less than 23 partnership points, he will pass knowing that game is out of the question. Only if he counts more will he continue.

When raising your partner's suit to the 2-level you need:

- 3-card support (or better) when raising a major suit
- 4-card support (or better) when raising a minor suit
- At least 6 points
- Partnership points below 23

Do not raise a minor suit when you have a major suit which you can bid at the 1-level.

When your partner opens in a major suit, you are pleased to raise with 3-card support in your hand. Your partnership has a normal trump fit in a major, which is the best place to play the hand. But when your partner opens in a minor suit, your first thought is to look for an opportunity in the majors. If your hand gives you a choice, you would rather respond to your partner's opening 1

DIAMOND with 1 HEART or 1 SPADE rather than with 2 DIAMONDS.

When it is not feasible to bid a major, you consider raising your partner's minor with 4-card support. If you were to raise a minor with only 3-card support, and then found your partner also with three cards, your partnership would be in the woeful position of holding only six trumps while the opponents hold seven. Even with the required 4-card support, your side may have only a 7-card fit, but usually your partner will have more than the minimum length of three cards.

Your partner has opened the bidding with 1 SPADE. Should you respond 2 SPADES with the following hands? Be sure to check both your fit and your strength.

♠ Q 9 3 ♡ K 2 ◇ Q 5 3 ♣ J 8 7 5 2	You have a normal spade fit and 9 points. The partnership points come to 22 (your 9 plus your partner's promised 13). You are in the right range for a single raise, so bid 2 SPADES.
♠ 7 6 5 ♡ 9 8 ◇ K 7 6 3 ♣ J 10 8 3	You have at least eight spades in the partnership. But in spite of your normal fit, you only hold a count of 4 points. That is not enough to bid, so you will have to PASS.
♠ A K ♡ 10 9 7 3 ◇ Q 8 3 ♣ 8 7 5 2	Your ace-king combination in spades is nice, but not long enough. There is no normal fit in spades. A raise cannot be your bid. (1 NOTRUMP would be correct.)
♠ 4 3 2 ♡ A 10 9 8 ◇ Q 6 5 4 ♣ 8 2	Now you have a normal spade fit and 6 points. This is a minimum, but still enough to bid 2 SPADES.
♠ 9 ♡ J 8 7 6 3 ◇ 8 5 4 ♣ 10 9 8 2	You should be very unhappy about your partner's spade bid. (Couldn't he have at least picked another suit?) You can't possibly bid with this terrible hand, so just PASS.

♠ A K 4 ♡ 8 3 ◇ J 6 2 ♣ A 9 7 3 2	You have an 8-card fit and a count of 13. That makes a total of 26 points in the partnership—too many for a bid of 2 SPADES. You will have to find other means of communicating the fit and the strength of this hand to your partner.

Your partner has opened 1 DIAMOND. Should you raise to 2 DIAMONDS with these hands?

♠ K 7 5 ♡ Q 2 ◇ 7 6 5 4 ♣ J 9 7 5	You have 6 points and at least a subnormal 7-card fit in diamonds. You have no major suit so you have to take your chances on 2 DIAMONDS. To pass would be wrong—with 6 points you always make a bid even if you have some reservations about it.
♠ A J 3 ♡ 8 5 4 ◇ A 8 7 ♣ 9 4 3 2	You have 9 points but no support for diamonds. You will soon find out that a bid of 1 NOTRUMP is right for this hand.
♠ A 2 ♡ Q 10 9 ◇ J 10 5 4 3 ♣ 9 4 2	Your diamonds provide at least an 8-card fit, since your partner must have at least three diamonds. You have 8 points and you see 21 partnership points. Bid 2 DIAMONDS.
♠ K 10 9 7 ♡ Q 5 ◇ Q 10 8 4 ♣ 9 8 5	You have 7 points and support for diamonds. But first you must sound out the possibility of a fit in spades by bidding 1 SPADE. If that does not work out, you will fall back on the diamonds.

REVALUATION

When you are able to raise your partner, you can rejoice that you have found a fit. If your hand provides a trump fit which is longer than eight cards, your hand becomes worth more than before. Furthermore, singletons and voids in your hand increase in value. If your side wins the contract in your partner's suit, your hand becomes the dummy. Your partner, as declarer, can probably use one or more of your small trumps to ruff some of the losing cards which he may hold in your short suit.

The process of adjusting your original point count upward because of a good fit with your partner is called REVALUATION. Sometimes a hand which does not originally have enough points for a response will acquire the necessary 6 points through revaluation.

Revaluate when raising your partner's suit by adding:

- 1 additional point for each card over 8 which you see in your partnership in the proposed trump suit

Providing that you hold at least 3-card support, also add:

- 1 additional point for each singleton
- 2 additional points for each void

What is each of the following hands worth before you hear your partner's opening bid? What is each worth if your partner opens with 1 HEART? In each case, should you raise to 2 HEARTS?

♠ K 3 ♡ 7 5 4 2 ◊ Q 9 8 5 ♣ 10 8 3	Before you hear your partner's bid, you have a count of 5. But if your partner opens with 1 HEART, you see a 9-card fit which is worth an extra point. Now you have 6 points and can raise to 2 HEARTS.
♠ 9 8 7 6 ♡ Q 5 3 ◊ A 10 9 8 4 ♣ 6	You have an original count of 8 points. If your partner opens with 1 HEART, you have a normal 8-card heart fit. Your singleton is now worth an extra point, bringing your revaluated total up to 9.

♠ 5 2
♡ K J 8 7 4
◇ 9 8
♣ 7 6 5 2

Your original 5 points shoot up to 7 when you see the 10-card heart fit. You can now bid 2 HEARTS. If your partner had opened in any other suit, you would have to pass with only 5 points.

♠ 10
♡ J 10 8 5
◇ A J 4 3
♣ 9 6 5 2

Your original count of 7 goes up to 9 when your partner opens in hearts. If he had opened in clubs or diamonds, you would (probably) have an 8-card fit, and the value of your hand would be unchanged. But if he had opened in spades, your hand would actually be worth a point less—a singleton (or void) in your partner's suit is not worth anything. Do you see how the value of your hand changes with the bidding?

RAISING A SUIT OVERCALL

When your partner has overcalled, as opposed to opening, you are very interested in raising his suit. The bidding has become a competition. If you have a fit, you can compete.

OPPONENT	PARTNER	OPPONENT	YOU
1 HEART	1 SPADE	PASS	2 SPADES

or perhaps

OPPONENT	PARTNER	OPPONENT	YOU
1 HEART	1 SPADE	2 HEARTS	2 SPADES

When you are the overcaller's partner, you can raise by following essentially the same guidelines as you would if you were the opener's partner. There are two differences:

• Any suit your partner overcalls in has five or more cards, so 3-card support is always enough—even to support a minor suit.
• Your partner may overcall with less strength or at a higher level

than when he is opening, so you will generally pass when you only hold 6 points, but you should not hold back a raise when you hold 7 points or more after revaluation.

If your partner overcalls and you cannot raise him, any other bid you might make will probably be wrong. So for now, simply pass when you cannot raise.

You may have gotten the feeling by now that bidding on the defensive is different from bidding on the offensive. It certainly is, although there are some similarities. We can't go into details at this point, but you can see that it involves being aggressive when you have a fit, and being cautious when a fit seems unlikely.

What do you bid on the following hands after the bidding has proceeded as indicated?

OPPONENT	PARTNER	OPPONENT	YOU
1 DIAMOND	1 HEART	2 DIAMONDS	???

♠ K 4 3
♡ Q 9 7 3
♢ 8
♣ 10 9 5 3 2

Your hand originally had 7 points but it is worth 9 now that your partner has bid hearts. Your singleton in the opponents' suit is particularly valuable. Raise with a bid of 2 HEARTS.

♠ A K 8 7 4
♡ 9 8 3
♢ 5 2
♣ J 10 8

You have 9 points and support for hearts. Do not bid spades, where a fit is speculative. Bid 2 HEARTS.

♠ K 9 8 4 3
♡ 3 2
♢ J 8 7
♣ A 4 3

Although you can count 9 points you should downgrade that to 8: queens and jacks in the opponents' suit tend to be worthless. You have no support for hearts so you must PASS. When both sides are bidding, you must be conservative without a fit.

♠ A 10 8
♡ Q 8 7
◇ 8 5
♣ 9 7 5 4 2

This is a minimum 7-point hand which just barely justifies a raise to 2 HEARTS. Your five small clubs are probably worthless—a weak side suit in a weak hand doesn't do much toward producing tricks.

OPPONENT	PARTNER	OPPONENT	YOU
1 SPADE	2 HEARTS	2 SPADES	???

♠ 9 7
♡ K 9 4
◇ A J 8 7
♣ 10 9 7 4

To raise your partner you will have to go to the 3-level. However you have 8 points and good support for your partner. So raise to 3 HEARTS, outbidding the opponents and leaving them to figure out what to do next.

Responding to the Opening Bid with a New Suit at the 1-level

When your partner opens the bidding in a suit, he is suggesting a possible trump suit. You may not be able to accept his suggestion simply because you do not support his suit adequately. Or, if his suit is a minor and you hold a major, you will want to make a counter-suggestion before settling on his suit. For example:

PARTNER	YOU
1 DIAMOND	1 HEART

Your 1 HEART bid is called a 1-OVER-1 SHIFT because you have bid at the 1-level over your partner's 1-level bid, and you have shifted from his suit to a NEW suit not previously bid by anyone.

To respond with a new suit at the 1-level you need:

- A 4-card suit
- 6 points or more

As long as you have at least 6 points, you can always bid a new suit at the 1-level. But with a minimum hand (partnership points below 23) you must rule out a *new* suit which can only be bid at the 2-level. For example, over your partner's opening 1 DIAMOND you must not respond 2 CLUBS as long as the partnership points are below 23. You will have to ignore your club suit with a minimum hand. However, you may raise your partner's suit with a bid of 2 DIAMONDS, even with a minimum, because you have a fit in diamonds.

As an opening bid you would choose a major suit only if it contained at least five cards. But after the opening bid you may choose a major as long as it has at least four cards. Minor suits chosen after the opening bid are normally at least four cards long. On rare occasions you may have to make do with a 3-card minor, but never a 3-card major.

When you have a choice of suits with which to respond, use the general guideline given before: The longer suit first, the higher ranking of equally long 5-card or 6-card suits, the cheapest of equally long 4-card suits.

Unlike a raise, a bid in a new suit is virtually unlimited in strength. It may be bid when your hand is minimum and also when it is much stronger. This solves the problem of what to do when you would like to raise your partner but your hand is too strong for a single raise. You must bid a new suit first and then show your support by raising later. This maneuver, like the mating dance of certain birds, creates a distraction at first, but the true intent will be shown later.

When the bidding starts with two suits, such as:

OPENER	RESPONDER
1 DIAMOND	1 HEART

each partner knows the minimum value which the other must hold (opener at least 13, responder at least 6), but neither knows even approximately how much additional the other may hold. Since neither can judge the full potential of the two hands, the bidding must not stop after two suits have been bid in succession. The opener must bid again unless the opponents intervene with a bid.

Your partner has opened the bidding with 1 HEART. Should you bid 1 SPADE with these hands?

♠ K Q 3 2 ♡ Q 2 ◇ 8 7 4 3 ♣ 10 7 6	You have 7 points and no support for hearts. A bid of 1 SPADE is quite clear.
♠ K Q 3 2 ♡ Q 6 2 ◇ 8 7 4 3 ♣ 10 7	This is like the previous hand but now you have heart support. Since you have a fit in a major, there is no sense in looking for a fit elsewhere. Respond with 2 HEARTS.
♠ K Q 3 2 ♡ Q 6 2 ◇ 8 7 4 3 ♣ A 7	Again we have the same hand with a difference: The count here is 11 points, putting the partnership total at 24 in the near-game range. You know you are going to play in hearts, but 2 HEARTS at this time would show a minimum hand. Save your heart raise for later and TEMPORIZE (bide time) with 1 SPADE. Your partner must not pass, and you will be able to reveal your heart fit later.
♠ Q 9 6 5 ♡ 8 2 ◇ A J 6 5 3 2 ♣ 8	You have 9 points. You have no support for hearts so you cannot revaluate your hand. The partnership points come to 22—still in the minimum range. You can and should bid 1 SPADE. You must ignore your longer diamond suit because you are not strong enough to make a bid at the 2-level.

Your partner has opened the bidding with 1 CLUB. What should you bid with these hands?

♠ 6 4 3 2
♡ J 3
◇ K J 8
♣ A 8 5 3

You must bid 1 SPADE with your 9 points and your 4-card spade suit. Raising clubs is wrong when there is a possible major fit. If the spades look weak, remember they will be just as weak if clubs are trump, and then they will have no ruffing power.

♠ K J 10 7
♡ J 9 8 6
◇ 8 4
♣ Q J 5

Here you have 8 points and a choice of suits. You choose a response of 1 HEART, the cheaper of the two 4-card suits. The strength of the suits is not a factor in our guideline for selecting among suits.

♠ 10 9 8 5 4
♡ A Q 8 7 2
◇ 4
♣ 5 2

You should be able to choose 1 SPADE fearlessly. The higher ranking of two 5-card suits is correct. Your points are 9, the partnership points are 22 as you see them.

♠ A 9
♡ Q 9 8
◇ A J 10 3 2
♣ 8 3 2

In this hand you have 12 points, bringing the total for the partnership up to 25. However you may still bid 1 DIAMOND because a 1-over-1 shift is not limited to use with minimum hands. Your partner will only know about 6 of your 12 points, but he must bid again, and you can carry on from there.

Responding with 1 NOTRUMP

You will find some minimum hands that do not lend themselves to raising your partner's suit or to bidding a new suit at the 1-level. The solution is to use the 1 NOTRUMP RESPONSE. For example:

PARTNER	YOU
1 HEART	1 NOTRUMP

As used by the *responder*, a 1 NOTRUMP bid is a bid of last resort. You will choose it only when no other bid is available. You may use it whether you are responding with a balanced hand or an unbalanced hand. Since the 1 NOTRUMP RESPONSE is a make-do bid, not necessarily very suitable for notrump, we will refer to it as the "flaky notrump." We will have to treat it somewhat differently from the normal notrump bid, which is based on a balanced hand and a positive liking for notrump.

When you use the flaky 1 NOTRUMP RESPONSE you are likely to find that your partnership does not have a normal notrump fit, either because your hand is unbalanced or because your partner's hand is unbalanced. When there is a danger of having no normal fit, you must stop counting any distribution points which you may have. In other words, you will count only your high-card points. This adjustment in point count is called DEVALUATION.

The 1 NOTRUMP RESPONSE, like the single raise, declares that your hand is minimum. You must see less than 23 partnership points to make this bid. The bidding may stop after a 1 NOTRUMP RESPONSE because it reveals a hand of limited value.

Sometimes you will be considering a 1 NOTRUMP RESPONSE when your partner's opening bid has been overcalled by a suit bid by your right-hand opponent. Whenever you bid notrump after the opponents have bid a suit, you must have a STOPPER (a high card which will take a trick) in the suit the opponents have bid. If you do not, you may have to pass, even holding 6 points.

When responding with the 1 NOTRUMP RESPONSE you need:

- 6 points after devaluation
- Less than 23 partnership points
- A stopper in any suit which the opponents have bid

Do not respond 1 NOTRUMP if you can find another bid.

Your partner has opened the bidding with 1 HEART. Should you pass, raise, bid a new suit 1-over-1, or bid 1 NOTRUMP with these hands:

♠ 9 3 ♡ Q 3 7 ◇ J 10 9 4 ♣ A 10 8 7	This 7-point hand contains support for your partner's heart suit. Bid 2 HEARTS.
♠ J 10 8 5 ♡ Q 4 ◇ K Q 8 7 4 ♣ 9 5	Here you have 9 points but no heart support. You cannot bid your diamonds at the 1-level, so that possibility is out. But you have a spade suit, so bid 1 SPADE.
♠ A 9 8 ♡ 4 2 ◇ A 10 9 8 ♣ 10 8 4 3	Now you have no heart support and no suit you can bid at the 1-level with your mini-mum 8-point hand. All of your points are in high cards, so they are all valuable for a response of 1 NOTRUMP.
♠ K J 3 ♡ 4 ◇ K 9 7 6 ♣ J 8 4 3 2	Again you have no alternative but 1 NOTRUMP. When you count only the HCP you still have 8 points left. Your hand is unbalanced, which is acceptable, even if not desirable, for the 1 NOTRUMP RE-SPONSE.
♠ 9 ♡ 5 2 ◇ K 9 8 4 2 ♣ Q 6 5 3 2	When you first look at this hand you count 8 points. If your partner were to open 1 DIA-MOND or 1 CLUB, you could manage a raise. But after his 1 HEART, your hand devaluates to only 5 HCP. You must PASS.
♠ A Q 3 ♡ 5 4 ◇ K 9 7 4 ♣ Q 7 6 4	This hand is to remind you that sometimes you are too strong to respond 1 NOTRUMP. Your 11 points bring the partnership total up to 24. If you were able to guess that 2 CLUBS should be your response, you did very well.

Responding with a New Suit at the 2-level

Suppose the bidding starts:

PARTNER	YOU
1 HEART	???

If you hold 6 points and cannot raise hearts, you may want to suggest another suit. Holding spades, you might bid 1 SPADE. Now two suits have been bid in a row, and your partner must continue bidding (unless the opponents intervene with a bid). Nevertheless, your side can end up as low as 1 NOTRUMP or 2 SPADES if both hands are minimum. All is well—you can stop at the 2-level.

But now suppose you hold diamonds instead of spades. To suggest diamonds you must bid 2 DIAMONDS, a 2-OVER-1 shift. Again, your partner must continue bidding in response to your new suit. His next logical bid might be 2 NOTRUMP or 3 CLUBS. Both of these bids are at the 3-level. Since your diamond bid at the 2-level may eventually push the partnership up to the 3-level, you must hold enough points to bring the partnership total up to 23. (Your partner opened with possibly only 13 points so you must hold at least 10 for bidding a new suit at the 2-level.)

Here we go, possibly to the 3-level, possibly without a fit! Your side may end up in notrump as the only playable place even though one or both hands are unbalanced! We have a general guideline which is particularly important when bidding a new suit at the 2-level:

With no support for your partner's suit, devalue your hand.

With no normal 8-card fit, you must count only high-card points. If you eventually find a normal fit, you can revive any distribution points.

Once in a while you will want to raise your partner's suit but find that you are too strong for a single raise. You must TEMPORIZE with a bid in a new suit. Now there is no question of fit. Even if your suit must be bid at the 2-level, you do not have to devaluate your hand. You know that you can bid your partner's suit later and have a normal fit.

It is very important to have a sound bid when you make a 2-over-1 shift. If you have exactly 10 points (partnership points just 23) and only a shaky 2-over-1 shift to bid, you will do better to pretend that you only have 9 points and bid accordingly. This is typical of the kind of judgment you have to use in bridge. You may upgrade or downgrade your hand by a point based on specific good or bad factors which you can identify in your hand.

Whenever you respond to an opening suit bid with a new suit, two suits have been bid in a row and your partner is required to bid again. He is relieved of this obligation only if the next opponent intervenes with a bid. But in either case you are guaranteed to get another chance to bid. That is why you can freely bid a new suit, even with a strong hand, and not have to worry that the bidding will die at too low a level before you have had the chance to explore the possibilities of a game.

To respond with a new suit at the 2-level you need:

- A 4-card suit
- 10 points or more (23 or more partnership points)

DEVALUATE YOUR HAND IF YOU DO NOT HAVE SUPPORT FOR YOUR PARTNER.

If you have a choice of suits, use the general guidelines which we gave before. On rare occasions you may have to make do with a 3-card minor, but never a 3-card major.

Your partner has opened with 1 HEART. How do you respond with these hands?

♠ A J 3 ♡ 8 5 ♢ A Q 9 8 5 ♣ 9 5 4	Here you have originally 12 points, but with no support for your partner the hand devaluates to 11 HCP. That brings the partnership up to 24 so you have no problem in bidding 2 DIAMONDS.
♠ 9 ♡ Q 2 ♢ A K 4 3 ♣ K J 10 8 7 6	This hand has 13 HCP plus 2 distribution points. Setting aside the distribution points for now, the 13 HCP are more than enough to bid your longest suit, 2 CLUBS.
♠ K 9 5 4 ♡ 7 ♢ Q 8 7 4 3 ♣ A J 9	Remember that you should bid your longest suit first whenever you can. In this case you can because of your 10 HCP. Bid 2 DIAMONDS. With a minimum hand you would ignore the diamonds and bid spades.
♠ A 10 9 8 ♡ A ♢ Q 8 4 3 ♣ 9 6 5 2	Now you have a choice among three 4-card suits. Your 10 HCP are enough to bid either at the 1-level or 2-level. The cheapest bid is your choice among 4-card suits: 1 SPADE.
♠ 7 5 ♡ 8 4 3 2 ♢ A Q 9 4 ♣ K J 4	Your support for hearts tells you that hearts is the suit. However, you have 11 points after allowing for the 9-card fit in hearts. This is too much for a single raise so you respond first with 2 DIAMONDS.
♠ 9 3 ♡ 10 ♢ A Q J 8 5 ♣ K 9 6 4 3	This distribution gives you a choice of two long suits, and of course your choice will be the higher-ranking, 2 DIAMONDS, for your first response.

C

Limited and Unlimited Bids

You have seen that some bids are LIMITED to a narrow range of a few points. All bids in notrump fall into this category. So also do all bids in a suit which your side has bid before. That leaves only the bids in a NEW SUIT (one which your side has not already bid). New-suit bids are based on some minimum number of points but are virtually UNLIMITED as to how high they may range.

The Forcing Concept

If your partner makes any of the limited bids, and game is not in sight, you may pass. This is your normal action when you have a minimum hand. But if your partner bids a new suit, which is an unlimited bid, you cannot tell whether your side has a game or not. We have already said that after two suits have been bid in a row, the bidding must not stop. The new-suit bid by your partner FORCES (requires) you to bid again unless your right-hand opponent intervenes with a bid. Either way, your partner is guaranteed another chance to bid. The principle is:

> The responder has FULL FORCING POWER: A new suit by the responder is forcing.

NOTE: There is an exception to the principle which we will come to later but which should be mentioned now. When an opening 1 NOTRUMP is followed by a response in a suit, this is not a case of two suits being bid in succession. A minimum new-suit response to an opening 1 NOTRUMP is a weak, limited bid and is not forcing. Since the opener is also limited, he always passes such a bid.

The Effect on Bidding Space

You can see in the following pictures how limited bids fit within the 2-level.

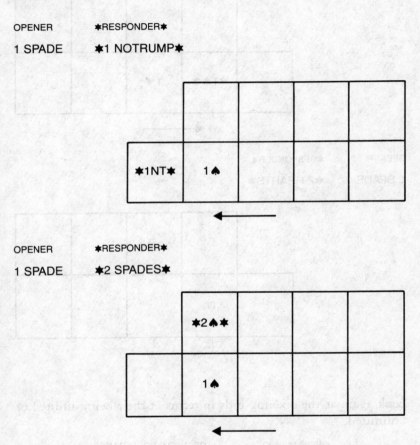

OPENER   ★RESPONDER★

1 SPADE   ★1 NOTRUMP★

OPENER   ★RESPONDER★

1 SPADE   ★2 SPADES★

Can you also see in the pictures below that the 1-over-1 leaves plenty of room to continue bidding within the 2-level whereas the 2-over-1 does not?

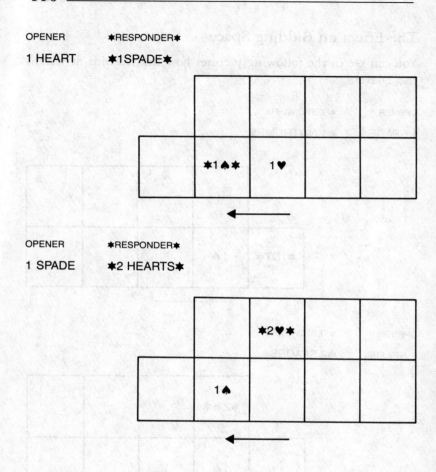

OPENER   ★RESPONDER★

1 HEART   ★1SPADE★

OPENER   ★RESPONDER★

1 SPADE   ★2 HEARTS★

Look again at the opening bids in terms of their being limited or unlimited.

OPENER'S BID	OPENER'S POINT RANGE	
1 NOTRUMP	limited	16,17,18
1 in a SUIT	unlimited	13 up

And now look at the responses to 1 in a SUIT.

RESPONDER'S BID	RESPONDER'S POINT RANGE	
1 NOTRUMP	limited	6,7,8,9
single raise	limited	6,7,8,9
1 in new SUIT	unlimited	6 up
2 in new SUIT	unlimited	10 up

You can see that 1 NOTRUMP and the single raise are appropriate only when the responder has a minimum hand and therefore sees partnership points below 23. The 1-over-1 shift can be used with any responding hand, minimum or above minimum, as long as it has enough points to bid at all. The 2-over-1 shift must be reserved for hands which at least bring the partnership points up to 23.

Chapter 5 ///

THE REBIDS

///

Now we are going to put you back into the opener's seat. When you bid for the second time, much of your bidding will be based on what you have already learned. However, we need to look at two cases: Your partner has made a 1-over-1 response, and your partner has made a 2-over-1 response.

A

Rebidding after a 1-over-1 Response

Suppose you have opened in diamonds and your partner has responded in hearts:

YOU	PARTNER
1 DIAMOND	1 HEART
???	

Your partner has made a 1-over-1 shift, introducing a second suit into the bidding. When the bidding starts with two suits bid one after the other, the opener must make another bid following the principle that:

A new suit by the responder is forcing.

While your partner has only promised 6 points, he could have a lot more. So this is no time to stop bidding.

To determine the partnership points as they appear to you as the opener, add your own points to the 6 points promised you by your partner. If these partnership points number less than 23, there is no game in sight as yet. Your hand is classified as MINIMUM. In fact, you will have 13, 14, 15, 16 points (with more you would reach 23 partnership points). You will have to make a conservative bid, keeping the bidding low while searching for a fit. In the example above, you might bid:

- 2 HEARTS, raising your partner's suit
- 2 DIAMONDS, rebidding your own suit
- 1 NOTRUMP, showing a balanced hand and real notrump interest
- 1 SPADE, bidding a new suit at the 1-level
- 2 CLUBS, bidding a new suit which is lower-ranking than your opening suit and therefore has to be bid at the 2-level

Now we can look at each of these.

Raising the Responder's Suit

You have opened the bidding and your partner has responded with a 1-over-1 shift. You are considering giving a single raise in your partner's suit, for example:

YOU	PARTNER
1 DIAMOND	1 HEART
2 HEARTS	

This is very similar to the raise we have already looked at. You are promising a fit and a limited minimum hand. You can revaluate your hand and apply essentially the same guideline as before:

When raising your partner's suit to the 2-level, you need:

- 3-card support (or better) when raising a major suit
- 4-card support (or better) when raising a minor suit
- Partnership points below 23 after revaluation

When your partner *opens* in a major, he is promising a 5-card suit. But this is not true of a subsequent bid in a major. In the example, your partner's response of 1 HEART promises only four hearts although five or more are also possible. You raise with three hearts in the hope that your partner may have more than four—you don't want to miss the possibility of an 8-card major fit. But you are aware that your partnership may have only a 7-card subnormal fit.

Rebidding the Opening Suit

After you have opened the bidding, you may consider rebidding your own suit at the 2-level.

YOU	PARTNER
1 DIAMOND	1 HEART
2 DIAMONDS	

Like a raise to the 2-level, this bid is made only with a minimum hand. But there is no question of revaluation since no fit for your partner's suit is involved.

When you rebid your own suit at the 2-level, you need:

- A 6-card suit (or longer)
- Partnership points below 23

Do not rebid a minor when you have a major which could be bid at the 1-level.

In contemporary bidding it is quite rare to rebid your own suit before your partner has supported it (by raising it) unless your suit contains at least six cards.

Bidding Notrump After Opening the Bidding

A balanced hand often leads to a notrump contract. With a balanced hand you want to suggest this by bidding notrump as soon as you can. Only a normal 8-card fit in a major takes precedence over a normal notrump fit. Here is a broadened guideline to use when you open the bidding with a balanced hand:

When opening the bidding with a balanced hand:

- With 13, 14, 15 points, open in a suit and next bid notrump unless an opportunity in the majors presents itself.
- With 16, 17, 18 points, open immediately with 1 NOTRUMP.

Here again you see the common device used in bidding. Since there are not enough bids to show all possible notrump ranges at once, with some ranges you temporize by bidding a suit first and then bidding notrump later. For example:

YOU	PARTNER
1 DIAMOND	1 SPADE
1 NOTRUMP	

The delayed notrump bid by the opener is a normal notrump bid, not to be confused with the somewhat flaky 1 NOTRUMP RESPONSE, bid by the responder. As the responder you may bid 1 NOTRUMP even with an unbalanced hand, but as the opener you must not if you can avoid it.

Summary of the Opener's Limited Rebids

The three rebids for the opener which we have just discussed are all limited bids. They declare that the opener has a minimum hand, and the responder may pass.

After the responder bids 1-over-1:

- The opener rebids his own suit with 13,14,15,16.
- The opener raises his partner's suit with 13,14,15,16.
- The opener bids a delayed notrump with 13,14,15.

The first two are limited for use when your hand has no more than 16, which keeps the partnership points below 23. The delayed notrump is limited to a top of 15 because with more you would have opened with 1 NOTRUMP. As a matter of fact, it is typical for raises of one's partner's suit and rebids of one's own suit to be limited to a 4-point range, and for notrump bids to be limited to a 3-point range. (The flaky 1 NOTRUMP response, being a pariah, falls with the suit bids and has a 4-point range of 6,7,8,9.)

Pictorially the bidding looks as follows:

OPENER	★RESPONDER★

1 DIAMOND	★1 HEART★
2 HEARTS	

		2♥	
		★1♥★	1♦

←

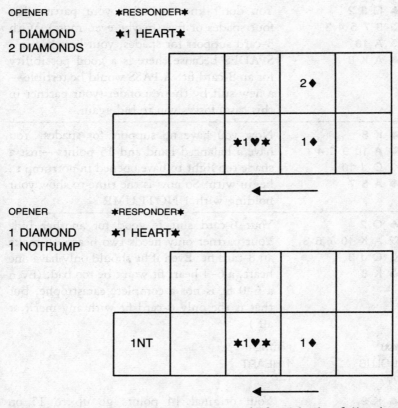

OPENER   ♣RESPONDER♣

1 DIAMOND   ♣1 HEART♣
2 DIAMONDS

OPENER   ♣RESPONDER♣

1 DIAMOND   ♣1 HEART♣
1 NOTRUMP

You are the opener. What is your rebid with the following hands?

YOU   PARTNER
1 HEART   1 SPADE
???

♠ J 9 8 7   Your partner must have at least four spades,
♡ K Q J 7 5   so you see an 8-card fit and contemplate a
◇ A J 8   raise. Your singleton club revaluates to an
♣ 5   additional point. Now with 15 points (21
     partnership points) you are not too strong to
     bid 2 SPADES.

♠ Q 3 2
♡ 9 7 5 4 3
◇ A 10
♣ A K 8

You don't know whether your partner has four spades or five (maybe even more). With 3-card support for spades, your best bid is 2 SPADES because there is a good possibility for an 8-card fit. A PASS would be terrible— a new suit by the responder (your partner in this case) forces you to bid again.

♠ K 8
♡ A 10 9 5 4
◇ Q J 10
♣ A 8 7

Now you have no support for spades. You have a balanced hand and 15 points—just a shade too light to have opened in notrump to begin with. So now is the time to show your holding with 1 NOTRUMP.

♠ Q 2
♡ A K 10 7 5 3
◇ Q J 3
♣ K 8

Your 6-card suit is good for another bid. Your partner only needs two hearts to make an 8-card fit. Even if he should only have one heart, a 6–1 heart fit won't be too bad. (Even a 6–0 fit is not a complete catastrophe, but that is the only 6-card fit with any merit at all.)

YOU	PARTNER
1 CLUB	1 HEART
???	

♠ K 9
♡ 10 8 3 2
◇ 9
♣ A K Q 8 5 3

Your original 14 points go up to 15 on revaluation for play in hearts where you have at least an 8-card fit. You must learn to ignore your minor suit when there is a fit in a major. Bid 2 HEARTS.

♠ A 10 9
♡ 8 4
◇ K 4 3
♣ A J 10 4 2

With 13 points and a balanced hand, your rebid is 1 NOTRUMP. You should not rebid your clubs because they are only five cards long.

♠ A 4 3
♡ 7
◇ A K 7
♣ 9 8 7 6 4 3

Again 13 points and you have only one choice. Rebid your clubs: 2 CLUBS. Do not pass out of fright—your partner's new suit requires you to bid again. He may have lots of strength, he may have help for clubs, he may bid diamonds next. Then again, you may get stuck with a poor contract in clubs, but if so, that is probably the least of the evils.

Introducing a Third Suit

After a 1-over-1 response by your partner, you may consider introducing a third suit into the bidding. For example:

YOU ·	PARTNER
1 DIAMOND	1 HEART
1 SPADE	

Whereas the bidding cannot stop after the *second* suit is introduced by the responder (your partner), it may stop after the *third* suit by the opener (you). Your partner could pass after your spade bid if he feels that spades is the best place to play the hand, but he will do this only with a very poor hand. You have seen that the responder has full forcing power, leading to the principle that:

A new suit by the responder is forcing.

But the opener has only LIMITED FORCING POWER. A new suit by the opener is not forcing except under special circumstances.

You may introduce a third suit at the 2-level, even with a minimum hand, providing this suit is lower ranking than your opening suit.

YOU	PARTNER
1 DIAMOND	1 SPADE
2 CLUBS	???

Perhaps you held five diamonds and five clubs. You know that you should start with the higher-ranking suit, so your first bid was

1 DIAMOND. After your partner's 1 SPADE, you introduced your clubs as the third suit. When your second bid is in a lower-ranking suit than your opening bid, your partner can stop the bidding satisfactorily at the 2-level if his hand is minimum. If he feels that your partnership has more clubs than diamonds, he may pass. But if he feels that the partnership has more diamonds than clubs, he can bid 2 DIAMONDS. A picture will help show this.

YOU	♣PARTNER♣
1 DIAMOND	♣1 SPADE♣
2 CLUBS	♣PASS ???♣ or
	♣2 DIAMONDS ???♣

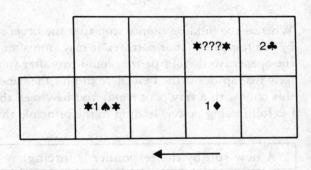

But suppose that you held four diamonds and five clubs. Now you will not bid your higher-ranking suit first because your lower-ranking suit is longer. To bid them both, you will have to bid them in the reverse of the usual order.

> **When your second bid is in a higher-ranking suit and at a higher level than your opening bid, you have REVERSED.**

For example:

YOU	♣PARTNER♣
1 CLUB	♣1 SPADE♣
2 DIAMONDS	♣3 CLUBS ???♣ or
	♣3 DIAMONDS ???♣

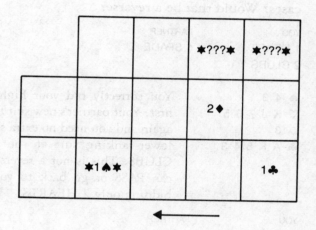

Your bid of 2 DIAMONDS is a reverse. A reverse asks your partner to choose one of your suits and *not* to pass.

> **The opener has LIMITED FORCING POWER: A new suit *reverse* by the opener is forcing.**

You can't reverse with a minimum hand because you are pushing the bidding up to the 3-level at the least. You must see at least 23 partnership points before you can introduce a third suit at the 2-level when the suit is higher ranking than your opening suit. When you have no support for your partner, you must (as usual) devaluate your hand before figuring the partnership points.

A reverse made at the 2-level usually forces the partnership up to the 3-level and thus is acceptable only when the partnership has at least 23 points.

Can you afford to rebid in your second suit in the following cases? Would that be a reverse?

YOU	PARTNER
1 HEART	1 SPADE
2 CLUBS ?	

♠ 4 3
♡ K J 7 6 5
◊ 8
♣ A K 8 4 3

You correctly bid your higher-ranking suit first. Your partner's new suit forces you to bid again and you need no extra strength to bid a lower-ranking suit at the 2-level. Bid 2 CLUBS. This is not a reverse. Your partner can PASS or go back to your first suit by bidding only 2 HEARTS

YOU	PARTNER
1 CLUB	1 SPADE
2 HEARTS ?	

♠ A 4
♡ K 10 8 6
◊ K 3
♣ A K 8 3 2

You correctly bid clubs first because it was your longest suit. For that reason you could not bid your higher-ranking suit first. Now if you bid hearts, it will be a higher-ranking suit bid at the 2-level. This is a reverse and your partner may be forced up to the 3-level. Since your partnership points total 23, even after you devalue your hand, you will go ahead and bid 2 HEARTS.

YOU	PARTNER
1 CLUB	1 HEART
1 SPADE ?	

♠ K Q 8 2
♡ J 3
◇ 8 7 5
♣ A Q J 8

Bid 1 SPADE. A 1-level bid is never a reverse because it is at the same level as your opening bid. Your partner could pass, but usually he will bid 2 CLUBS or 2 SPADES or 1 NOTRUMP.

YOU	PARTNER
1 DIAMOND	1 SPADE
2 HEARTS ?	

♠ 5 3
♡ K 8 3 2
◇ A K 9 7
♣ K 5 4

2 HEARTS would be a reverse, and you are not strong enough for a reverse. But your balanced hand is fine for 1 NOTRUMP. Besides, if your partner holds hearts, he will bid them at his next turn.

B

Rebidding after a 2-over-1 Response

Limited Rebids

When you can make a limited rebid, your considerations after a 2-over-1 response are not much different from what they are after a 1-over-1 response. Suppose the bidding goes:

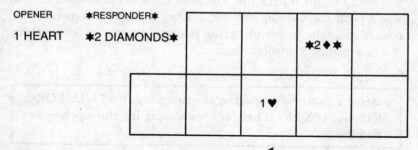

OPENER	✴RESPONDER✴			
1 HEART	✴2 DIAMONDS✴		✴2♦✴	
		1♥		

Your limited rebid as the opener might be:

- 3 DIAMONDS, raising your partner's suit
- 2 HEARTS, rebidding your own suit
- 2 NOTRUMP, showing a balanced hand, too weak (13, 14, 15) to have opened 1 NOTRUMP to begin with

The fact that your partner was able to respond with a new suit at the 2-level means that he already sees 23 points in the partnership. He is counting on 13 from you plus 10 or more in his own hand. Anything extra which you hold will bring the partnership points up toward the game level. A limited bid is appropriate after a 2-over-1 response only when the partnership points as you see them are below the game level. Remember that the bidding can stop after you make a limited bid, and you don't want that to happen when your partnership has a possible game.

For a good chance to succeed at the game level (4-level) you need 26 partnership points, but you should go along with 25 when you have a possible fit in a major suit. Remember to revaluate or devaluate your hand as appropriate when you are figuring the partnership points.

Unlimited Rebids

Sometimes after a 2-over-1 response you cannot make a limited rebid, either because you have the wrong kind of hand or because you hold too much strength. The solution is to bid a new suit if it won't push the bidding too high. After a 2-over-1 response, the opener gains the same full forcing power as the responder. So there is a new principle involved here:

> After a 2-over-1 response, the opener gains FULL FORCING POWER. Then any new suit by the opener is forcing.

If your new suit can be bid at the 2-level, your partner will have room to bid again and not go above the 3-level. But if you must bid your new suit at the 3-level, you may be forcing your partner up to the 4-level! Just as you had to watch out when responding with a 2-over-1 shift, you have to be careful when your rebid is a 3-over-2-over-1 shift. For example:

OPENER	★RESPONDER★
1 HEART	★2 DIAMONDS★
3 CLUBS	

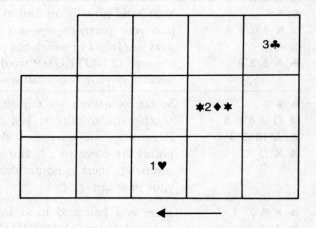

Your partner is forced to bid, and you can see that his most logical next bid may be 4 CLUBS or 3 NOTRUMP, both of which are at the 4-level.

When you think about bidding a new suit, it is generally because you have no fit. When you have no fit, you must devalue your hand and count only HCP. After devaluation as necessary, you would like to see 26 points before forcing the bidding to the 4-level, but 25 will do—especially if you see a possible game in a major suit.

What is your next bid after the indicated bidding?

YOU	PARTNER
1 HEART	2 CLUBS
???	

♠ A 8 5 ♡ A 10 9 8 6 4 3 ◇ 3 ♣ K 8	Even with your strong distribution, your points only come to 14 originally, and devaluate to 11 after your partner bids 2 CLUBS. Make the obvious limited bid of 2 HEARTS.
♠ 7 5 ♡ K J 8 5 4 ◇ A 7 ♣ A 8 3 2	Your hand is really minimum but you cannot pass your partner's new-suit bid. 3 CLUBS puts you into a fit which has probably 8 cards or more. 2 NOTRUMP would be dangerous because of your two small spades.
♠ 9 8 ♡ Q J 8 6 5 ◇ A 10 8 9 ♣ K Q	So far, you don't see any fit. But you have another suit to suggest: bid 2 DIAMONDS. Because of devaluation, the partnership points are down to 22. But since you aren't reversing, there is no problem with bidding your new suit.
♠ K 8 7 ♡ A Q 9 5 2 ◇ K J 3 ♣ 7 4	Here is a balanced hand in the minimum range. A bid of 2 NOTRUMP expresses both of those facts. You hope that your partner's hand will be suitable for notrump or for hearts.
♠ K 8 7 6 ♡ A Q 9 5 2 ◇ K J 3 ♣ 7	Your second suit is spades and is higher ranking than your hearts. Since your partner responded 2-over-1, he has 10 good points to go with your 13 HCP giving the partnership 23 in spite of your devaluation. You can reverse with 2 SPADES.

NOTE: Traditionally, Standard American has required that a reverse always be based on additional strength. However we will follow newer thinking which permits a reverse as long as you can still see 23 partnership points after devaluating your hand as necessary. If you are playing serious bridge, discuss this with your partner so that you will both use the same yardstick. In social bridge, the difference may not matter much.

The Problem Hands

Sometimes when you want to bid a new suit, you will find that you just don't have enough points to do it. Worse yet, when you have to devaluate your hand, it may become worth less than the original 13 that you counted when you opened.

♠ 8
♡ A Q 7 6 4
♢ 5 3
♣ A 9 8 7 5

You open 1 HEART and your partner responds 2 DIAMONDS. Now your hand devaluates to only 10 HCP, so the partnership points only total 20. Help! You don't dare bid 3 CLUBS. What do do?

In such cases, you must try to make a limited bid, even if you don't have quite the distribution which the guidelines call for. Bidding 2 HEARTS is the least of the evils in the above case. It is better to make a bid for which you have slightly the wrong distribution than to make a bid for which you do not have the strength.

NOTE: There are times when no bid seems right. When this happens, you just have to bid as best you can. When you are able to call this "inspired bidding" instead of "muddling through" you are on your way toward becoming an expert!

Because the opening hand may become devaluated, you must limit this effect by following the guideline:

> **An opening bid must include at least 10 HCP.**

You can see that the hand above just barely qualifies for an opening bid.

Summary of the Opener's Unlimited Rebids

A reverse at the 2-level can force the bidding up to the 3-level, so you must see at least 23 points (after any necessary devaluation) before making such a bid.

A 3-over-2-over-1 bid can force the bidding up to the 4-level, so you must see at least 25 points before making such a bid.

When you are too weak to bid your second suit, make the best limited bid that you can, even if you don't have quite the right distribution to do so.

C

Responding for the Second Time

Now we are going to put you back in the responder's position again. Suppose the bidding starts with three suits in succession. You may find that you have a problem in making your second response.

The Preference Bid

PARTNER	PARTNER	YOU	YOU
♠ 8	1 HEART	1 SPADE	♠ A 9 7 5 2
♡ A Q 9 3 2	2 CLUBS	???	♡ 8 6
◇ 5 3 2			◇ 9 8 6 4
♣ K Q 8 7			♣ A 9

Your partner has bid two suits, ignoring your suit completely. You are being asked which you prefer, hearts or clubs. You must make a

PREFERENCE BID based on where you think the best (longest) fit is. Sometimes you will see a good fit for one of your partner's suits. Sometimes, as in the example, you will not—you will simply have to choose the lesser of the two evils.

When making a preference bid:

- **Prefer the suit in which you have the most length.**
- **In case of tie, prefer the first-bid suit since your partner may have more cards in that suit.**

You can see from the example that you won't always have real support for the suit you prefer, but you will normally have at least 2-card support. With a minimum hand, if you prefer your partner's last-bid suit, express this by passing. But if you prefer his first-bid suit, express this by bidding it. In the example you would bid 2 HEARTS and hope for the best.

The example also shows another fact of life at the bridge table. When your partner bids two suits, he is likely to be short in the other suits. Even if you had six spades in the example hand, you would only have a 7-card fit. So don't refuse to make a preference bid, rebidding your own suit instead, unless this will probably give your partnership a better fit even opposite a singleton. And don't refuse to make a preference bid in favor of bidding a fourth suit where you probably don't have a fit either. (Bidding a fourth suit is appropriate only with extra strength—and you must devaluate your hand, counting only high-card points, unless you happen to have a normal fit in one of your partner's suits.)

- **Whenever it appears that there is no normal fit, you must devaluate your hand.**
- **When there is no normal fit and a scarcity of points, quit bidding early.**

Those who keep bidding, only because they have no fit, end up at a higher contract and usually still have no fit.

NOTE: When you are showing a preference between a major suit and a minor suit, and you are playing duplicate, it is sometimes better to choose the major even if the minor fit may be longer. But you should be sure that the major represents at least a 7-card fit and you should be able to contribute a high card to bolster the strength of the trump suit.

The Preference Bid When You Cannot Pass

Sometimes you will be making a preference bid when you cannot pass. You may be forced to bid because of one of the principles which you just learned:

- Your partner has reversed, so you are forced to bid.
- Your first response was 2-over-1, so any new suit by your partner is now forcing.

Except for the fact that you cannot pass, the situation remains basically the same as before.

PARTNER	YOU
1 HEART	2 CLUBS
2 DIAMONDS	???

Your normal rebid will be a preference bid of 2 HEARTS or 3 DIAMONDS.

What is your second response after the indicated bidding?

YOU	PARTNER
	1 DIAMOND
1 SPADE	2 CLUBS
???	

♠ K Q 4 3
♡ J 2
◇ Q 9 8 3
♣ 10 8 5

You must choose diamonds or clubs. You have more diamonds than clubs and a minimum hand (you see less than 23 partnership points) so you bid 2 DIAMONDS. When your partner bids diamonds and then clubs, he will usually have at least five diamonds (although four is also possible). You probably have a 9-card diamond fit.

♠ A 8 6 5 3
♡ Q 9 7 5 2
◇ 8
♣ 10 8

This is a sorry situation. You would like to be in one of the major suits. But unless you limit your bidding to a simple preference, your partner will think you have a better hand than you do. Then, instead of a minor mess, you will have a major catastrophe. You must pass and keep your fingers crossed.

♠ 10 9 8 5 3
♡ 10 4
◇ A 5 3
♣ A 8 7

Now you have no problem. You tried to find a fit in spades, but apparently that is not to be. So you can be perfectly happy to bid 2 DIAMONDS. You have as many clubs as diamonds, but partner bid diamonds first. He probably has five diamonds and four or five clubs.

♠ K J 8 7 6
♡ A 8 3 2
◇ 8 3
♣ 6 4

The only thing to do is to go back to your partner's first suit, bidding 2 DIAMONDS. Your hand has devaluated to 8 points. You would need several more high-card points to attempt 2 NOTRUMP. That is a 3-level bid and needs 23 partnership points.

YOU	PARTNER
	1 HEART
2 CLUBS	2 DIAMONDS
???	

♠ 9 7 6
♡ K 2
◊ 7 5 3 2
♣ A K J 3

Your 11 points allowed you to make your first response a 2-over-1 shift. Now you must not pass when your partner introduces a third suit. Since you prefer diamonds you will bid 3 DIAMONDS.

♠ J 4
♡ 10 8 3
◊ A 9 2
♣ A J 9 4 3

You would have raised hearts as your first bid but you were too strong. Now, given a choice between hearts and diamonds, you still choose hearts. Bid 2 HEARTS.

♠ 8 4 3
♡ 5
◊ K 7
♣ A K 10 8 5 4 2

Here you have good reason to insist on your own suit. Your partner is likely to have five hearts and four diamonds. But your seven clubs are good ones and you may very well have an 8-card fit. Bid 3 CLUBS.

D
Bidding Patterns

Leading Up to a Limited Bid

Probably you didn't realize it, but what we have been looking at is bidding patterns which lead up to a limited bid:

• The opening bid is a limited bid (notrump).
• An opening suit bid is followed by a limited response (a raise, or notrump, or a pass).

- Two suit bids in succession are followed by a limited rebid by the opener (a raise, a rebid of the opener's suit, or notrump).
- Three suit bids in succession are followed by a limited bid by the responder (usually a preference bid).

The Forcing Principle

The forcing principle says that certain bids require the bidder's partner to bid again unless an opponent intervenes with a bid.

- **The responder has FULL FORCING POWER; any new suit by the responder is forcing.**
- **Initially the opener has LIMITED FORCING POWER; a new suit *reverse* by the opener is forcing.**
- **After a 2-over-one response, the opener gains FULL FORCING POWER; then any new suit by the opener is forcing.**

To understand this, suppose the bidding begins:

OPENER	RESPONDER
1 HEART	1 SPADE

The responder sees 13 points in his partner's hand and he may easily have another 13 to get to game with. He must be able to keep his partner from passing while he is searching for a fit. The opener, however, sees only 6 points and very seldom will have the other 20 needed for game. But after a 2-over-1 response, the opener is assured of 10 points. Now he need have only 16 points—a more likely occurrence—so he too gains full forcing power.

If you are the opener, you are forced whenever your partner bids a new suit. But if you are the responder, you are forced only when your partner has reversed, or when you have bid 2-over-1 and your partner, now with full forcing power, continues by bidding any third suit.

NOTE: You might note again the side remark that we made to the effect that after an opening 1 NOTRUMP, a minimum response in a suit is not forcing—in fact it almost demands that the opener pass.

NOTE: The two defenders start with no forcing power. None of the bids which you might make as a defender are forcing.

Chapter 6

PHASE-TWO BIDS

A
Phase-Two Notions

Getting to Game

At all stages of bidding, the principal questions you must ask yourself are:

- Where is our fit?
- Do we have a game?

and for stronger hands:

- Do we have a slam?

In the early part of the bidding, the emphasis is on finding a fit. In the latter part, the question of game or slam becomes more important.

When your partnership points reach 26, your probability of being able to make a game is good, providing you can find a fit. With 25 points, your probability of making game is fair. With less than that, your probability is very poor. In the minor suits, where a game is at the 5-level, 29 points gives you a good probability of making game and 28 gives you a fair probability.

The Captain

When your partner makes a limited bid, you become the captain for the partnership. Because your partner has limited his hand, you can judge the prospects for your partnership. First you must make the PRIME DECISION—whether to stop the bidding because game is out of the question, or whether to continue because game is at hand or at least close at hand. It is up to you as captain to guide the bidding once you decide to go on.

When you are the one who first makes a limited bid, it is your partner who becomes the captain. Then he will take the lead and it is up to you to become strictly a follower. If he decides to stop the bidding and signs off, usually by passing, you must trust his judgment and not carry the bidding to higher levels if you get a chance to bid again. If his bidding amounts to asking you a question, you must merely answer the question in the prescribed way. In short, you must not take the initiative, but you may respond to your partner's initiative with the proper show of enthusiasm or lack of interest.

Once a captain is elected, the forcing power is redistributed between the captain and his partner, the LIMIT BIDDER.

- **The captain normally has FULL FORCING POWER: any new suit by the captain is forcing.**
- **The limit bidder has NO FORCING POWER: no further bid by the limit bidder is forcing.**

The Bidding Phases

Most of the time we can look at the bidding as having two phases. The first phase is the bidding leading up to the point where a limited bid is made. The typical first phase consists of one or more new-suit bids in succession, followed by a limited bid which is:

- A notrump bid
- A raise of one's partner's suit
- A rebid of one's own suit

Sometimes the bidding starts with a notrump bid, so that the limited bid is reached even before any suit is bid. But in general, when nothing unusual happens, the picture is:

THE BIDDING:	THE QUESTIONS:
OPENING BID	
First-phase bids	FIT ?
LIMIT BID	
Decision by captain	QUIT ?
	TRY FOR GAME ?
	TRY FOR SLAM ?
Second-phase bids (if any)	

So far you have read about first-phase bids leading up to a limit bid. In the first phase you concentrated on keeping the bidding low while searching for a fit. Now you are going to see how the bidding gets carried on toward game when the captain sees game possibilities. For the time being, we will ignore the possibility of slam, reserving that consideration for later on.

More about Revaluation

When your partnership finds a fit in a trump suit, both hands may be worth more because of a long trump suit and short side suits. With better than an 8-card trump fit, each additional trump is worth an extra point to the partnership. Either partner may count these extra points, allowing for any points already counted by his partner.

You know already that singletons and voids take on extra value when they are in the short hand (the hand with the fewest trumps, usually the dummy), provided they are accompanied by at least three trumps for ruffing with. In the long hand, singletons and voids also take on the same extra value provided that they are accompanied by at least *six* trumps. With fewer than six trumps, the opponents may force you to ruff in the long hand and leave you too short to draw trumps.

The following is the guideline which we gave to use when you have a fit for your partner's suit and you will be the short hand:

Revaluate, when you have support for your partner's suit, by adding:

- **1 additional point for each card over 8 which you see in your partnership in the proposed trump suit**

Providing that you hold at least 3-card support, also add:

- **1 additional point for each singleton**
- **2 additional points for each void**

The following guideline applies when your partner has a fit for your suit and you will be the long (at least equally long) hand:

Revaluate, when your partner has support for your suit, by adding:

- **1 additional point for each card in the trump suit which your partner cannot know about and therefore will not include in his count of trump length**

Providing that you hold at least 6-card trump length, also add:

- **1 additional point for each singleton**
- **2 additional points for each void**

You will very shortly see where this guideline can be used in phase-two bidding.

With the following hands you open the bidding with 1 HEART. How many points is your hand worth before and after your partner responds 2 HEARTS?

♠ K 3 ♡ A Q J 4 3 2 ◇ K 8 4 ♣ 10 7	Before hearing your partner's bid, you counted 14 points. When he revaluated his hand for his raise, he counted on you for five hearts. Since you actually have six, the fit is longer than your partner would think, so take another point for the extra trump, making 15 points.
♠ 8 ♡ K Q J 10 8 ◇ K 7 5 2 ♣ A J 7	Your fit is exactly what your partner thinks it is. And your singleton does not take on extra value when you only hold five trumps. So your count was and still is 16.
♠ A Q J ♡ K 8 7 5 4 3 2 ◇ A 8 ♣ 4	Now you have two extra trumps and your singleton is also worth an extra point. You originally had 17 points, now you have 20.

B
After a Raise

After an Opening Major Suit Is Raised

When the bidding starts with 1 in a SUIT, the response may be a raise. This is a limited bid, ending the first phase of the bidding. For example:

	YOU	PARTNER
	1 HEART	2 HEARTS
	???	

You have become the captain of the team and must make the prime decision: go on or quit. This involves asking yourself:

• Where is our fit?
• Do we have a game?

Fit? Your partner has promised a normal trump fit (3-card support to go with your five hearts). Since a normal trump fit in a major suit is the best place to play the hand, it is now decided that your partnership will play in hearts (regardless of any future bidding).

Game? Your partner has promised 6 points, but his range is 6, 7, 8, 9 and thus could include as many as 3 extra points. First you revaluate your hand based on the fit. Then you compute the partnership points, as you see them, by adding your points to your partner's promised 6. If that total comes to 23 or more, your partner's undisclosed extra points could be enough to reach the 26-point game level. If the total comes to 25 or more, you should go on to game. It is true that 25 is slightly below the game level and only gives you a fair chance for game. But opposite a 4-point spread, you cannot be completely accurate and you must take your chances when 25 is reached.

When your partner has limited his hand with any bid which ranges over 4 or more points:

- **If you see 25 partnership points, go for game.**
- **If you see 23 partnership points, invite game.**
- **If you see less, PASS.**

This guideline tells you how to continue in the example case where your partner raises you to 2 HEARTS. If you see 25 points, bid game with 4 HEARTS, hoping your partnership really has 26 points for a better chance at making your contract. If you see 23 points, invite game with 3 HEARTS. If you see less than 23 points, simply PASS.

Accepting an Invitation. Now look at it the other way—supposing that it is you who has given the raise and it is your partner who has given the invitation.

PARTNER	YOU
1 HEART	2 HEARTS
3 HEARTS	???

The general idea when you are offered an invitation is that you refuse if you are at the bottom of the range for your bid and you accept if you are at the top of it.

When your partner makes a game invitation after you have limited your hand with a bid which ranges over a 4-point spread:

- Decline if you have the very minimum for your bid or if you have 1 extra point.
- Accept if you have 2 or 3 extra points.

In the above case, if you have only 6 or 7 points, you will PASS. If you have 8 or 9 points, you will bid 4 HEARTS.

NOTE: Actually, your partner would be inviting game if at his second turn he said anything except PASS. There is no reason for him to continue the bidding unless he sees a chance for game. More sophisticated methods use various bids, but the simple, straightforward way to invite game is to bid the heart suit again.

What is your rebid in the following cases?

YOU	PARTNER
1 SPADE	2 SPADES
???	

♠ A 7 6 4 3
♡ Q 5 3 2
◇ 6
♣ A K Q

Your 17 points plus your partner's promised 6 add up to 23 so you should bid again to invite game. Spades has been agreed on as the trump suit (an 8-card major fit has been found) and you can invite game with 3 SPADES.

♠ K Q J 9 7 5
♡ A K Q 2
◇ 4 2
♣ 3

Your original count of 17 has gone up to 19 now that you see a 9-card fit. The partnership total comes to 25, enough to bid game, 4 SPADES.

YOU	PARTNER
	1 HEART
2 HEARTS	3 HEARTS
???	

♠ 4 3
♡ K Q 2
◇ J 9 8 5
♣ 6 5 4 2

You barely had enough points to give a raise, so you must decline your partner's invitation with a PASS. You must always decline with only 6 or 7 points. Don't be mislead into bidding again because of your strong hearts.

♠ 4
♡ 8 7 6 4
◇ A Q 10 7
♣ 6 4 3 2

Your original count was 7, but after your partner opened in hearts, your count went up to 9. Now that your partner has invited game, you can accept with 4 HEARTS.

After an Opening Minor Suit Is Raised

If the bidding starts:

YOU	PARTNER
1 DIAMOND	2 DIAMONDS

you have found a fit, but it is in a minor suit. As captain, you will pass unless you see partnership points of 23 or more. But if you are at least at the near-game level, you should start thinking about notrump. Of course if your hand is unbalanced, you will have to stick to diamonds, giving up on notrump.

If your hand is balanced, look to see what kind of strength you have in the other three suits. A high card (ace, king, queen or jack) or even four small cards will do unless the opponents have bid the suit. In that case you want a full stopper (usually an ace, a king or a queen-jack combination).

Except for an opening bid in notrump, or an overcall in notrump, don't make a normal notrump bid unless your partnership has length or some strength in all four suits, including a stopper in any suit bid by the opponents.

If you meet the conditions of the guideline, then in the example 2 NOTRUMP is the best game invitation and 3 NOTRUMP is the best game bid.

What if your hand is balanced, is strong enough to bid again, but has a weak suit or two? You can work toward notrump by bidding any new suit in which you have some strength. With a choice of suits, generally make the cheapest bid. The suit may have only three cards in it, but your partner should understand that you are only showing where your strength is. Bidding a new suit in phase two is not always for the purpose of suggesting a trump suit.

Furthermore, your partner cannot pass because the captain has full forcing power and any new suit by the captain is forcing.

If your partner has length or strength in the other two suits, and if his hand is balanced, he can now bid notrump. If not, he may also bid a new suit where he has strength, or he may go back to diamonds if his hand is unbalanced.

> **After a minor suit has been bid and raised, a bid in a new suit is a move toward notrump.**

What is your rebid in the following cases?

YOU	PARTNER
1 CLUB	2 CLUBS
???	

♠ 7 6 5
♡ A K 2
◇ K Q 8
♣ A K J 3

Partnership points come to 26 (20 + 6). Notrump is a possible place for game but your spades are weak. Move toward a game in notrump by bidding 2 DIAMONDS. If notrump doesn't work out, your partnership may have to play in clubs.

♠ A 10 8
♡ A 7
◇ K J 8
♣ A K 9 7 6

Partnership points again spell game, but this time you have strength in all of the three unbid suits. Go directly to 3 NOTRUMP. Your fit in clubs will be an advantage in notrump since it will give you some easy, fast tricks.

♠ K 3
♡ Q J 7
◇ K 9
♣ A K Q 8 7 4

Here your tremendous fit in clubs will give you even more fast tricks. An unbalanced hand with a solid minor suit can often be played advantageously in notrump, as long as the opponents can't take too many tricks in some other suit. Bid 3 NOTRUMP rather than try to get to 5 CLUBS.

After a Response Is Raised

Now consider that you are the responder and the bidding has gone:

PARTNER	YOU
1 DIAMOND	1 HEART
2 HEARTS	???

You recognize of course that you have become the captain.

With Five Hearts. Your partner has promised 3-card support. If you have five hearts, you see a normal fit and have only to decide between PASS, 3 HEARTS and 4 HEARTS, according to the level of the partnership points.

With Four Hearts. If you only have four hearts, you would prefer to be in notrump unless your partner has more than three hearts. If you are not strong enough to invite game, you have no choice but to pass and accept your fate, whatever it may be. But given the strength to go on (at least 23 partnership points), you should begin by assuming that your partner has only 3-card support. With some strength or length in the unbid suits, you can bid 2 NOTRUMP or 3 NOTRUMP according to the level of the partnership points. With strength or length in only one of the other two suits, bid that suit, moving toward notrump in the way we discussed before.

- When a suit has been raised and you can only be sure of a 7-card fit, do not bid that suit again until your partner does.
- When a suit has been raised, your partner may then take the bidding in another direction. If you know there is an 8-card fit and you wish the partnership to play in that suit, you must rebid the suit. You will always do so for a major suit and sometimes for a minor suit.

Over your notrump invitation, if your partner really has 4-card support he will return to hearts. He will reject your game invitation by bidding 3 HEARTS and accept it by bidding 4 HEARTS. Over your 3 NOTRUMP game bid, your partner will take out to 4 HEARTS if he has 4-card support. But whenever your partner has only 3-card support, he will usually be content to play in notrump, although he might find some other bid if his hand is so unbalanced that notrump is out of the question.

NOTE: If your partner plays 4-card majors, his opening bid in a major only promises a 4-card suit. You may raise his suit with 3-card support, but do not pursue the suit further unless he bids it again. However, if you raise with 4-card support and your partner continues the bidding in another direction, rebid the major suit.

What is your next bid in these cases?

YOU	PARTNER
	1 CLUB
1 HEART	2 HEARTS
???	

♠ K Q 10 2 ♡ K 8 4 2 ◇ Q J 8 ♣ 5 4	You count partnership points at 24, enough to invite game. Your partner may only have three hearts, so you will avoid rebidding hearts at this time. Bidding 2 NOTRUMP may lead to a contract in hearts (if your partner has four of them) or in notrump.
♠ 8 ♡ K J 10 4 3 ◇ K 9 8 ♣ A J 5 4	Now you count partnership points at 27. Even if your partner only has three hearts, you have an 8-card fit. So bid 4 HEARTS.
♠ 10 5 4 ♡ Q J 10 8 ◇ A K 3 ♣ A 8 5	Again you see game but the bidding is a little tougher. 3 HEARTS would suggest that you have five hearts. You can't raise clubs with only 3-card support. 3

NOTRUMP would be fine if you had a stopper in spades. Bid 3 DIAMONDS for now, as a move toward notrump.

YOU	PARTNER
	1 CLUB
1 DIAMOND	2 DIAMONDS
???	

♠ Q J 7
♡ K 6 5
◇ K 9 8 4 3
♣ J 2

Game is a possibility since you can count 24 points in the partnership, but it will have to be in notrump, not diamonds. Bid 2 NOTRUMP. Your diamond fit will be an asset at a notrump contract.

♠ 7 6 3
♡ K J 7 5
◇ K 10 9 5
♣ A 7

Again you have 24 partnership points and want to get to notrump if possible. You have no high card in spades, so a notrump bid would be unsound. Bid 2 HEARTS, hoping that your partner can bid notrump. Since your partner skipped over hearts to raise your diamonds, he can't be expected to hold four hearts.

After A Preference Bid

Generally the cases we have already looked at will guide you in proceeding after any raise. However it may be well to give a look at the case where preference must be shown. For example:

YOU	PARTNER
1 HEART	1 SPADE
2 DIAMONDS	???
???	

Your partner must normally show preference. He could respond with 2 HEARTS or PASS, showing minimum strength and possibly only 2-card support. He could invite game by bidding 2 NOTRUMP, if notrump is appropriate, or by bidding the fourth suit (3 CLUBS), or by raising diamonds to 3 DIAMONDS with real support. (He could have shown mere preference for diamonds simply by passing.) As long as you recognize the difference in these bids, you will be able to continue the bidding sensibly.

NOTE: Remember that a bid in the fourth suit always shows extra strength.

C
After the Opener Rebids His Suit

After a Rebid in a Major

PARTNER	YOU
1 HEART	1 SPADE
2 HEARTS	???

As captain you have an easy time as long as you hold at least two hearts—with your partner's 6-card length you have a normal trump fit in a major suit. You simply choose between PASS or 3 HEARTS (game invitation) or 4 HEARTS (game). With less than 2-card support for hearts and a minimum hand you will do best to pass. A poor fit is not so bad if one hand has six trumps—even a 6-0 fit is not a total disaster. And remember the guideline about not bidding on if you have no points and no fit.

If you hold enough points to invite game but have no fit for your partner's hearts, you might bid a new suit. Your partner will then have to show his preference between your two suits without passing. Remember that a new suit by the captain is forcing. Or you might rebid your spades if you have six of them, hoping to find your partner with two more.

After a Rebid in a Minor

If the bidding were:

PARTNER	YOU
1 DIAMOND	1 SPADE
2 DIAMONDS	???

you now have the additional consideration that notrump may be your best bet for a game. Your partner's hand cannot be balanced, but it may be necessary to compromise in order to reach game. In that case your partner should go along with notrump with 6-3-2-2 ("semi-balanced") distribution, or even with a singleton if it is in your spade suit. Of course it may not be necessary to compromise on notrump if you can find a fit in spades or hearts.

What is your next bid?

YOU	PARTNER
	1 CLUB
1 DIAMOND	2 CLUBS
???	

♠ 8 7 5 ♡ 7 6 3 ◇ A Q 9 8 7 2 ♣ 2	There is no hope for game. Be thankful you aren't completely void in clubs. PASS.
♠ 9 2 ♡ K J 9 ◇ A Q 10 4 3	You can see 26 partnership points. Bidding 2 HEARTS moves your partnership toward notrump, but you can't really know where

♣ Q 8 7	you will end up until you hear more from your partner.
♠ K 8 3 ♡ J 5 4 ◇ A 10 9 3 2 ♣ K 6	Your 12 points make game a possibility if your partner can tolerate notrump and has a little extra strength. Invite game with 2 NOTRUMP. Give up if your partner comes back with 3 CLUBS or 3 DIAMONDS.
♠ J 9 8 ♡ J 3 ◇ K 9 8 5 3 ♣ A Q 3	Your poor holdings in hearts and spades prevent you from bidding notrump. But you see 25 partnership points and you have support for clubs. Bidding 3 CLUBS may yet get you to 3 NOTRUMP if your partner has stoppers in both of the major suits.

The Bidding Direction

A limit bid by one partner automatically elects the other partner as captain. If the captain decides not to pass, bidding enters the second phase. The strategy for the second-phase bidding which you have seen so far is:

- If an 8-card major fit has been found, the bidding normally continues in that suit. (However, any other bid is intended to lead toward game in that major.)
- If a 7-card major fit or a minor fit has been found, the bidding usually turns toward notrump.

D

After an Opening 1 Notrump

Continuing in Notrump after an Opening Bid of 1 NOTRUMP

When your partner opens the bidding with 1 NOTRUMP, you become the captain immediately. You must ask yourself the two questions:

* Where is our fit?
* Do we have a game?

Fit? Since your partner is proposing a notrump contract, you look first for a normal notrump fit. Your partner has promised a balanced hand. If your hand is also balanced, notrump is a satisfactory place for the final contract.

Game? Having decided that the partnership should play in notrump, you now consider the partnership prospects for game. Remember that your partner's 1 NOTRUMP bid promises 16 points with possibly 1 or 2 additional points. Add your own points to the 16 promised by your partner to get the partnership points

---

When your partner as the opener bids 1 NOTRUMP, and your hand is balanced, and you wish to play in notrump:

* With 26 (or more) partnership points, bid 3 NOTRUMP.
* With 24 or 25 partnership points, bid 2 NOTRUMP.
* With less, PASS.

which are known to you. If these partnership points reach 26 or more, your partnership is at the game level. If the total is 24 or 25, you realize that your partner may have the 1 or 2 additional points needed to bring the partnership total up to 26. Your partnership is at the near-game level. However, if the partnership points are below 24, your partner cannot have enough additional points to reach 26. Your partnership is at the minimum, no-game level.

If you are the one who is the opener and bid 1 NOTRUMP, then your partner is the captain. If he passes or bids 3 NOTRUMP, he has made a final decision. This is the final bid for the partnership and you must not bid again. But if he bids 2 NOTRUMP, he is making a GAME INVITATION, inviting you to go on to game if you have more than the minimum 16 points. With 17 or 18 points you will accept the invitation and bid 3 NOTRUMP. Or with a 5-card major you may bid 3 HEARTS or 3 SPADES as appropriate, leaving it to your partner to make the final bid of 3 NOTRUMP or 4 HEARTS or 4 SPADES. With only 16 points you will pass.

When your partner invites game after you have bid a normal notrump:

* Decline the invitation when you have only the minimum number of points.
* Accept the invitation when you have 1 or 2 extra points.

After your partner has opened 1 NOTRUMP, what is your response?

YOU

♠ K 4 2
♡ Q 10 4 3
◇ 10 9 6 5
♣ Q 8

Your hand is balanced so notrump is a good contract. With 7 points in your hand, the partnership total comes to 23. There can't be enough points to make 3 NOTRUMP so there is no point in bidding further. Simply PASS and play at 1 NOTRUMP. If your partner had opened with 1 in a SUIT, you couldn't know that game was out of the question, so you would bid.

♠ J 10 8
♥ 7 6 3
♦ A J 4 3 2
♣ A 8

Your balanced hand and 11 points add up to 27 points for the partnership. Bid 3 NOTRUMP. There is no future in the diamond suit—you always prefer notrump to a minor when you have a normal notrump fit.

♠ K 5 2
♥ 9 8 4
♦ K J 9
♣ J 9 8 5

Now you count 24 partnership points. You are near enough to game to make a game invitation. Bid 2 NOTRUMP and let your partner go on to 3 NOTRUMP if he has an extra point or two. If he has only 1 extra point, the partnership will have only 25 points, but it can't be helped. You have a fair chance of making your contract anyway.

♠ A K 3
♥ 7 5 3
♦ 9 6 4
♣ Q 10 7 6

The 25 partnership points are not quite enough to bid game directly, but you can invite game with 2 NOTRUMP. Now if your partner has even 1 extra point, your chances of making 3 NOTRUMP are good. (Unlike bidding for a trump contract, you should avoid a notrump game contract with only 25 points—notrump is more difficult. Only when you can't find out whether or not your side has 26 do you have to take your chances on a known 25.)

Taking Out into a Suit after an Opening Bid of 1 NOTRUMP

Fit? Sometimes, after your partner opens the bidding with 1 NOTRUMP, you will find that you have a hand which is unsuitable for notrump, usually because it is unbalanced. In that case, if you have a suit of *five* cards or more, you will want to take your partner out of notrump into your long suit. More often than not, your partner will have at least 3-card support for your suit, giving you an 8-card fit. At worst, you will have a 7-card fit (since your partner must not bid notrump with a singleton or void).

Game? As usual, you will determine the partnership potential by adding your own points to your partner's promised 16. But first revaluate your hand on the assumption that your partner will provide 3-card support. Six cards in your trump suit make a presumed 9-card fit, which is worth an extra point on revaluation. (Your partner will only expect you to have five trumps, so you have to be the one to count the additional points.) If you also have a short side suit to go with your six trumps, it will increase the value of your hand (1 extra point for each singleton, 2 extra for each void, accompanying a 6-card or longer suit).

No Game. If the partnership total is less than 24, there can be no game potential. (Remember, your partner has only 1 or 2 undisclosed points, so unless you see 24 partnership points, there is no hope of reaching 26.) Although your partnership is at the no-game level, your side will be better off in a suit because of your unbalanced hand. So you bid your suit (five cards or longer), for example:

PARTNER	YOU
1 NOTRUMP	2 HEARTS

Since you have taken your partner out of notrump into a suit, your bid is called a TAKEOUT bid. Notice that you have not increased the level of the bidding (1 NOTRUMP is already at the 2-level). A minimum takeout, which does not increase the level of bidding, is based strictly on distribution and a lack of enough points to be at the near-game level. In fact, in an extreme case you may not have any high-card points at all, merely a distribution which makes trump play more satisfactory than notrump play.

PARTNER	PARTNER	YOU	YOU
♠ A K 3	1 NOTRUMP	2 HEARTS	♠ 9 8 5
♡ K Q 10			♡ 9 8 7 5 3 2
◇ K 10 9			◇ 6 5 4
♣ Q 6 4 3			♣ 7

Your hand is a disaster! (A hand with no honors, not even a ten, is called a Yarborough.) Your side cannot make 1 NOTRUMP. But you can turn your six lowly hearts into six lovely trumps by bidding 2 HEARTS. Now you might even make your contract. But even if you are set, you will go down by less than you would have at notrump. After playing a few rounds of hearts to exhaust the opponents' trump holdings, some hearts will still remain in your hand. At a notrump contract these hearts cannot be used because there is no way to get the lead into your hand. At a heart contract, the remaining hearts are always good and provide a way to get the lead into your hand.

> With a genuine choice of contracts, if one hand is weak, the best choice is usually in a suit belonging to the weak hand.

Even in the example above, with your terrible hand, you become the captain of the partnership as soon as your partner bids notrump. Your minimum takeout bid is a SIGNOFF bid—a command to your partner to PASS. (Some say it tells your partner to "drop dead.") Now you understand why a minimum new-suit response to 1 NOTRUMP is not forcing.

> After your partner has bid 1 NOTRUMP, a takeout into 2 of a SUIT is a signoff—it shows little or no strength and serves only to take the partnership out of notrump.

Game. Sometimes, after your partner has opened 1 NOTRUMP, you will count 26 partnership points. With a long major suit (5 cards or more) you will show the game-level strength of the partnership by making a JUMP TAKEOUT, for example:

PARTNER	YOU
1 NOTRUMP	3 HEARTS

A (single) jump means that you bid one level higher than necessary. (You skipped over 2 HEARTS to make your 3 HEART bid.) If you can find a normal 8-card major fit, this will be superior to playing in notrump. Therefore your partner will bid 4 HEARTS if he has three hearts (or more) and 3 NOTRUMP if he has only two hearts. He may not pass until game is reached because you as the captain have full forcing power and your response has told him that your partnership has enough strength for game. This illustrates another forcing principle:

> When you have FULL FORCING POWER, any single jump bid you make is forcing to game.

Problem Cases. If you should hold a 5-card minor suit and a balanced hand, you should ignore the minor and go for notrump, which is much the better contract. Rarely, you will hold a long minor suit and an unbalanced hand. With a little extra strength you can go for a 5-level minor game contract. Otherwise you will have to choose between playing below game in your minor or compromising on 3 NOTRUMP in spite of your lack of a normal notrump fit.

How do you respond to an opening 1 NOTRUMP with these hands?

♠ K 10 9 5 4 ♡ — ◇ J 8 7 5 ♣ 5 4 3 2	With an unbalanced hand and five spades, you want to play in spades. You can count only 7 points in your hand so you are not near to game. Sign off with 2 SPADES.
♠ A 5 ♡ J 10 8 5 2 ◇ A 8 6 ♣ J 5 3	Your 11 points give a partnership total of 27. Bid 3 HEARTS. Whether your partner's next bid is 3 NOTRUMP or 4 HEARTS, you will PASS.
♠ K Q 8 7 5 3 ♡ A 3 ◇ 5 2 ♣ K 8 7	Your original 13 points can be revaluated to 14, putting the partnership points at 30. Bid 3 SPADES. If your partner then bids 3 NOTRUMP you will bid 4 SPADES. You might ask, why not bid 4 SPADES to begin with? The lower bid leaves bidding room to test for slam possibilities, as you will see later.
♠ 9 ♡ J 8 2 ◇ A Q 8 5 4 ♣ 9 7 3 2	You have 9 points if you play in diamonds, but game in a minor is out of the question with only 25 partnership points. At best, your partner can only bring the total up to 27 if he holds 18. If you play in notrump with no normal notrump fit, your hand devaluates to 7 points, so game in notrump is also out of the question. Sign off at 2 DIAMONDS.

General Guideline for Responding to 1 NOTRUMP

Now we can replace the previously given guidelines for responding to 1 NOTRUMP with a more general one.

When your partner has opened 1 NOTRUMP:

- With 26 partnership points, respond with 3 NOTRUMP or 3 in your LONG SUIT (usually a major).
- With 24 or 25 partnership points, respond with 2 NOTRUMP, or if you can't stand notrump, fudge a little:

  - Treat 25 points as if they were 26.
  - Treat 24 points as if they were 23.

- With fewer partnership points, respond with PASS, or 2 in your LONG SUIT (a signoff).

When responding with more than one long suit, follow the usual guideline. Bid the longer one first or, in case of tie, bid the higher-ranking one first. With a singleton and no long suit (4-4-4-1 distribution) you may have to pretend that your hand is balanced until you learn more advanced methods.

NOTE: Today it is considered standard to reserve the takeout response of 2 CLUBS as an artifical bid known as the STAYMAN convention (explained later). If you agree with your partner in advance *not* to use Stayman, then 2 CLUBS is a signoff like two of any other suit. If you have not discussed this matter with your partner, as may happen in a social game but not in a serious game, you will simply have to avoid the bid since you do not know whether your partner will take 2 CLUBS as a natural signoff bid or as an artifical Stayman bid.

If your partner makes a 1 NOTRUMP OVERCALL, you become the captain with full forcing power, and you respond in the same way as if the notrump were an opening bid. However, before you plan to play in notrump, take a good look at your holding in the opponents' suit(s). A small doubleton in one of their suits is a strong warning that you may be defeated in notrump. They may be able to take too many tricks in their long suit.

How do you respond after your partner has opened with 1 NOTRUMP?

♠ K 9 8 3 2
♡ K Q 9 5 3
♢ Q 4
♣ 9

Your 13 points give a partnership total of 29, so you want to play in game at 4 HEARTS or 4 SPADES. Start by bidding 3 SPADES. If your partner then bids 4 SPADES, well and good. If he bids 3 NOTRUMP, you will bid 4 HEARTS. Your partner must have three cards in one of the two suits. There is no need to devaluate your hand when you know you have a fit.

♠ Q J 8 3
♡ 6
♢ Q J 9 7
♣ 8 7 5 4

You aren't too fond of notrump, but you have no 5-card suit to bid. Your 7 points devaluate to 6 at notrump. You will simply have to PASS.

♠ K Q J 3 2
♡ 8 7 4
♢ 9 3
♣ 10 9 5

Here you have a balanced hand which could play at 1 NOTRUMP, but you also have a 5-card major suit which would allow you to play at 2 SPADES. Most of the time it is better to play in the major, so bid 2 SPADES.

♠ 9 3
♡ 8 7 4
♢ K Q J 3 2
♣ 10 9 5

This is the same hand as before but with spades and diamonds interchanged. Now your 5-card suit is a minor, so you will do best to PASS and play in notrump.

You open with 1 NOTRUMP with the following hand. Considering the various bids your partner might make, what is your second bid?

♠ A Q
♡ A J 10
◇ Q 7 5 4
♣ K 9 8 4

YOU	PARTNER	
1 NOTRUMP	2 HEARTS	Apparently your partner has an unbalanced hand which will not play well in notrump. His minimum takeout is a signoff. You must PASS.
	3 HEARTS	Your partner's jump in hearts indicates that your side has enough strength for game. He has five hearts and you have three. So bid 4 HEARTS. You must not pass the captain's forcing jump.
	3 SPADES	Again your partner is out for a game, but this time in spades if there is a fit there. Since you only have two spades, bid 3 NOTRUMP.
	2 NOTRUMP	With no hope for game your partner would have passed. With game assured, he would have bid it himself (3 NOTRUMP). Your partner is inviting game. Since you have only the minimum of 16, you must decline with a PASS. (With an additional point you

could accept the invitation with 3 NOTRUMP—minor suits are best ignored, and besides, you must not introduce a 4-card suit on your own initiative.)

3 NOTRUMP	Your partner has picked the final contract. He is the captain—under no circumstances should you bid.

Again consider what your second bid will be after your partner makes the various responses given below.

♠ K J 8 7 4
♡ 8 2
◇ A J 8
♣ A Q J

YOU	PARTNER	
1 NOTRUMP	2 HEARTS	Your partner may have a difficult time playing at 2 HEARTS, but it is the only thing his hand is good for. Obey the captain's signoff and PASS.
	2 SPADES	Your partner is signing off in his 5-card spade suit, but a rather unusual fit has developed which he could not foresee. When you take an extra 2 points for the 10-card fit, your strength becomes 19 points. Only because your hand revaluates to more than 18, and only because a major suit is involved, invite game

with 3 SPADES. If your partner has a maximum (6 or 7 points) he will go on to 4 SPADES. This illustrates the point that even when a guideline says "always" or "never," common sense may tell you that an exception is in order.

2 NOTRUMP

Your partner is inviting game. Since you have 17, which is more than a minimum, you should accept the invitation. You could bid 3 NOTRUMP, but it is better to investigate the possibility of a spade fit by bidding 3 SPADES. (You would not do this if you held only four spades or if your suit were a 5-card minor—you would simply bid 3 NOTRUMP.) Your partner will carry your 3 SPADES on to 4 SPADES if he has at least three spades, otherwise he will bid 3 NOTRUMP.

E

After Other Notrump Bids

After one partner has bid 1 NOTRUMP, no matter how that bid was arrived at, the other partner (the captain) can sign off by passing or by bidding a suit without jumping or reversing. Other bids show interest in going to game.

After a Delayed Notrump by the Opener

When you hear your partner open with a suit bid and later follow up with a (nonjump) notrump bid, he is showing a normal balanced notrump hand which was too weak for an opening bid of 1 NOTRUMP. For example:

PARTNER	YOU
1 DIAMOND	1 HEART
1 NOTRUMP	???

In principle, you respond as if he had opened in notrump except that you know that your partner has 13, 14, 15 points and so you count the partnership points based on 13 in your partner's hand instead of 16. However, there are more possibilities for playing in a suit because of the fact that both of you have bid before. Generally you will take out into a suit when your hand is unbalanced and will be content to play at some level of notrump when your hand is balanced.

Signoff. A pass is the most obvious kind of signoff. However, if you take out into a suit without jumping and without reversing, you are also signing off. In that case your partner is expected to pass or make a preference bid. Your suit bid tells him clearly that notrump is unsuitable. Your takeout for signoff (in the example case) may be in:

Your own suit	2 HEARTS
Your partner's suit	2 DIAMONDS
A new, lower-ranking suit	2 CLUBS

If your bid is 2 CLUBS, your partner is expected to show preference by passing or by bidding 2 HEARTS.

Invitation. If you raise your partner's notrump, you are inviting game (because otherwise you would have passed). If you take out with a reverse, you must have at least enough extra strength to invite game. Since your reverse is forcing, you will have another chance to clarify your strength. Invitations are based on 24 partnership points (your points plus the 13 promised by your partner). The figure 24 is used because your partner can only have 1 or 2 extra points to get to 26 with. In the example case the invitations are:

A raise in notrump	2 NOTRUMP	
A new, higher-ranking suit	2 SPADES	(a reverse, forcing)

Game Force. If you make any jump bid, you are announcing enough partnership points for game. A jump by the captain forces both partners to continue bidding until game is reached:

A jump in notrump	3 NOTRUMP
A jump in your own suit	3 HEARTS
A jump in your partner's suit	3 DIAMONDS
A jump in a new suit	3 CLUBS

What do you bid next as responder after your partner bids a delayed notrump?

PARTNER	YOU
1 CLUB	1 SPADE
1 NOTRUMP	???

♠ K Q 8 3 2
♡ K 4 3
◇ 8 7
♣ 6 4 2

Your 9 points added to your partner's 13 come only to 22. Your partner can only have 1 or 2 extra points so you cannot think about game. You have no better bid than to PASS. Notrump is fine for your balanced hand.

♠ K 10 9 5 3
♡ Q J 6 5
◇ 8
♣ 5 4 2

You don't want to play in notrump with a singleton diamond. You want to play in spades or hearts. You indicate this by bidding 2 HEARTS. Your partner's delayed notrump is a normal balanced notrump so you are guaranteed at least a 7-card fit in one of your two suits, and maybe better.

♠ K Q J 10 4 3
♡ 10
◇ 8 3 2
♣ 5 4 3

It should be fairly obvious to sign off with 2 SPADES where you will have at least an 8-card fit.

♠ K J 10 8
♡ J 8 7
◇ Q 9 7
♣ A 5 4

You can count 24 partnership points and you are satisfied to play in notrump. You invite game with 2 NOTRUMP. With any fewer points, you would have passed. With a couple more, you would go directly to 3 NOTRUMP.

♠ A Q 10 9 5 3
♡ K Q 8 4 2
◇ 9
♣ 3

Your 15 opposite your partner's 13 is good for a game at least. You want to suggest hearts as an alternative to spades. You know that 2 HEARTS is a signoff but 3 HEARTS is forcing to game (a jump by the captain), so the latter is your bid. Since you will find a fit in one of your two suits, you do not have to devalue your hand.

♠ K 8 7 5 4
♡ A 6
◇ 8
♣ A J 9 8 7

Again you are headed for game. Since your spade bid did not get support from your partner, and since your hand is not suited for notrump, you jump to 3 CLUBS. If your partner now bids 3 NOTRUMP you will pass since that may be your only chance for game. Even after devaluation, your hand is still worth 12.

After the Flaky 1 NOTRUMP RESPONSE

Another similar case occurs when your partner responds to your opening bid with the flaky 1 NOTRUMP RESPONSE.

YOU	PARTNER
1 HEART	1 NOTRUMP

Your next bid is based on the possibilities for fit and the fact that your partner promises 6 points. Since the flaky notrump response has a 4-point spread (6,7,8,9), you will invite game with 23 partnership points, signing off with less and going to game with 25 or more.

The flaky 1 NOTRUMP RESPONSE may show as little as 6 points and it denies a fit in your suit. You are unlikely to see a game and yet a flaky captaincy has been shoved onto you anyway. In this one case you become the captain without gaining full forcing power. Instead you retain the limited forcing power that you, as opener, already had. However, the limited forcing power of the opener is broader than we have already said. A full statement is:

When the opener bids with limited forcing power:

- A new suit *reverse* is forcing.
- A jump into a *new suit* is forcing to game.

Other (single) jumps are non-forcing game invitations.

Unbalanced 1-Suiter. Continuing with the example above, if you have six hearts you can sign off by bidding 2 HEARTS. With 23 partnership points, you will bid 3 HEARTS. With 25 partnership points you must go directly to 4 HEARTS. However, you must remember that the 1 NOTRUMP RESPONSE does not promise a balanced hand or any support at all for your suit, so you must devaluate your hand. And even then, unless your suit is strong enough to play opposite a singleton, you must be cautious about jumping to game.

Unbalanced 2-Suiter. Holding two suits, you bid (for example) 2 DIAMONDS to sign off in either diamonds or hearts according to your partner's preference. But you bid a forcing 3 DIAMONDS (a jump in a new suit) with game-level values. If your second suit were spades, you would need to see at least 23 partnership points to bid 2 SPADES. This reverse forces your partner to bid, and you will end up at the 3-level at least. Of course you can then carry on to game if your hand warrants it.

Balanced Hand. If you like notrump, you may sign off with a pass, or invite game with 2 NOTRUMP, or get to game with 3 NOTRUMP.

In all the above cases your partner should decline a game invitation with 6 or 7 points and accept with 8 or 9.

What is your next bid in the following cases?

YOU	PARTNER
1 HEART	1 NOTRUMP
???	

♠ K 10
♡ A Q J 5 4
◇ Q 7 5 4 3
♣ 7

You have 15 points if you can find a fit in hearts or diamonds. Adding 6 points minimum from your partner, you get only 21 partnership points. Bid 2 DIAMONDS and let your partner choose between passing or possibly bidding 2 HEARTS where you will leave the contract.

♠ A 8 7 4
♡ J 10 9 3 2
◇ K J 8
♣ A

Your original count was 15, but if you have to play in notrump, your hand devaluates to 13. In either case there is no game potential. To look for a fit in spades by bidding 2 SPADES would be wrong for two reasons: if your partner had four spades he would have bid 1 SPADE instead of 1 NOTRUMP, so there is no 8-card fit there; besides, 2 SPADES is a reverse and you may end up at the 3-level without the strength for it. Since your partner is short in the majors, he must have some length in the minors. A pass leaves you at only 1 NOTRUMP, so you will probably make your contract even with shortness in clubs. The least of the evils is a PASS.

♠ K J 8
♡ A K 9 5 4 3
◇ A 3 2
♣ 4

Now you hope to get to game because you can count 21 partnership points in HCP alone, or 24 if you find a fit, so bid 3 HEARTS. This invites your partner to bid 4 HEARTS, holding two hearts and 8 or 9 points. With only one heart and a maximum, he might still gamble on 4 HEARTS or even 3 NOTRUMP. Either may work out as long as your side has a good supply of high-card points.

♠ K Q
♡ A Q J 10 8
◇ Q 4 2
♣ A 7 6

You were too strong to open in notrump so you started with hearts. Now you can count 25 partnership points and you jump right to 3 NOTRUMP.

More about the Bidding Direction

Here is a more complete statement about the direction the bidding takes in phase two:

> • If an 8-card major fit has been found, the bidding normally continues in that suit. (However, any other bid is intended to lead toward game in that major.)
> • If a 7-card major fit or a minor fit has been found, the bidding usually turns toward notrump.
> • If the limit bid was 1 NOTRUMP:
>
>> • Additional bidding in notrump takes the partnership to or toward a game in notrump.
>> • A minimum takeout bid in a suit (not a reverse) is a signoff leading to a trump contract.
>> • Reverse and jump suit bids lead to or toward a game, usually in a trump contract.

F

Forcing Versus Full-value Bidding

Forcing

Forcing allows you to make a low-level bid and still be sure that your partner will not pass. When it is your partner who makes a forcing bid, he is absolutely counting on getting a chance for another bid. You must bid unless the opponent between you and your partner comes in with a bid. In that case you have the option of passing because the bidding will get around to your partner again. Also, you are not forced to bid again if your side's bidding has already reached the game level.

The ordinary forcing bid only requires that the bidding be kept open for one round, so that the partner who makes the forcing bid will get one more chance to bid. These forcing bids are called ROUND FORCING.

Any bid which promises enough strength for the partnership to reach game requires both partners to continue bidding until a game bid is made. These bids are called GAME FORCING. (However, most game-forcing bids promise only enough partnership points for the 4-level. Occasionally the bidding has to stop at 4 CLUBS or 4 DIAMONDS because there are not enough extra points to support a 5-level contract, and 3 NOTRUMP or 4 SPADES or 4 HEARTS must be ruled out.)

The fundamental principle in using forcing bids is:

> The partner who sees game must either bid game or make forcing bids so that the other partner will not pass.

Forcing Power

Once the bidding has been opened, you can identify four positions at the table.

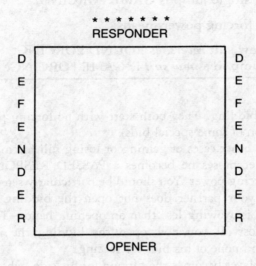

The stars over the responder signify that the responder starts with full forcing power in Standard American bidding. The opener starts with only limited forcing power, and the defenders start with no forcing power.

Full forcing power is advantageous to a bidder who is likely to see game, but is disadvantageous otherwise. The responder, sitting opposite a 13-point hand (or better), is likely to see game. The opener is not likely to see game unless his partner reveals a holding of at least 10 points. Therefore the opener starts with limited forcing power but gains full forcing power after a 2-over-1 response. The defenders are not likely to have a game since the other

Full forcing power means:

- Any new suit is ROUND FORCING (except a simple suit takeout after 1 NOTRUMP).
- Any single jump is GAME FORCING.

Limited forcing power means:

- A new suit *reverse* is ROUND FORCING.
- A jump in a *new suit* is GAME FORCING.

side is also bidding. They both start with no forcing power (with the exception of some special bids).

There are other cases of gaining or losing full forcing power. If the responder passes he becomes a PASSED RESPONDER and loses full forcing power. You should be particularly sensitive to the case where your partner does not open the bidding but passes instead. He is avowing less than an opening hand—12 points at the very most. If you now open the bidding, he is a passed responder and none of his bids are forcing.

When a player becomes the captain for his side, whether on the offense or the defense, he gains full forcing power and his partner loses it. This assists the captain in taking charge of any further bidding. However, when the opener becomes captain after a flaky 1 NOTRUMP RESPONSE, he gets only limited forcing power because of the uncertain situation.

Full-value Bidding

When you are the responder, you can keep the bidding alive with low-level forcing bids. But when you are the opener with limited forcing power, or a defender with no forcing power, you must frequently bid the full value of your hand as soon as you see a fit—otherwise your partner might pass, not knowing the real worth of your hand.

YOU	PARTNER
1 DIAMOND	1 HEART
???	

If you have 4-card support for hearts and can see 25 partnership points, you must go directly to 4 HEARTS. With only 23 partnership points, you must bid 3 HEARTS, which is invitational. Now your partner becomes the captain. He may pass, or with two or three extra points he may go on to game.

The same principle also applies when you as opener want to rebid your own suit. Given the same first two bids as above, you may now want to rebid your diamonds. If you see 23 partnership points, you must jump to 3 DIAMONDS in order to bid the full value of your hand.

If you are the opener and your partner responds with a 2-over-1 bid, the situation is different because you now have full forcing power.

YOU	PARTNER
1 HEART	2 CLUBS
???	

Your partner's bid has already promised enough strength for the partnership to reach 23 points. There is no reason for you to take drastic action unless you see that the partnership is at the game level. Therefore if you want to rebid your hearts with less than game strength, 2 HEARTS is sufficient. But with game strength you can bid a forcing 3 HEARTS, allowing room for your partner to say 4 HEARTS or 3 NOTRUMP or possibly some other bid. Even though you were the one to create the game force, he becomes the captain. You have limited your hand, and only your partner can tell whether there are slam possibilities.

Summary of Forcing Principles

FULL FORCING POWER	LIMITED FORCING POWER	NO FORCING POWER
New suit ROUND FORCING except simple takeout (nonjump,nonreverse) after 1 NOTRUMP Single jump GAME FORCING	New suit reverse ROUND FORCING Single jump in new suit GAME FORCING	
Phase 1	Phase 1	Phase 1

Full power

```
+--------+              +----------+
|        |  <-----------|  OPENER  |
+--------+              +----------+
```

after 2-over-1

```
+-----------+                    +-----------+
| RESPONDER |------------------->|           |
+-----------+    No power        +-----------+
               if he passes
```

```
                                +-----------+
                                | DEFENDERS |
                                +-----------+
```

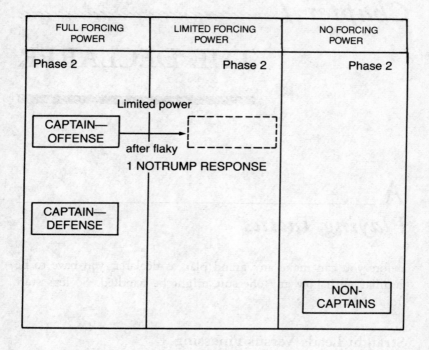

FULL FORCING POWER	LIMITED FORCING POWER	NO FORCING POWER
Phase 2	Phase 2	Phase 2

Chapter 7

THE DECLARER

A
Playing Tactics

Before you can make any grand plan as declarer, you have to be familiar with how any one suit might be handled. So let's start from there.

Straight Leads Versus Finessing

Suppose, playing at notrump, you hold:

YOU (DECLARER)	DUMMY
♠ K 3	♠ A 2
♡ 4 3 2	♡ A 6 5
◇ A K Q 6	◇ 5 4 3 2
♣ A Q J 6	♣ 5 4 3 2

In diamonds you have a sequence of three touching honors—the ace, king and queen. In clubs you also have three honors but the king is missing, leaving you with a tenace. Three honors are usually enough to control the suit and you can plan on using one of them on each of the first three rounds (tricks) played in that suit.

In diamonds, you can proceed with STRAIGHT leads, leading out your three high honors in succession. If you were a defender, you would lead your king first to signal your ace-king holding to your partner. If you did this as declarer, your opponents would see the king win and would guess that you also held the ace. As declarer, you want to conceal your holding from the defenders, so when you are playing from high cards which are equal to each other, you always play them from the top down (in this case, ace then king then queen). By the time your three high cards have been played, the opponents should be out of diamonds, setting up your small six as a long trick.

In clubs, you want to use your tenace for a finesse. You must ENTER the dummy, getting the lead into the dummy hand by taking a trick with one of the dummy's cards. The ace of spades and the ace of hearts are ENTRIES into the dummy. Once you get the lead into the dummy, you can lead the two of clubs, finessing (playing) the queen if the second hand plays low. If the queen wins, the opponents still have the king. You must reenter the dummy and repeat your finesse against the king. Lead the three of clubs and finesse the jack if the second hand plays low again. That's the end of your finessing, but if the opponents' clubs have split 3–2, then they only have one club left, perhaps the king. If you simply play the ace of clubs, their last card will drop under your ace, leaving your six as a long trick. Again you had three high cards to use on the first three rounds of play.

When you are the declarer and are working with a sequence which is only two cards long, straight leads generally are not the best procedure.

DUMMY

♠ K Q 7 6

OPPONENT
♠ A J 8

YOU

♠ 5 4 3 2

You could play the king, losing to the ace. Later you would win the second round with queen and lose the third round to the jack. But if the ace is favorably placed, you can do better than that by finessing. Lead the two from your hand, and if the second hand plays low, play your king. If that wins, enter your hand and lead spades again toward your queen. No matter when your left-hand opponent plays his ace, you will make tricks with both your king and queen, and the opponent's jack never will take a trick.

NOTE: It is customary, when showing three or four hands, to place the declarer at the bottom (the "South") position. From now on, the customary arrangement will be used.

Common Finesses

Here are a few of the most common finesses. You will see many other situations which are similar.

The holdings in the declarer's hand and the dummy hand are as shown. If the second hand does not play low, use the lowest available card which will cover the second hand's card. If you can't cover, then discard the lowest card.

ONE HAND	OTHER HAND	PROCEDURE WHEN SECOND HAND PLAYS LOW
4 3 2	A K J	If possible, play the ace first (to drop a singleton queen). Then lead low to the jack.
4 3 2	A Q	Lead low to the queen.
4 3 2	A Q J	Lead low to the queen, then low to the jack.
4 3 2	A Q 10	Lead low to the *ten,* then low to the queen.
4 3 2	A J 10	Lead low to the jack, then low to the ten.

4 3 2	K Q 5	Lead low to the king, then low to the queen.
4 3 2	K J 5	Lead low to the *jack,* then low to the king.
4 3 2	K J 10	Lead low to the jack, then low to the ten.
4 3 2	K 5	Lead low to the king.
4 3 2	Q J 5	Lead low to the queen, then low to the jack.
4 3 2	Q 10 5	Lead low to the *ten,* then low to the queen.

When you have two honors, one in each hand, here is how to attack the suit.

A 3 2	Q 5 4	Lead the ace first (to drop a singleton king). Then lead low to the queen.
K 3 2	Q 5 4	Either lead low to the queen or low to the king. If that succeeds, the ace is badly positioned for playing the other honor—either give up on further play in this suit or play low from both hands and hope the ace drops. (It will if it was in a doubleton.)
K 3 2	J 5 4	You will do better if you let the opponents lead this suit first. If you have to BREAK (start) the suit yourself, lead low toward either honor.

		Then lead low toward the other honor.
Q 3 2	J 5 4	Again you will do better if you let the opponents break this suit. Otherwise, lead low toward either honor. Then lead low toward the other.

When you have four honors, split between the two hands, you can often afford to waste one. When that is the case, you may be able to begin your finesse advantageously by leading an honor. As you will see, this may result in your playing two honors on the same trick, but you will still have enough honors to use one on each of the first three rounds of the suit.

Q J 10	A 5 4	Here you have four honors, which gives you one to spare. Lead the *queen*. If it is covered by the king from the second hand, PUT UP (play) the ace. But if it is not covered, DUCK (play low) from the other hand—if the queen wins, the lead is still in the same hand. (That is one of the advantages of finessing by leading an honor, but you need a spare honor to do it.) Now lead the jack for a repeat performance.
J 10 9	A 5 4	Lead the jack, then lead the ten, in similar fashion to the previous example. The nine substitutes for a fourth honor.
J 10 9	K 5 4	Lead the jack and duck if it is not covered.

It is not always necessary for you to lead a suit to take a finesse—sometimes the opponents do it for you. For example, the dummy holds:

YOU	DUMMY
♠ 8 7 5	♠ K 6 3

Your left-hand opponent leads a small spade. You would have played low toward the dummy and finessed the king if you had to lead the suit yourself. You accomplish the same thing now by playing the king. It wins if your left-hand opponent has the ace.

YOU	DUMMY
♠ A Q 7	♠ 9 6

Your left-hand opponent leads a small spade and you are delighted. If your right-hand opponent holds the king and plays it, you will top it with the ace and be left with a good queen. If your right-hand opponent does not play the king (maybe he doesn't even hold it), you will play your queen and still have your ace. When you are the fourth hand to play to a suit, and you hold a tenace in that suit, you get a FREE FINESSE—so called because the finesse cannot fail.

Ruffing High, Ruffing Low

Sometimes you have a choice of trump cards to ruff with. You want to use as high a trump as you can afford whenever there is a possibility that an opponent might OVERRUFF (ruff with a higher trump than you used).

YOU	DUMMY	
♠ K Q J 10 2	♠ A 8 4	← SPADES are trump
♡ 9 7 6 5	♡ 3 2	

Your left-hand opponent begins by leading first the king of hearts, then the ace and then the queen. Naturally you are going to ruff the queen but you are worried that your right-hand opponent may also be able to ruff. You see that you can afford to ruff with the ace of spades (because you also hold the king, queen, jack and ten), so you go up with the ace. If you were not able to spare the ace, you would use the eight.

YOU	DUMMY	
♠ A K Q J 10	♠ 8 4	← SPADES are trump
♡ A 9 7 6 5	♡ 3	

You want to use both of your small spades in the dummy to ruff hearts with. You will use first the four of spades and then the eight. The danger of being overruffed gets greater as you make successive ruffs, so you will start ruffing with the smaller spade and save the larger one for the second ruff.

Notice that if you draw trumps first, you will make five spade tricks and no ruffs. But if you first take two ruffs in the dummy, you will make seven tricks with your spades. If you make a ruff in your own hand, you do not increase the number of tricks which you can take with your spades. It is generally true that you will make additional tricks by ruffing in the short hand (the hand with the fewest number of trumps). But you should not ruff unnecessarily in the long hand—you may need those trumps to get the lead back from the opponents at a later time.

YOU	DUMMY	
♠ K Q 10 9 3	♠ A 8 4	← SPADES are trump
♡ A K 3	♡ 7 5	

You find that you must ruff your small heart in order to make your contract, but you wonder if you will be overruffed on the third round of hearts. Since you only need one trump for ruffing, you can play two rounds of trumps first, winning with the ace and king of spades. That will leave only one opponent with any trumps. Now you will play your ace, king and low heart. You will use your eight to ruff with. If one of the opponents is out of hearts at the time, he may be the one who is also out of spades and thus won't be able to overruff you.

YOU	DUMMY	
♠ J 10 9 7 6	♠ 8 4 3	← SPADES are trump
♡ A K 3	♡ 8 5	

You want to ruff your three of hearts and you realize you must do it immediately. If the opponents get the lead, they could play the ace, king and queen of spades, leaving you none in the dummy to ruff with. Since you are only planning to make one ruff, you will use the highest available trump. In this case, it's all right with you if an opponent overruffs—he will have to use the ace, king or queen to do it with!

Making Long Cards Good

Both in the trump suit and in long side suits you can usually establish some long cards. You must begin by determining how many cards the opponents hold in the suit to be established, and then watch to see when all those cards have been played.

> The most probable way for the opponents' cards to split between the two of them is a slightly uneven division.

The following will give you a good idea of how many times you will usually have to play a suit in order to clear the opponents of their holdings. (The fractions given are approximate—and you certainly don't need to remember them.)

YOU HAVE	OPPOSING SPLIT	ROUNDS NEEDED TO CLEAR THE SUIT
7-card fit	4–2	4 rounds are needed ½ of the time.
	3–3	3 rounds will do ⅓ of the time.
8-card fit	3–2	3 rounds are needed ⅔ of the time.
9-card fit	3–1	3 rounds are needed ½ of the time.
	2–2	2 rounds will do ⅓ of the time.
10-card fit	2–1	2 rounds are needed ⅔ of the time.

In establishing long cards, you may have to lose some tricks on the way.

YOU	DUMMY
♠ 8 5	♠ A 9 6 3 2

Here you can win the first round and will lose the second round. At notrump you would lose the third round and probably the fourth round, barring a lucky 3–3 split. But at a heart contract you may be able to ruff the dummy's spades on the third round, and perhaps also on the fourth round if necessary. The use of ruffing when setting up long cards is a common technique which you should keep in mind. This is one case where ruffing in the long hand may be effective if you can spare the trumps to do it with. The ruffing does not create additional tricks, but it keeps the opponents from gaining the lead while you are setting up your long cards.

YOU	PARTNER	
♠ A K Q J 4	♠ 7 5 2	Your contract is 4 SPADES.
♡ Q 4 3 2	♡ 9 8 5	The opening lead is the ♠3.
◇ K 5	◇ A 9 8 4 3	
♣ 4 3	♣ A K	

You should be able to draw trumps in three or four rounds, leaving one or two trumps in your hand. Then you can win with the king of diamonds for the first round of diamonds, followed by the ace on the second round. On the third round you can lead a small diamond and trump it in your hand. If that does not exhaust the opponents' diamonds, and you still have a trump left, you can go to the dummy and trump still another diamond. With any kind of luck you will have established one or possibly two small diamonds as long tricks.

B
Planning the Hand

Bidding and defensive play are both highly cooperative activities. But declarer play is a solo activity. How well you do as a declarer is directly related to your ability to recognize your opportunities and to plan to make best use of them. Your planning must begin as soon as you see the opening lead and the dummy—before you play a single card.

The Goal in Declarer Planning

In most forms of bridge, your prime objective as declarer is to make the contract which you and your partner have arrived at. If you are not playing duplicate, you will look for the safest way to make your contract, giving up on any possible overtricks if that will make the contract any surer. However you will frequently find that you can make the overtricks at no risk to your contract and will do so.

On the other hand, if you play duplicate, your success depends on doing better on each hand than others do who play the exact same hand. If you bid and make 4 SPADES while others make the same contract with an overtrick, you have done very badly. At duplicate you must make every trick which you reasonably can. However you will not normally jeopardize your contract unless the chances for an extra trick are fairly good.

Counting Losers at a Trump Contract

When you are the declarer, you may tend to look for your winning cards (WINNERS). But if you are playing at a trump contract it is even more important to recognize your losing cards (LOSERS). At a trump contract you can often prevent these cards from losing, using methods which are not available at notrump.

First of all you must count the losers in the *long hand*—the hand which has the most trumps. In the following examples, assume that you (the declarer) hold the long hand since that is usually the case anyway.

How many losers do you count in your hand in the club suit in the following cases? Do not count a small card in your hand as a loser if it will be played on a winning card in the same suit from the dummy.

YOU	DUMMY	
♣ 3 2	♣ 5 4	You expect both your three and your two to lose, so you count two losers.
♣ 3 2	♣ A K	Since both of your small cards will go on winning tricks taken by the dummy's ace and king, they are not counted as losers. You have no losers in clubs.
♣ A 2	♣ 5 4	Only your two will lose—one loser.
♣ 3 2	♣ A 4	You have one loser.
♣ A 2	♣ 6 5 4	You have one loser, the two. Remember that you are counting against your own hand because it has the most trumps.
♣ A 3 2	♣ 5 4	Now you have two losers, the three and the two.

Eliminating Losers by Ruffing

You have already seen one of the ways to eliminate losers. Sometimes they can be ruffed by trumping them in the short hand.

```
YOU                DUMMY
♠ A K Q 7 5 3      ♠ 6 4       ← SPADES are trump
♣ 3 2              ♣ —
  L L
```

At first you might perceive the two small clubs (marked L) as losers, but you will soon realize that they can be ruffed with small trumps from the dummy. If this is done, they will no longer be losers. You note mentally that you are planning to ruff these two clubs if possible:

```
YOU                DUMMY
♠ A K Q 7 5 3      ♠ 6 4       ← SPADES are trump
                     W W
♣ 3 2              ♣ —
  R R ←
```

The two small clubs to be ruffed have been re-marked with an R, and the trumps which will convert them into winners have been marked with a W. You will have to take these ruffs before drawing trumps—otherwise the dummy's trumps will be gone.

```
♠ A K Q 6 4 2      ♠ 9 8 7 5      ← SPADES are trump
♣ A 7 5            ♣ K 6
```

You have a loser in clubs which you can ruff in the dummy. But you can draw trumps first—even if one opponent should have all three outstanding trumps, you can lead trump three times and still have one left in the dummy. When you can afford to do it, you must go after your trumps first. Suppose instead that you take the king of clubs, then the ace of clubs, then lead the five for a ruff. If one of the opponents had only two clubs, he may now ruff your five with the ten or the jack, so your loser loses in the end. And think what would happen if one opponent had only one club. There is no need to take these risks when you can draw trump first.

♠ Q J 10 9 8   ♠ 5 3 2   ← SPADES are trump
♣ A 7 5   ♣ K 6

Now if you start to draw trumps first, the opponents may help you out by playing the ace, king and another trump. The dummy will have no trumps left to ruff with and that ruins your plan for your loser. In this case you must go after your ruff first, before drawing trumps, or you may never get the chance later. You do face some risk of having an opponent outruff you, but this time you can't get around it.

Although you as declarer will usually hold the long hand, sometimes the dummy will hold the long hand. If both hands have the same number of trumps, you can pick either one to be the "long hand," but if you plan to do some ruffing, pick as the long hand the one containing the losers to be ruffed. After counting your losers in the long hand, compare that number against the number of tricks you can lose and still make your contract. For example, at the common contracts of 4 HEARTS and 4 SPADES you can afford to lose only three tricks.

In the following hands, count your losers. Can you get rid of any of them by ruffing? If so, will you draw trumps before or after ruffing?

YOU	DUMMY	
♠ A K Q J 5	♠ 6 3 2	Your contract is 4 SPADES.
♡ A 8 6	♡ 9	The opening lead is the ♡K.
◇ K 8	◇ A 7 5 4	
♣ 9 7 5	♣ A 8 6 3 2	

You count probably no losing spades, two losing hearts and two losing clubs. The two hearts can be ruffed in the dummy, but you cannot draw trump first. Take the opening trick and immediately ruff a heart. Reenter your hand by taking the ace of spades (the surest way) and ruff another heart. Then return to your hand via the king of diamonds and draw the remaining trumps.

YOU	DUMMY	Your contract is 4 SPADES.
♠ A K Q J 10	♠ 7 5 4 3	The opening lead is the ♠6.
♡ A 3	♡ 5	
◇ Q J 10 4	◇ K 8 7 5	
♣ 7 6	♣ Q 8 5 3	

You can count one loser in hearts, one in diamonds and two in clubs, but you can ruff the heart loser. You can afford to play trump up to three times. That should exhaust the opponents' trumps, but whether it does or doesn't, you will then play hearts twice and take your ruff while you still have a trump left in the dummy.

Eliminating Losers by Discarding

Sometimes you will have a situation like this:

YOU (LONG HAND)	DUMMY (SHORT HAND)	
♠ A K Q J 4	♠ 8 7 5	← SPADES are trump
♡ 3	♡ A K	
◇ K Q 7 5 4	◇ A J 3 2	
♣ A 2	♣ 8 6 4 3	

You are the long hand because you have the most trumps. You can see only one loser in the long hand—in clubs. But look at the hearts. Your small heart will go on the ace of hearts. The king of hearts in the short hand is called an EXTRA WINNER because it will take another heart trick *after* the hearts in the long hand are exhausted. Since your hearts will be gone, you can discard your losing club on the king of hearts. Pictorially we might show this as:

```
♠ A K Q J 4      ♠ 8 7 5        ← SPADES are trump
♡ 3              ♡ A K
                        W
◇ K Q 7 5 4      ◇ A J 3 2
♣ A 2            ♣ 8 6 4 3
        D ←
```

The two of clubs has been marked D because it is slated for discard on the winning king of hearts, marked W. There is no reason not to draw the trumps first, after which you will play the hearts and take your discard.

Assuming that your hand is the long hand and that hearts are a side suit (not the trump suit), how many extra winners can you find in the heart suit? Are there any losers in the heart suit?

YOU	DUMMY	
♡ A 3	♡ K Q 4 3	After two rounds of play, the queen will be an extra winner, but the remaining small card will not. There are no losers in hearts—you count only the long hand for losers.
♡ 5	♡ K Q	If the opponents play their ace on the first round, you will have one loser and one extra winner. But if they hold up their ace until the second round, you will have no loser but also no extra winner. Either way will usually amount to the same thing.
♡ —	♡ A K	You have two extra winners and no losers.

♡ A 9 4	♡ K Q 8 7 3	After the first three rounds, the opponents will probably be out of hearts, so the long cards left in the dummy will become extra winners. But you must draw trumps first or the opponents will start ruffing.
♡ 6	♡ A Q	If you play the ace on the first round, you will have no loser but also no extra winner. If you take the finesse on the first round, you may or may not have a loser (depending on the success of the finesse), but you will always have an extra winner.
♡ 6	♡ K 3 2	You must lead the six, and if the second hand plays the ace, you have one loser and one extra winner. If the second hand has the ace but does not play it, you have no loser (your king wins) but no extra winner. If the king loses to the ace in the third hand, you have one loser, no extra winner and tough luck.

Using Extra Winners

YOU	DUMMY	
♠ K Q J 5 4 3	♠ 10 8 7	← SPADES are trump
♡ 3 2	♡ A K Q	
◇ K Q 7	◇ A J 3	
♣ 9 3	♣ 8 6 4 2	

You can see one loser in spades and two losers in clubs. And if the opponents begin by leading clubs, their ace and king will prevail. But the defense doesn't always get off to the right lead. If they start with hearts or diamonds, you can make use of your extra winner in hearts to discard one of your clubs. But you cannot draw trumps first—they will win with the ace and get a second chance to find the club lead.

Now let's put the ace of clubs into your hand.

♠ K Q J 5 4 3	♠ 10 8 7	←SPADES are trump
♡ 3 2	♡ A K Q	
◇ K Q 7	◇ A J 3	
♣ A 3	♣ 8 6 4 2	

If the opponents begin with a club lead you can take your ace, but then your three of clubs is naked. If you let the opponents get the lead while the three is exposed, they can win with their king of clubs and the three loses. To prevent that you must immediately play hearts to get your discard in clubs.

On the other hand, if the opponents begin with a diamond or a heart lead, you can start to draw trump. They will win a spade trick, getting the lead, but your ace of clubs is still there to protect your three. When you get the lead back, you can finish drawing trumps and then go to hearts for your discard. The difference is based on what damage the opponents can do to you if you give them the lead.

Now let's look at one more variation on this hand.

♠ K Q J 5 4	♠ 10 8 7	←SPADES are trump
♡ 3 2	♡ K Q J	
◇ K Q 7	◇ A J 3	
♣ A K 3	♣ 8 6 4 2	

You still have an extra winner in hearts, but you will have to lose to the ace of hearts before you can establish it. You count one loser each in spades, hearts and clubs. If the opponents begin leading clubs, your ace goes on the first trick. You can lose a heart trick next and when the opponents continue clubs your king will win. Now you can take your extra winner in hearts, discarding your losing three of clubs. You can't go about drawing trump before you take the discard because that gives the opponents the lead one more time than you can afford.

To eliminate losers you need a suit where the cards are unevenly distributed between you and the dummy. To ruff in the dummy you need a suit with more cards in your hand than in the dummy. To find a place to discard your losers, you need a suit with more cards in the dummy than in your own hand. As declarer you should look for the suits which are unevenly distributed to find these possibilities.

The preceding hands illustrate that when you are making your plans as the declarer, you must ask yourself:

- Can I draw trump immediately or must I wait?
- Whan can happen to me if I give up the lead?

In the following hands, count your losers. Can you get rid of any of them on extra winners? Will you draw trumps before or after using your extra winners?

YOU	DUMMY	Your contract is 4 SPADES.
♠ A K 8 7 4	♠ Q J 6	The opening lead is the ♠3.
♡ 8 6 2	♡ 5 4 3	
◇ 7 5	◇ A K Q 4	
♣ A 8 3	♣ K 5 2	

You have three losers in hearts and one in clubs. But you have an extra winner in diamonds. Draw the trumps and then play diamonds three times, discarding a club or a heart.

YOU	DUMMY	
♠ 5	♠ K Q J 2	Your contract is 4 HEARTS.
♡ K Q J 7 4	♡ 9 8 6	The opening lead is the ♣ J.
◇ A K 3	◇ 5 4 2	
♣ K 7 4 3	♣ A Q 6	

You have a loser in each of the four suits. However, you can establish two extra winners in spades. Win the opening lead with the king of clubs and start drawing trumps. The opponents will win a trick with their ace of hearts (and with their ace of spades, if they wish, but that is all right with you). But then they will have to give you the lead back. Assuming that the ace of spades is still in the opponents' hands, you will play spades until they decide to play their ace. After that you will have to get back to the dummy to continue playing spades—do you see that you must save the ace or queen of clubs for that very purpose?

YOU	DUMMY	
♠ 7 6 5	♠ J 3 2	Your contract is 5 CLUBS.
♡ 3	♡ A K Q	The opening lead is the ◇ 8.
◇ A Q J	◇ K 9 6	
♣ K Q J 10 4 2	♣ 9 8 7 5	

If the opponents had started with spades, they would have set you immediately. You can't let them have the lead again without doing something about your three spade losers. Besides that you have a club loser. Fortunately you can discard just enough of the spade losers on the heart extra winners. But you can't draw trumps first because that would give up the lead and give the opponents another chance to find the heart lead. First play your three hearts, discarding spades. Then draw trump.

Planning for Entries

Up till now we have been assuming that you can get the lead back and forth between the declarer's and dummy's hands as needed. This COMMUNICATION between hands is not always available, or it may need some planning to make it available. Here are some examples where communication is readily available if you play your cards in the right order.

Assume SPADES are trump and that there is no possibility to take a trick in the "other" hand except as shown. How do you proceed?

THE LEAD IS IN THIS HAND	THE OTHER HAND	THE OBJECTIVE	
♡ A Q J ◇ 4 3	♡ 8 7 5 ◇ A K	To finesse hearts	Lead the small diamond to get the lead into the other hand. Lead the small heart to finesse the queen of hearts. If the finesse succeeds, lead the other small diamond so that you can finesse again in hearts.
♡ A Q 4 ◇ 7 5	♡ J 10 7 ◇ A 2	To finesse hearts	Lead the small diamond to the ace. Then lead the jack for a finesse. If the finesse succeeds, you are in the right hand to finesse hearts again.

♠ 5 4 ♡ — ♢ 3 2	♡ 8 7 ♢ A K	To ruff the hearts	Lead a diamond to the other hand and return a heart for a ruff. Then repeat a second time.
♡ A K Q ♢ 4	♡ J 8 6 4 3 ♢ A	To use the long hearts	After trumps have been drawn, play off the ace, king and queen of hearts. Then lead a diamond and continue with hearts. The high hearts BLOCK the heart suit—hearts cannot be continued without first shifting to another suit.
♡ A ♢ 8 6 4	♡ K 4 ♢ A	To discard a diamond on the ♡K	First play the ace of hearts which is blocking the heart suit. Then lead a diamond to the ace and play the king of hearts, discarding a diamond.

Establishing and Saving Entries

Sometimes you have to take some action to establish the needed entries.

Given the same assumptions as before, how can you establish an entry in the "other" hand?

THE LEAD IS IN THIS HAND	THE OTHER HAND	
♣ 4 3	♣ K Q	Lead a small club. If the opponents do not play their ace, you have entered the other hand. If they do, you have established an entry for later on.
♣ A 5 3	♣ Q J	You can't start by leading the ace and still accomplish your objective. Lead a small club to the queen, which will either win or will establish the jack as an entry.
♣ 6 4	♣ K 2	Unlike the previous cases, there is no guaranteed entry here. Lead the small club and finesse the king. If the ace is in the second hand, the king will supply an entry.
♣ A 4	♠ 8 ←TRUMP ♣ 5	Lead the ace and then ruff the four.

Sometimes the entries are already there—but you have to be careful not to use them up before you really need them. Here are some cases, following the same pattern as before.

♠ A K J 8 7   ♠ Q 4 3

Sometimes the only entry to the other hand is in the trump suit. You must save the queen until you are ready to enter the other hand. The ace and king may be played earlier, but that will only partially draw the trumps.

♡ 3 2   ♡ A K 8 5 4

Sometimes the only entry to the other hand is in the long side suit which you are trying to establish. If you play the ace and king first, you have used up your only entries. When you lose the third round of hearts you will have no way to reenter the other hand. Instead, you must duck (play low) from the other hand on the first round. Later you will lead the other small heart and win with the ace. Now you can continue with the king—if you are lucky, that will exhaust the opponents' hearts and you can make your long hearts good. If the hearts split 4–2 or worse, that's just too bad.

◇ A 2   ◇ K 2

If the opponents lead diamonds, and you will need an entry into the other hand, you must take the trick with the ace. But if you will need the entry into the first hand, then you must take the trick with the king. Think first, play later!

How will you play these hands so as to manage your entries properly? Be sure to count your losers and to determine when you will draw trumps.

YOU	DUMMY	
♠ A J 10	♠ 6 3 2	Your contract is 4 HEARTS.
♡ A K 9 4 3	♡ 8 7 5	The opening lead is the ♣Q.
◇ A 4 3	◇ Q J 7	
♣ K 9	♣ A 4 3 2	

You have up to two losers in spades, a third in hearts (at least), and a fourth in diamonds. There are no ruffing or discarding possibilities, so your main concern is to limit your spade losses to one. That means that you must lead spades twice from the dummy. Fortunately you can get to the dummy twice, once with the ace of clubs and once with queen-jack of diamonds. The safest approach is to win the first trick with the king of clubs, play three rounds of hearts, and then go after the spades. If you were to take the opening trick with the ace of clubs, you would have to take a spade finesse immediately, before drawing trumps. When you can get into the dummy a limited number of times, you must use each occasion to maximum advantage.

YOU	DUMMY	
♠ A K Q J 8	♠ 4 3 2	Your contract is 4 SPADES.
♡ 8	♡ K Q J 4	The opening lead is the ♠5.
◇ 7 6 4	◇ K 8 2	
♣ K Q J 2	♣ 9 7 6	

You expect no losers in spades, but you have one in hearts, a second, a third and possibly a fourth in diamonds, a fifth and probably a sixth in clubs. However, you have two extra winners in hearts, and your king of diamonds or your fourth club may win. If that takes care of three losers, you can afford the other three without going down. A heart lead will establish the extra winners, but then you will need an entry to get to them. The king of diamonds is the only entry available, so it had better win! Since you do not need trumps for this plan, you can play spades first. Then you will play hearts to set up your extra winners. After the ace of hearts is played, you will have to lead toward your king of diamonds, keeping your fingers crossed.

YOU	DUMMY	Your contract is 4 HEARTS.
♠ A K	♠ Q J 8 6 5	The opening lead is the ♣K.
♡ K Q 5 3 2	♡ A 7 6	
◊ A 10 8 5	◊ 7 4 2	
♣ 5 3	♣ 8 7	

You can see that you are going to lose two clubs right away. Also, you have a third, fourth and fifth loser in diamonds. However, you have long spades in the dummy which will give you three extra winners on which to discard the three diamond losers. But the spade suit is blocked, so you will need an entry to get into the dummy to continue after the first two rounds of spades. The ace of hearts is conveniently available for that purpose. You can draw two rounds of hearts using the king and queen. Then you must play the ace and king of spades. Be sure you see why. Then you can play the third round of hearts, winning with the ace so that you can continue with the spades and throw off the diamond losers.

YOU	DUMMY	Your contract is 6 HEARTS.
♠ —	♠ A K Q J 4	The opening lead is the ◊K.
♡ A K 9 8 7 6	♡ 5 4 3 2	
◊ A 10 3	◊ 8 5	
♣ A 8 7 5	♣ 9 4	

You can count on no losers in spades or hearts, two in diamonds and three in clubs, making five in all. But you can see those big extra winners in the dummy spade suit, just sitting there and grinning at you. The spade suit is blocked so you need to get to the dummy via another suit. Then you notice that you can ruff a diamond, getting rid of a diamond loser that way and also entering the dummy. So you will win the opening trick with the ace of diamonds and play the ace and king of hearts, hoping that will exhaust the opponents' trumps. Then you can lose a diamond trick—the opponents can do you no damage. Whatever the opponents lead, you will get the lead back and will ruff your third diamond. Then away you go, RUNNING (playing in succession) the top spades and throwing off your losing clubs.

YOU	DUMMY	Your contract is 4 SPADES.
♠ A K Q J 7	♠ 6 3 2	The opening lead is the ♠8.
♡ A 8 4	♡ 7 6 3	
◇ 6 4 3	◇ A K 8 7 2	
♣ A 7	♣ 8 6	

With no losers in spades, you count two losers in hearts, a third in diamonds and a fourth in clubs—one too many for 4 SPADES. But you have extra winners in the dummy's diamond suit if you play it carefully. After drawing trumps, you tackle the diamonds. You will have to lose one round of diamonds if they divide 3-2 and two rounds if they should divide 4–1. You will lose one round immediately, playing a low diamond from each hand, in order to keep your entries. The opponents can then take a club trick and may play hearts, forcing you to win with your ace. Now the heart losers are exposed so you cannot give up the lead again. You will take the ace and king of diamonds, and a normal split will give you two long cards for an overtrick.

NOTE: If the opponents do not force out your ace of hearts, you can deliberately lose a second round of diamonds. Then you will have only one long card, but a 4–1 split cannot hurt you. This SAFETY PLAY will make your contract surer but gives up the opportunity for an overtrick. At duplicate you must try for the overtrick because you will probably succeed, but at other forms of bridge the safety of your contract is more important than an overtrick.

YOU	DUMMY	Your contract is 4 HEARTS.
♠ A Q 7	♠ 8 5 3	The opening lead is the ♣K.
♡ Q J 7 6 4 2	♡ A K	
◇ A Q	◇ 9 7 6 4	
♣ A 6	♣ 8 5 3 2	

Your trumps are solid but you have one or two losers in spades, a possible third in diamonds and a fourth in clubs. With no ruffing or extra-winner possibilities you must count on making at least one finesse. You will enter the dummy with a high heart and immediately take one of your finesses. As soon as you can, you will reenter the dummy with your other high heart and take the other finesse if needed. (At duplicate you would always take the second finesse.) Only after that can you completely draw trumps.

Summary for Trump Contracts

When making your plans as declarer at a trump contract, you must:

- Count the losers in the long hand.

- Look for opportunities to eliminate the losers by:

  - Ruffing them in the short hand
  - Discarding them on extra winners in the short hand

- Decide the best sequence of play:

  - Can you draw trumps first?
  - Can you afford to give up the lead?
  - Do you have the entries for a given line of play?

When you and the dummy hold the same number of trumps, you can pick either hand to be the "long" hand—but if you plan to do some ruffing, pick the hand containing the losers to be ruffed.

Winners at Notrump

As the declarer at a trump contract, you planned how to eliminate your losers. This worked because once you had discarded or ruffed the losers from some suit in the long hand, you were in a position to trump the opponents if they threatened you by playing in that suit. As the declarer at notrump, you do not have the protection of a trump suit—you have to plan your play by counting your winners and by assessing what damage the opponents can do to you when they have the lead.

YOU	DUMMY	
♠ K Q J 6 5	♠ A 10	Your contract is 3 NOTRUMP.
♡ A 4 3	♡ K Q J 2	The opening lead is the ♡10.
◇ K Q J	◇ 9 5 4 3	
♣ 8 2	♣ 6 5 3	

First count your winners in *both* hands—in spades you have five, in hearts you have four, and in diamonds you have two after losing to the ace. When you come to clubs, you see your big weakness. The opponents have eight clubs, including all the high ones. If they had started with a club lead, they could have taken at least four club tricks and the ace of diamonds to set you before you even got the lead!

The good news is your nine winners in spades and hearts—enough to make your contract. You will grab those tricks first. After that you can play the king of diamonds and not have to worry

---

At a notrump contract, when you have established enough winners to complete your contract, check all four suits to see if the opponents can damage you if you give up the lead.

- If so, take your tricks immediately.
- If not, try to establish one or more overtricks.

what happens next. If you were to play the diamonds before taking your nine tricks, the opponents would get the lead, giving them a second chance to set you with their club tricks.

YOU (DECLARER)	DUMMY	Your contract is 3 NOTRUMP.
♠ A K	♠ J 9 5	The opening lead is the ♠4.
♡ K 7 3	♡ A 5 4	
◇ 6 4 3	◇ A J 7 5	
♣ A Q J 7 8	♣ 5 4 2	

In spades you can take the first two tricks—after that the opponents can take the rest of the spades. A first guess is that your left-hand opponent has led from five spades headed by the queen. You can count two more tricks in hearts and one in diamonds, making five tricks so far. In clubs you see possibilities for finessing and for establishing long cards, probably giving you the additional four tricks needed to complete your contract.

The very first thing you must do after winning the opening spade trick is to start working on your club suit. Remember the principle of first establishing the additional tricks which you need to make your contract. You must hold on as long as possible to your aces and kings which are already established. Then, if you lose the club finesse, you can take the next trick and gain the lead back, no matter whether the opponents continue the spade suit, as they probably will, or whether they shift to hearts or diamonds.

In order to finesse in clubs, you need to get the lead into the dummy. Necessarily that means using one of the dummy's high cards as an entry. Since you have two stoppers in hearts, you will lead the three of hearts and win with your ace of hearts. Now you can lead the two of clubs and finesse the queen. If the queen wins you will want to go into the dummy again to repeat the finesse. This time you will use your ace of diamonds as an entry, lead a low club and finesse the jack.

As soon as you have finished playing the clubs, you will have to win immediately with all your remaining aces and kings. You will see that you cannot lose the lead again without giving the opponents a chance to take too many tricks in the suits which you no longer have stopped.

Impeding the Opponents at Notrump

Declarer play at notrump is a combination of establishing tricks for yourself and impeding the opponents so that they do not set you. If your partnership has bid wisely, you will usually have one natural impediment—at least one trick in each of the suits. But there is more you can do. Suppose at a contract of 3 NOTRUMP the spades are divided as follows:

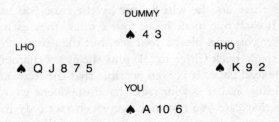

DUMMY

♠ 4 3

LHO

♠ Q J 8 7 5

RHO

♠ K 9 2

YOU

♠ A 10 6

Your left-hand opponent makes an opening lead of the seven of spades. Suppose you take the trick with the ace. Since you can rarely make your contract without giving up the lead, sooner or later you will have to let one of the opponents take a trick. Whichever opponent wins that trick now will play spades. The opponents will proceed to take four more tricks in spades, setting your contract.

Suppose instead that you do not play the ace of spades on the first round of spades, or on the second round either. You HOLD UP your ace until the third round, when of course you have to play it. But now your right-hand opponent is out of spades. If he later gets the lead, he cannot continue playing spades.

YOU	DUMMY	
♠ A 10 6	♠ 4 3	Your contract is 3 NOTRUMP.
♡ 7 6 3	♡ A J 4	The opening lead is the ♠7.
◇ K Q J	◇ 8 7 5	
♣ A K 7 8	♣ Q 10 5 3 2	

You can see that you can only take one trick in spades, after which the opponents will have the field to themselves. You plan to hold up your ace of spades until the third round. Counting your winners, you find you have nine, assuming that the club suit will yield five tricks. But in order to make your queen and jack of diamonds good you will first have to give up the lead to the ace. You can only hope that your right-hand opponent has the ace and that he is out of spades at that time.

Since your side holds five spades, the opponents hold eight. If your left-hand opponent started with five, your right-hand opponent holds three and he will be out by the time you have played your ace. If each opponent holds four spades, they each will have one left after you have played your ace, but then they can only take one more spade trick (three in all) plus the ace of diamonds before you get the lead back. It is even possible that the lead came from a 3-card holding and it is your right-hand opponent who holds five spades. In that case you can make your contract only if your left-hand opponent is the one who holds the ace of diamonds.

YOU	DUMMY	Your contract is 3 NOTRUMP.
♠ A Q 8	♠ 10 6 5 4	The opening lead is the ◇ K.
♡ 9 5	♡ A Q 4	
◇ A 4 3	◇ 8 7	
♣ A Q 9 7 6	♣ K J 3 2	

The opening lead looks ominous since it may have come from five diamonds headed by the king-queen-jack. That opponent, on your left, holds the DANGER HAND—if possible you want to prevent that hand from getting the lead later on and running the diamonds. By holding up your ace of diamonds as long as possible, you hope to exhaust the diamonds in the hand on your right, making it safe for that hand to obtain the lead. You can count eight winners which you can take without losing the lead, but to get a ninth trick you will have to take a finesse in either spades or hearts. If the spade finesse loses, the danger hand will get the lead, but if the heart finesse loses, the SAFE HAND will get the lead. So you plan to take the heart finesse first and not even try the spade finesse if the heart finesse succeeds.

Summary for Notrump Contracts

As you plan the hand for a notrump contract:

• Count your winners in both hands.
• If you do not have enough winners to make your contract, look for the best way to establish the needed winners.
• Determine which opponent holds the danger hand.

As you play the hand:

• Hold up your high cards in the opponents' long suit for as long as you can without causing your high cards to lose unnecessarily.
• When you must give up the lead, try not to give it to the danger hand.
• When you have established enough winners to complete your contract, check all four suits to see if the opponents can damage you if you give up the lead.

    • If so, take your tricks immediately.
    • If not, try to establish one or more overtricks.

Chapter 8 ///////////////////////////////////////

THE
DEFENDERS

///////////////////////////////////////

A
Leads and Plays

When the opponents win the contract, your side becomes the defense during the play period. The declarer can see his partner's hand (the dummy) but you as a defender cannot see your partner's cards. You must try to overcome this disadvantage by playing your own cards in such a way as to SIGNAL to your partner what your true holdings are.

Even though you can't see your partner's hand, you can read the signals which he gives you by the way he plays his hand. Besides that, you can see one of the opponent's hands (the dummy), which will help you in making your LEADS (the first card played to a trick) and PLAYS (any subsequent card played to a trick).

Leading from a Sequence

When you hold a 3-card sequence headed by an honor, you have a strong combination. The first three rounds of play in a suit are usually controlled by high cards, and you have three high (or fairly high) cards available to use, one on each of those rounds. This makes a high-card lead appropriate.

When you hold a 2-card sequence headed by an honor and backed up by a third card which almost forms a 3-card-sequence, you also have three high cards. Again a high-card lead is appropriate.

The following examples will illustrate the various cases and the correct card to lead to properly signal your holding to your partner.

♠ A K̲ Q	Lead the king from any ace-king combination. The ace, king and queen are already established tricks.
♠ K̲ Q J	Lead the king from the top of your 3-card sequence. If it loses to the ace, you will have established your queen and jack. If your partner holds the ace, so much the better.
♠ Q̲ J 10 2	Lead the queen from the top of your 3-card sequence. You are working toward establishing your ten, and if your partner holds the ace or the king, your side will get additional tricks.
♠ A K̲ J 2	Your top two cards form a 2-card sequence, and your third card (the jack) is only one card away from making it a 3-card sequence. This is called a BROKEN sequence, in contrast to the SOLID sequences above. Lead the king because you are leading from an ace-king combination.
♠ J̲ 10 8	Notice that this is also a broken sequence, headed by an honor. You will lead the jack because it is at the top of the two cards which are strictly in sequence.
♠ K J̲ 10 4	Again the jack and ten are in sequence, but this time they are not at the top of your suit. This is called an INTERIOR sequence be-

cause it starts with an honor (the jack) which is inside your suit. But again you lead the jack because it is at the top of the two cards which are in strict sequence.

When you hold a simple 2-card sequence headed by an honor, you do not have the strength assured by any of the sequences we just looked at. How you lead from a 2-card sequence depends on whether you are defending against a trump contract or against a notrump contract.

Trump Contract. At a trump contract, you depend mainly on your high cards to take whatever tricks you can. Furthermore, the declarer or the dummy may start ruffing after a few rounds of your suit have been played, so you need to use your aces and kings in the earliest rounds of the suit. With a 2-card sequence including the king, the lead of the king accomplishes that objective and does you some immediate good: From ace-king it takes a trick, or from king-queen it establishes your queen.

Leading from the lower 2-card sequences (queen-jack, jack-ten, ten-nine) is of more questionable value. You will need to find one or two high cards in the same suit in your partner's hand to help you out. When your suit is long enough, it is best for you to lead your fourth-highest card and let your partner play his high cards first, since he probably has the short holding. But when your suit is only two or three cards long, then you have the short holding and should play your own high cards first, leading from the top of your sequence.

Notrump Contract. At a notrump contract, your primary goal is to set up some long cards. If you can, you will generally start leading from a 5-card (or longer) suit, or possibly from a strong 4-card suit. If the suit is headed by three cards which form a solid sequence or broken sequence or interior sequence, you will start leading from the sequence. With any lesser holding, you will start with a fourth-highest lead. Because you are trying to set up long cards, you want your partner, with the short holding, to play his high cards first. You do not have to be in a hurry to play your own high cards because they cannot be trumped later.

A K 5 2	At notrump, lead the two. At a trump contract, lead the king.
K Q 5 2	At notrump, lead the two. At a trump contract, lead the king.
Q J 5 2	At all contracts lead the two—this is a low 2-card sequence.
J 10 2	At all contracts lead the jack—there is no fourth card.

SUMMARY

The conventional lead from a sequence headed by an honor is:

- King from ace-king or king-queen
- Top of the sequence from other combinations

For a two-card sequence when a fourth-highest lead is possible

- At notrump, fourth-highest from all two-card sequences
- At trump, fourth-highest from low two-card sequences (queen-jack, jack-ten, ten-nine)

Following Suit from a Sequence

You already know to lead the top card from a sequence such as:

♠ Q J 10 2

But if someone else leads the spades and you plan to play a high card, either because you will take the trick or because you will force the opponents to play a higher card, you must follow suit with the *ten,* picking the lowest card from your sequence. There is a reason for this:

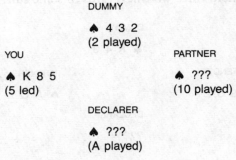

```
                     DUMMY
                   ♠ 4 3 2
                   (2 played)
    YOU                          PARTNER
  ♠ K 8 5                       ♠ ???
  (5 led)                       (10 played)
                    DECLARER
                   ♠ ???
                   (A played)
```

It might occur to you to wonder why the declarer did not take the trick with the queen or the jack, both of which are lower than your king. Of course he would have if he held either one of them. It must be your partner who holds these cards! He followed suit from the bottom of his queen-jack-ten sequence, allowing you to deduce in this particular case where the other honors are. Even if this logic seems beyond you at your present skill level, you can still get into the right habit for your partner's benefit:

> **When selecting a card from a sequence headed by an honor lead high and follow low.**

Leading from a Worthless Suit

When you lead from a worthless suit, not even containing a ten, you can tell your partner that you have nothing by leading the highest of your small cards.

> **When leading from a worthless holding (without even a ten), lead top of nothing.**

When you are leading the trump suit, top of nothing does not apply. Trumps are too valuable to use a high one for routine signaling. For now, if you decide to lead from two or three small trumps, lead your lowest.

LEAD THROUGH STRENGTH

Suppose you hold three worthless cards in some suit:

	DUMMY	
	♠ K 4 3	
YOU (DEFENDER)		PARTNER
♠ 9 5 2		♠ A Q 6 ???
	DECLARER	
	???	

You certainly can take no tricks in this suit, but how about your partner? You can't see your partner's hand, but you can hope that it looks as shown.

Your partner is dying for you to lead spades so he can take a finesse. The finesse is going to work, because the king is on your left. When you hold worthless cards and see one or two high cards on your left, that is often a good suit to lead. Just picture your partner holding one or two of the missing high cards.

Now suppose the dummy is on your right:

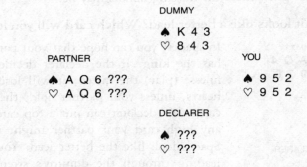

DUMMY

♠ K 4 3
♡ 8 4 3

PARTNER

♠ A Q 6 ???
♡ A Q 6 ???

YOU

♠ 9 5 2
♡ 9 5 2

DECLARER

♠ ???
♡ ???

If you lead spades now and your partner has the ace-queen, he cannot make his queen good because the king is on your right. But if your partner should hold some combination such as the ace-queen in hearts, his finesse will work because any high cards which the opponents hold must be in the declarer's hand. You can see that you are more likely to be successful when your lead goes around to your partner through strength in the second hand. This general principle is stated as:

Lead through strength. A lead from a worthless hold-ing may work well:

- If the dummy is on your left and holds one or two high cards in that suit.
- If the dummy is on your right and holds no high cards in that suit.

Before leading a suit because the strength is favorably located for your side, consider what the declarer may want to do with the suit. If the dummy has a long enough holding for the declarer to establish long cards, there is no point in helping him by leading the suit. Or if the dummy holding is short, the declarer may want play off the cards in that suit for a later ruff. Don't assist him— consider a trump lead instead.

Perhaps you get the idea now that a defender has to think just as hard as a declarer does. Your defender play will improve when you begin to imagine where the missing honors may be.

Which suit looks like a better lead? Which card will you lead?

DUMMY
♠ A Q 4
♡ 9 7 6

YOU
♠ 8 3
♡ 8 3

DECLARER
???

In spades, you can hope that your partner has the king. If the declarer decides to finesse (play) the queen, it will lose. In hearts, unless your partner holds the top cards, the declarer can put a top card on any high card your partner might play. Spades look like the better lead. You are leading through the dummy's strength. Lead the eight of spades (top of nothing).

DUMMY
♠ 7 6 4
♡ A 7 3

YOU
♠ 5 2
♡ 5 2

DECLARER
???

If you lead spades, any finesse which your partner takes will lose. But if your partner holds the king of hearts, he wants you to lead that suit. Then if the dummy plays the ace, your partner's king becomes established. If the dummy plays low, your partner can win with his king. Lead the five of hearts.

DUMMY
♠ A J 10
♡ 7 6 5

YOU
♠ 4 3 2
♡ 4 3 2

In spades, if your partner has the king or the queen, the dummy's ace will top it. But in hearts, the dummy cannot beat your partner's high cards. If the declarer has high cards, he must play them before your partner. Hearts look like the better lead. You are leading through any strength the declarer may have, up to the dummy's weakness. Lead the four of hearts.

DUMMY
♠ K J 10 9 4
♡ 10 8 2

YOU
♠ 7 5 3
♡ K Q J 3

DECLARER
???

A spade lead might give your partner a finesse if he has the ace-queen. But leading the dummy's long suit seldom pays. The declarer will lead that suit all too soon. Instead, you must get to your own tricks as quickly as possible. Lead the king of hearts. A 3-card sequence is the strongest and surest combination to lead from in almost any case.

Leading from an Honor

Suppose you have the opening lead. You have decided to lead a low spade from:

YOU (DEFENDER)

♠ K 3 <u>2</u>

You must hope that your partner also has a high card or two in spades for this lead to succeed. But if he doesn't have any honors in this suit, your lead may work out badly. For this reason a lead from an honor, not in a sequence, is not a favored lead, but it is not a really bad lead either. The more likely it is that your partner has some strength in the suit, the better the lead is.

HOLDING THREE OR MORE CARDS

When you lead from an honor, or from several honors not in sequence, you lead your lowest card, but initially not lower than the fourth-highest card in your holding.

K 9 5 <u>4</u> 3   Lead the four as your
first lead.

When you hold the ace of a suit without the king, you will generally avoid leading this suit. However, if you suspect that your partner holds the king of the suit, then this lead becomes more attractive. If you really need to lead this suit at a trump contract, lead the ace itself—it may be trumped if it is not led right from the beginning.

<u>A</u> 4 3 2   Lead the ace at a trump contract, if you *must*
lead this suit.

At a notrump contract the ace cannot be trumped, so a low lead is best.

NOTE: Even at a trump contract, a sophisticated player may make a low lead when he can tell from the dummy that the ace will be good later.

If you lead away from a tenace (two honors not in sequence), you are depending heavily on your partner to fill in the gap in your honor holding. If he does not, you are likely to lose a trick which you could have won by finessing. That requires that someone else lead the suit first.

Lead low from an honor, or honors not in sequence (your fourth-highest card if available, otherwise your lowest), but don't underlead an ace at a trump contract.

You are defending against a *heart* contract and have decided to make the opening lead in spades. What card do you lead from these holdings?

YOU

♠ K J <u>2</u>	Lead the two. Low from honors not in sequence. This is a lead to avoid.
♠ J 10 5 <u>2</u>	Lead the two. Fourth highest from a low 2-card sequence.
♠ <u>Q</u> J 4	Lead the queen. No fourth highest available.
♠ <u>9</u> 5 3 2	Lead the nine. Top of nothing.
♠ J 8 5 <u>3</u> 2	Lead the three. Low from an honor. The three is the fourth-highest card in your holding.
♠ 10 3 <u>2</u>	Lead the two. Low from an honor—remember that the ten is an honor.
♠ <u>10</u> 9 8 4	Lead the ten. Yes, this is a 3-card sequence headed by an honor.
♠ <u>A</u> 9 7 4	Lead the ace since this is a trump contract. But remember this is a poor suit to lead.
♠ <u>3</u> 2	Lead the three. Top of nothing—but not very high for a top card, so you partner may think that you have led low from an honor. Signals are not always clear. Perhaps you can lead another suit and not confuse your partner.
♠ Q 9 <u>8</u>	Lead the eight. Low from an honor. Again your partner may misread this as top of nothing, but it is the best you can do—you have nothing lower.

NOTE: A variation in Standard American calls for leading the fourth-highest card from four or more small cards. There is no unique standard, but top of nothing should work best for you in most cases since it discourages your partner from continuing the suit. But if you are in a notrump contract and feel that you can establish a long card in a worthless suit, a fourth-highest lead can be used to induce your partner to continue in that suit.

DOUBLETON AND SINGLETON HONORS

You will virtually never lead from a high card when it is in a doubleton or singleton such as:

$$\underline{K} \ 2 \qquad \underline{Q} \ 2 \qquad \underline{J} \ 2 \qquad \underline{K} \qquad \underline{Q} \qquad \underline{J}$$

When you do, it will be because your partner has bid the suit or you are otherwise convinced that your partner has high cards in that suit. Then you will follow the rule that *all* doubletons are led from the top, as marked above. With a singleton, of course, there is no choice.

You might think, for instance, that the singleton king will not take a trick because it will drop under the ace when the ace is played. Frequently that is not what happens.

DUMMY

♠ A Q 3

PARTNER   YOU

♠ 4 (played)   ♠ K (singleton)

DECLARER

♠ 2 (led)

The declarer naturally finesses his queen, hoping the king is on his left. You put your king on the queen, secretly smiling. The declarer didn't know that the king was a singleton or of course he could have played the ace. Similar situations can be shown for other holdings.

If you hold the ace with one small card, you will be reluctant to lead from that suit—unless you are trying to get a ruff. Then you would lead first the ace and then the small card, hoping that your partner will be able to lead the suit again before your trumps are drawn away from you. If you see your partner break a suit by leading an ace and then a small card, you can be fairly sure that he has led from a doubleton and wants you to help him get a ruff. Similarly, if you see your partner lead first the ace and then the king, you will know that he holds only those two cards in the suit. Otherwise he would have lead the king first.

When your Partner Leads

Now let's look at what happens when your partner is the one who leads. You are the third hand in that case.

DUMMY

♠ 9 5 3

PARTNER   YOU (DEFENDER)

♠ 2 (his lead)   ♠ Q 8 4

Suppose that after your partner leads the two of spades, the hand on your right plays the three. You are the third hand to play to this trick. You must play your queen. Your partner's low lead tells you that he has a high spade. Perhaps it is the king. Playing your queen will force the declarer to play the ace if he wants to take the trick. That will set up your partner's king (if he has it) to be a trick. We describe this method of play with a slogan:

> If you are a third hand to play to a trick, play **THIRD HAND HIGH** *if* that will win the trick or will force a higher card from the fourth hand than your partner's card will.

However, there are some times when this slogan will not give you the best results. Here is the principal case where the slogan does not apply:

DUMMY
♠ K 8 3
(3 played)

PARTNER   YOU
♠ 4 (led)   ♠ A J 2

Your ace is sitting behind the dummy's king ready to cover it. But the dummy did not play the king. So hold your ace and play your jack. The jack may even win if your partner has the queen. Later you will use your ace to kill the king.

In any similar case, where you are sitting behind the dummy, it is better for you to hold on to a higher honor until the dummy plays his lower honor. When you are the third hand, as above, then you should play your next lower card providing that it is high enough to force an honor from the declarer. If your next lower card isn't that good, you may as well come up with your high honor right away.

Your partner leads the indicated card. The second hand plays the *two*. As third hand, what do you play? What do you expect your partner to hold?

DUMMY
♠ 7 5 2

PARTNER   YOU
♠ 4 (led)   ♠ Q 3

(Same dummy for the first six cases)

Play the queen. Your partner appears to be leading from an honor—you hope it's the king or the jack. Your queen will force out a high honor to help establish a trick for your partner.

♠ 4 (led)   ♠ A 8 6 3

Play your ace. Then lead your three of spades. Your partner probably has some honor in spades which will take a trick eventually, if not immediately.

♠ Q (led)	♠ A 8 6 3	Your partner does not have the king (he would have led it if he did). Play your ace and continue with your low spade, leading toward the jack which your partner almost certainly has. (A lead from queen-small or queen alone would be possible but unusual.)
♠ 9 (led)	♠ A 8 6 3	Play your ace. However, your partner's lead is probably top of nothing. So your best next lead will probably be in another suit.
♠ 4 (led)	♠ Q J 8 3	Play your jack—third hand high, but follow suit with the lowest of equals.
♠ 8 (led)	♠ 6 4 3	Very sad. Your partner is apparently leading top of nothing, and nothing is what you have too. Play the three since you can't do any better than the eight.

DUMMY
♠ K 2
(2 played)

PARTNER   YOU
♠ 3 (led)   ♠ A Q 5

Play the queen. In that way you make a finesse against the dummy's king. Third hand high, but not too high! You can follow that with the ace if you wish, dropping the dummy's king. Your partner probably holds the jack or the ten.

DUMMY
♠ K 5 2
(2 played)

PARTNER   YOU
♠ 4 (led)   ♠ A 9 6

Play the nine and keep the ace to top the king with later. The nine will force the declarer to play an honor to win the trick. (If you couldn't force the declarer to play an honor, you would do best to play your ace.) Your partner probably holds one or two honors out of queen, jack and ten.

DUMMY
♠ A 8 5

YOU   PARTNER
♠ Q 10 3   ♠ 4 (led)

DECLARER
♠ 2 (played)

You can see that if you play the three, the dummy will take the trick with the eight. You must force the dummy to play his ace. It is not necessary to play your queen to do this, the ten will suffice. Your partner probably holds the king or the jack or both.

Signaling attitude when your partner leads

PARTNER (DEFENDER)   YOU (DEFENDER)

♡ K (his lead)   ♡ Q 8 3

Suppose your partner breaks the heart suit by leading the king. Since you hold the queen, your partner must have led from an ace-king combination. The question on your partner's mind is whether or not to continue playing the suit. You can answer this question for him.

Your partner's king will take the trick, and you could discard either of your small cards on the trick. Actually you choose the *eight.* You discard as high as you can afford to in order to tell your partner that your ATTITUDE toward hearts is positive—you would like your partner to continue playing hearts. He continues with his ace, taking a second trick while you play your three. Your HIGH-LOW sequence of discards makes it even clearer that you want a continuation in hearts. Your partner then plays a low card giving you a third trick with your queen.

PARTNER (DEFENDER)	YOU (DEFENDER)
♡ K (his lead)	♡ 9 8 3

Now you hold nothing but small cards. Your attitude toward hearts is negative. You discard your smallest heart, the three, to discourage your partner from further play in hearts unless his own hand justifies it.

When your partner breaks a suit, your first *discard* shows your attitude toward that suit.

- **Discard as high as you can afford to if you want your partner to continue with that suit.**
- **Discard your lowest card if you have no reason for your partner to continue with that suit.**

This is probably the most important signal there is in the game of bridge. Unfortunately, many beginners and other uninformed players do not use this simple device to direct their partner toward the best line of play. You should give this ATTITUDE SIGNAL whenever you do not have to play a high card to take the trick or to force the opponents to play a higher card. Here are some specific cases where you will use the attitude signal.

Your side is defending. *Spades* are trump. **How do you play?**

DUMMY
♥ 5 4 3
(3 played)

PARTNER
♥ K (led)

YOU
♥ A 7 2

The lead must be from a king-queen combination. You signal positively by discarding your seven. When your partner sees your signal, he knows that he can continue the suit safely. If instead of the ace you had the eight, you would signal with the two to tell your partner that you have no trick in hearts.

DUMMY
♥ Q 6 4
(4 played)

PARTNER
♥ K (led)

YOU
♠ 5 4 2
♥ 6 3

With only two hearts you will soon be able to ruff. Play your six so that your partner will continue hearts. On his ace you will play the three. If he had any doubt whether your six was high or low, he will know for sure when he sees you discard high-low. Now he will continue with a small heart and you will ruff the dummy's queen. Very pleasant.

DUMMY
♥ J 8 4

YOU
♥ K 7 5 3

PARTNER
♥ 2 (led)

DECLARER
♥ A (played)

You can't beat the ace, played by the declarer, so you will simply discard. But you will carefully discard the seven to tell your partner that you would like a continuation in hearts. If he gets the lead later, he can lead hearts for you to make your trick with the king. Then you will continue hearts with the three because your partner's original low lead (the two) suggests that he may have the queen.

DUMMY
♡ 8 7 4
(4 played)

YOU   PARTNER
♡ A K J   ♡ ???
(K led)   (3 played)

You broke the heart suit by leading the king. Your partner signaled low so he doesn't want you to continue. Who has the queen? The declarer, of course. Later, if your partner is able to lead a heart to you, you will be able to finesse against the declarer's queen. For now, look for another suit to lead.

DUMMY
♡ Q 7 4
(4 played)

YOU   PARTNER
♡ A K 3   ♡ ???
(K led)   (9 played)

Your partner has signaled with a high small card. Since he doesn't have the queen, which you can see in the dummy, he must hold a doubleton and want to get a ruff. (These are the only two reasons for him to signal high.) Lead your ace next, since that is a sure trick, then lead your three for a ruff.

DUMMY
♡ 6 5 2
(2 played)

YOU   PARTNER
♡ K Q 3   ♡ ???
(K led)   (4 played)

DECLARER
♡ (7 played)

Your king has won, so you might think that your partner has the ace. Or could it be that the declarer has it but didn't play it? Look at your partner's signal. He played the lowest heart he had (you can see the two and the three elsewhere). You should assume that he doesn't hold the ace or the jack either. You must shift to another suit and let someone else lead the hearts. The declarer is probably trying to trap you into leading into his ace-jack.

Signaling Attitude When Not Following Suit

Signaling can be used, no matter who leads, when you cannot follow suit. If you are not going to ruff, you must discard something. You can make your discard say something to your partner:

When discarding because you cannot follow suit:

- Discard as high a card as you can afford in a suit which you would like your partner to lead.
- Discard your lowest card in a suit which you do not want your partner to lead.

When signaling, be careful not to throw away a card which you will need later. Sometimes you will need all the cards in the suit you want led, so you will have to signal with a low card in some other suit.

What discard would you choose in the following cases where you cannot follow suit? The contract is in NOTRUMP.

DUMMY
♡ K 8

PARTNER   YOU
♡ ???   ♡ A Q J 9 3
♢ K (led)   ♢ —

You want a heart lead so you can finesse against the dummy's king. If you discard the nine of hearts, your partner will get the message unless he is a rather poor player.

DUMMY
♡ Q 7 3
♢ Q J 8 7

PARTNER   YOU
♡ ???   ♡ A K J 10
♢ K (led)   ♢ —
♣ ???   ♣ 5 4 3

You very much want a heart lead. If you discard the jack of hearts, you will give a loud message (the ten and jack are equal so pick the higher), but you will also lose a trick. If you can set the contract anyway, shout with the jack of hearts. But if you need that extra trick, discard the three of clubs. Your partner will know that you

are not interested in a club lead.
That leaves hearts and spades.
Maybe he can figure out which
one of the two to lead.

When an Opponent Leads

When the opponent on your left leads to a trick, you will be the
fourth hand to play to the trick. This is the catbird seat—how to
play is usually obvious. If you can take the trick, you will do so
with as small a card as will suffice. If you cannot take the trick, or
if your partner has already played high enough to take the trick,
you will simply discard your lowest card. You will not use the
attitude signal when discarding in a suit led by the opponents—
they hope to make tricks in that suit, so why tell them where the
high cards are?

NOTE: Later you will learn to use the COUNT SIGNAL when an
opponent leads to the trick.

When the opponent on your right has the lead and you are
therefore the second hand, you will follow the guidelines already
given:

> If you are the second hand to play to a trick, play
> second hand low, except to cover an honor with an
> honor.

When you are the second hand, your partner will play after you as
the fourth hand. In that case it is better to let your partner take the
trick if he can. Besides, you want to hold any high card until you
can play it on a lesser high card held by your right-hand opponent.
But if your right-hand opponent leads a honor, covering it with
your own honor can do your side some good in many cases—you
should cover, even if it means sacrificing your own honor, unless

you can absolutely see that covering cannot set up a later trick for you or your partner.

As second hand, defending against a notrump contract, how would you play?

DUMMY
♠ Q 6 5
(5 led)

YOU
♠ A 4 3

DECLARER
♠ ???

You are the second hand, so don't jump up with your ace unless you can see some pressing reason to do so. Play low for now. You want to slaughter the dummy's queen when it is played later. Perhaps the declarer has the king-ten and will finesse the ten, losing to your partner's jack! Perhaps the declarer has only the jack, losing to your partner's king. You stand to gain by playing second hand low.

DUMMY
♠ 7 6 5
(5 led)

YOU
♠ A 4 3

Again play low. Let your partner take the trick if he can.

DUMMY
♠ Q 6
(Q led)

YOU
♠ A 4 3

DECLARER
♠ ???

Cover the queen with your ace. This will be the only opportunity for your ace to catch a high card. If your partner should hold four spades to the ten, or three to the jack, your covering will set up his honor to take a trick.

DUMMY
♠ Q 6
(Q led)

YOU
♠ K 4 3

DECLARER
♠ ???

The declarer probably holds the ace, jack and ten and is finessing against your king. Cover the queen with your king and make the declarer put his ace on his own queen if he wants to take the trick. By accelerating the fall of the honors in this way you may set up a trick for your partner if he holds three spades to the ten, or even four spades to the nine.

Summary of Conventions

In bridge, a convention is an artificial way of bidding or playing in order to convey a specific message to your partner. Of course your partner must understand what the message is. The signals which we have looked at are all standard conventions. You can assume that your partner will use them and understand them unless he is quite untrained in bridge. Be sure that you take the time to learn them also.

When breaking a suit, the conventional lead is:

- High from any doubleton
- King from ace-king (not a doubleton) or king-queen
- Ace from ace without the king (trump contract)

Otherwise:

- Top of a sequence (headed by an honor)
- Top of nothing
- Low from an honor (fourth-highest when available)

For a 2-card sequence when a fourth-highest lead is possible:

- At notrump, lead fourth-highest from all 2-card sequences.
- At trump, lead fourth-highest from low 2-card sequences.

When *discarding* in a suit led by your partner, or in any suit you select because you can't follow suit:

- Discard as high a card as you can afford to encourage your partner to play that suit.
- Discard your lowest card to discourage your partner from playing that suit.

When *following suit* from a sequence with the intent to take the trick or to force the opponents to play a still higher card:

- Follow with the lowest card from the sequence.

Note that you are discarding when you are free to play any convenient card. You are not discarding when you must play a high card, either to take the trick or to force the opponents to play a still higher card.

Summary of Tactics

Some of the ideas we have introduced are tactics. There is nothing conventional or artificial about them. They are not a way of communicating with your partner but a way of taking tricks. The slogans to suggest these tactics were:

- Lead through strength,
- Second hand low,
- Third hand high,
- Cover an honor with an honor.

Slogans are over-simplifications and don't always work. There are two principles behind the slogans which are more reliable than the slogans.

> Work to establish tricks for your partner as well as for
> yourself.

Third-hand high tries to suggest taking the trick when possible, but otherwise forcing out a high card from the opponents so that your partner's high cards or your own high cards can be established. When you can't accomplish that, it may be better to play low.

Cover an honor with an honor suggests forcing out a second honor from the opponents. If there is no chance this will establish some other card for your side, it is better not to cover.

> • Try to put your high cards on a lesser high card held
>   by your *right-hand* opponent.
> • Give your partner a chance to top the high cards held
>   by your left-hand opponent whenever it may be pos-
>   sible for him to do so.

Second-hand low suggests both letting your partner top the card played by the third hand and also saving your own high cards to top any high card held by your right-hand opponent. It also avoids having you play an ace only to find that your partner has no card to play but the king.

The exception to *third-hand high* is based on holding on to your high card until your right-hand opponent plays his lesser high card.

Lead through strength may set up a finesse for your partner, or it may drive out a high card from the second hand and establish a lesser high card in your partner's hand. Usually you will be leading from a worthless holding to make this effective.

B
Outmaneuvering the Declarer

Since the declarer can see both of the hands belonging to his side, he can make an overall plan for playing the hand. The defenders cannot do this. The declarer's goal is to make his contract, which involves taking more than half of the tricks. The defenders' goal is to set the contract, which may involve taking rather few tricks, all of which are vital. The defenders' battle cry is: COMMUNICATE, COOPERATE, SET THE CONTRACT.

Of course it is totally unethical to communicate by any word, gesture, tone of voice or facial expression. But you have already learned to use some elementary signals and conventional leads, which is perfectly proper.

Choosing the Opening Lead at a Trump Contract

Choosing which suit to lead from for the opening lead is a task that baffles experts at times. We can say only a little about it. Let's start with the case of a trump contract.

GOOD LEADS—TRUMP CONTRACT
Partner's Suit. Usually a suit which your partner has bid will be a good suit to lead because he is likely to have some high cards in that suit. Lead the *same* card from your holding that you would have led if your partner had not bid the suit.

An Ace-King. Leading the king from an ace-king or ace-king-queen combination is a favorite lead. Watch your partner's signal when you lead, and continue with the ace if he signals with a high discard. If he makes a low discard, at least you will be able to see the dummy before deciding on your next lead.

A 3-Card Sequence. An honor which heads a 3-card sequence or broken sequence is another favorite lead because it tends to set up a trick or two without losing anything that you wouldn't lose anyway. Again, watch for your partner's signal.

BAD LEADS—TRUMP CONTRACT

Opponents' Suit. Leading a suit which the opponents have bid usually turns out badly, especially if it is one of their long suits. They will want to make tricks with high cards and/or long cards in this suit, so don't assist them.

Ace Without the King. Try to avoid leading a suit containing the ace but not the king unless your partner has bid that suit. If you have to make the opening lead at a trump contract in such a suit, lead the ace first off for fear that it might be trumped if kept until later. But bear in mind that laying down an ace in this manner will help whoever holds the king.

Low from Honors Not In Sequence. A lead from a suit containing two honors which are not in sequence (for example a king-jack combination) is usually a poor lead unless your partner has bid the suit. You would like someone else to lead this suit so you can finesse.

Doubleton Honors. A lead from the top of a doubleton containing an honor (for example the king and a small card) is usually a poor lead unless your partner has bid that suit. However, the lead of the ace from ace-small, followed by the lead of the small card, is sometimes made for the purpose of setting up a later ruff in that suit.

Singleton Honors. A lead from a singleton honor other than the ace (for example holding the king alone) is usually a poor lead unless your partner has bid that suit—the higher the honor, the worse the lead. It may win a trick if you don't lead it.

OTHER LEADS—TRUMP CONTRACT

The other leads are usually reasonable and will very frequently be used when none of the good leads listed above are to be found in your hand, or when the situation suggests a particular kind of lead.

Low from an Honor. You hope your partner also has one or more honors in that suit so that together you can make a trick or two. If he does, you will be leading low toward his honor while preserving your own.

Lead from a 2-Card Sequence (not the ace-king). You lead the king from a king-queen sequence to establish your queen immediately. But with a two-card sequence headed by a lower honor, your main chance of setting up a trick comes when your partner also holds an honor in the suit. Thus a fourth-highest lead is used when the suit is long enough. Otherwise you lead the top of the sequence.

Small Singleton. You hope to get a ruff later. If your partner sees a lot of cards of that suit in his hand and in the dummy, he may guess that you have led from a singleton and you want a chance to ruff. But this lead may backfire unless your partner can take a trick so as to lead the suit back to you, and unless you still have a spare trump to ruff with at that time. Normally you will have a trump stopper when you make this lead, just so that your trumps cannot be drawn away from you before you have a chance to ruff.

Top of Nothing. You hope your partner needs a lead in that suit. If not, you hope no harm is done even though your side doesn't take the trick.

Low from Two or Three Small Trumps. Small trumps are too valuable to lead the top one. For now, lead the lowest. Later you will learn how to signal from this combination. You hope you will reduce the number of ruffs the declarer can take, since your lead will use up one of the trumps in the dummy's hand and one in the declarer's hand.

Long Suit plus Trumps. When you hold four or more trumps, it may be to your advantage to lead your long suit. If the declarer runs out of your suit and has to trump in the long hand (normally his own hand), you may shorten his trump holding until he has only as many as you do—or perhaps even fewer. This may also work when you have one or no trumps and suspect that your partner has four of them.

Choose an opening lead from your hand as shown below.

YOU	LHO	PARTNER	RHO
			1 DIAMOND
PASS	2 DIAMONDS		

♠ A K 4   Here you have two good leads—spades and
♡ Q J 10   hearts. It will take some work to make a
◇ J 8   heart good, so start there by leading the
♣ Q 8 4 3 2   queen of hearts.

YOU	LHO	PARTNER	RHO
	1 DIAMOND	2 CLUBS	2 SPADES
PASS	4 SPADES		

♠ 7 3   Your partner should have some high cards in
♡ Q 10 5 4   clubs. Lead the four of clubs.
◇ 9 5 3 2
♣ J 8 4

YOU	LHO	PARTNER	RHO
	1 CLUB	PASS	1 HEART
PASS	2 HEARTS	PASS	4 HEARTS

♠ K 8 4   Leading one of the suits bid by the opponents
♡ K 6 3   is not attractive—neither is a diamond lead
◇ K J 4   because of the tenace. That leaves spades,
♠ 9 8 5 4   where you hope your partner will have a high
card. Lead the spade four.

YOU	LHO	PARTNER	RHO
			1 SPADE
PASS	1 NOTRUMP	PASS	2 HEARTS

♠ K J 3
♡ 8 5
◇ A 8 5 4
♣ J 7 5 3

When the bidding shows that the declarer has two long suits, a trump lead from small trumps is often effective. A lead from an ace without the king is to be shunned, as is a lead from your spade tenace. Four cards to the jack is also a combination usually avoided. Lead the five of hearts.

YOU	LHO	PARTNER	RHO
			1 SPADE
PASS	2 SPADES	PASS	4 SPADES

♠ A 8 6
♡ 10 8 5 4
◇ 3
♣ K Q 8 4 3

A singleton lead may work out here. Even if the declarer wins the first trick, he can't take your trumps away from you immediately because you hold the ace. If your partner can take a trick and can figure out to lead a diamond back to you, you will be able to ruff with one of your small spades.

YOU	LHO	PARTNER	RHO
			1 HEART
PASS	2 HEARTS	PASS	4 HEARTS

♠ A 8 6
♡ 10 8 5 4
◇ 3
♣ K Q 8 4 3

This is the same hand as before, but hearts are now trumps. Leading your singleton is not so likely to work out because the declarer may be able to take the first trick and draw your trumps. But you may be able to force the declarer to ruff with the valuable trumps in his long hand if you start with the king of clubs.

YOU	LHO	PARTNER	RHO
			1 HEART
PASS	2 HEARTS		

♠ K 8

♡ Q 7 4

◇ A Q 6 3 2

♣ 7 5 2

Here a top-of-nothing lead in clubs avoids the less attractive leads in the other suits: a doubleton honor in spades, a single honor in the *trump* suit and a tenace in diamonds. Lead the seven of clubs.

Subsequent Play

If your partner makes the opening lead, notice carefully what card he leads. Look also at the dummy. From the two observations, try to deduce whether this will be a good suit for you to lead later if you get the chance. If you are the one to make the opening lead, notice carefully how your partner signals. Little by little, your side will pick up information about where you can take tricks.

If you get the lead, after the opening lead, you must decide whether to continue in a suit which you or your partner has led before, or whether to break a new suit. You will very seldom lead a suit that the declarer has led, because that is probably a suit which is favorable to him. But if you notice that the declarer seems to be avoiding a suit where the dummy is not particularly strong, that may be the one for you to lead, even if you have a tenace or some other unfavorable holding. A common situation arises when you hold the king and your partner holds the ace (or vice versa) and you both have been holding back from leading that suit.

It is generally not advantageous to break a new suit unless it is headed by a strong honor combination. When you do break a new suit, the guidelines for making the opening lead generally apply. But after the opening lead you will have the advantage of seeing the dummy. That will often tell you whether the suit may be favorable for your side or not, and whether you will be leading through strength or not.

Thwarting the Declarer

If you and your partner as defenders can tell what the declarer's plan of attack is, the two of you together may be able to prevent him from carrying it out.

Declarer Wants to Ruff in Dummy. If you see that the dummy has a very short suit and also some small trumps to ruff with, you must suspect that the declarer is going to play off the short suit until the dummy is void and then lead the suit again from his own hand for a ruff. If you are able to lead trump without spoiling your own trump holding, you can reduce his ability to ruff.

Once the dummy is actually void in some suit, you should virtually never lead that suit. You are only helping the declarer carry out his own plan to ruff. Furthermore, if the declarer should also be void in that suit, you are giving him a ruff which he could not make without your aid—after all, he had no card to lead to make the ruff with. Worse yet, the declarer can decide which hand to ruff in and then SLUFF (discard) a losing card from the other hand. Giving the declarer a ruff and a sluff is with rare exception one of the worst leads in bridge.

Declarer Wants to Draw Trumps. Once in a while you can make it difficult or impossible for the declarer to draw trumps by forcing him to trump in the long hand. If you play a side suit (not the trump suit) until the declarer has become void but the dummy has not, and then continue with a high card in that suit, he must ruff in his own hand (which probably is the long hand) in order to take the trick. Sometimes this will leave him short of trump and in trouble. This is called PUMPING the declarer. (But if the dummy is the long hand, you will want to pump the dummy.)

The reason the declarer wants to take out (draw) the trumps is so that your side will not be able to make any ruffs. If you can find a suit which your partner can ruff, and if you lead that suit before your partner has had his trumps drawn out, you can get a ruff in spite of the declarer's desire to the contrary. You may get this opportunity when you suspect that your partner has previously led a singleton.

Declarer Wants to Make Long Cards Good. When you see that the declarer has a long side suit, usually in the dummy, try to figure out how he must go about making the long cards good. Then see if there is anything nasty which you can do to stop him. The most common opportunity arises when the declarer has only one entry to the dummy and may need it later to make his long cards good. If you can force him to play the entry card too soon for his purposes, you foil his plans.

When you can't stop the declarer from making long cards good, your best action is to CASH (take immediately) all the tricks you can in the other side suits, before the declarer gets to using his long side suit. This is when it pays to play off your aces and other high cards quickly. You may even lead from a tenace or other such unfavorable holding in case your partner has a trick there which can be taken quickly. The reason is this: When the declarer is playing the long cards from one hand, he is throwing away from the other hand any losers he may have in the suit where your high cards are. After that he can trump your high cards when you finally decide to play them—too late.

Declarer is Struggling. When the declarer can't ruff in the short hand and has no long suit that you know of, he probably will have a struggle to make his contract. This is not the time to take any risks that may give away a trick which the declarer couldn't have gotten otherwise. Play it safe. Try not to break a new suit unless it is headed by a 3-card sequence. It is better to lead a suit which has been led before, even if you know that the declarer has all the high cards in that suit. In fact, any lead which lets the declarer take a trick which he is going to take sooner or later is a safe play when the declarer is struggling. This could be a lead which forces the declarer to trump in the long hand or even a lead from two or three small trumps.

You are defending against 4 SPADES (no other suit having been bid). You made the opening lead of the king of hearts, which won. What is the declarer's plan? What will you lead next?

```
                 DUMMY
              ♠ J 8 5
              ♡ 7 3
              ◇ A 7 3 2
              ♣ Q 6 5 4

YOU                        PARTNER
♠ 6 3
♡ K Q 4                    ♡ 8 (played)
◇ J 8 6 5
♣ J 9 3 2

              DECLARER
              ♡ 2 (Played)
```

Your partner's discard of the eight signals that he holds the ace. The declarer has no truly long suit in the dummy but he may want to ruff a heart or two. Leading a trump will limit his ruffing ability. Before he can ruff he will have to let your side win yet another heart and you can lead trumps again, allowing the declarer only one ruff.

```
                 DUMMY
              ♠ Q 7 3
              ♡ 8 6
              ◇ A K Q 7 5
              ♣ K J 3

YOU                        PARTNER
♠ 8 4 2
♡ A K 5 4 3                ♡ 2 (played)
◇ 9 8
♣ 9 7 2

              DECLARER
              ♡ 7 (played)
```

Your partner's two suggests that he does not want you to continue with hearts. Besides, the long diamonds in the dummy tell you that the declarer will soon be discarding the losers from his hand. You had better get to your own winners in a hurry. They can only be in clubs—your partner may have the ace or the ace-queen or even ace-queen-ten. Lead the nine of clubs to your partner. He knows that you have the ace of hearts and will lead hearts back to you later.

```
                 DUMMY
              ♠ A J 7
              ♡ 9 5 3
              ◇ A K 2
              ♣ Q 9 7 4
```

The dummy doesn't look menacing since it has neither ruffing nor long-card possibilities. Your partner has signaled high, so he either

```
YOU                    PARTNER
♠ 9 6 4 3
♡ A K 10 8 5     ♡ 7 (played)
♢ 3
♣ J 8 2

        DECLARER
        ♡ 2 (played)
```

has the queen of hearts or has a doubleton (even a singleton) and wants a ruff. Continue with the ace of hearts and then the five. Perhaps your partner will play the queen on that trick and the declarer will ruff. You have pumped the declarer who now may have only four trumps left, the same as you do. Then he may be in trouble—if he draws trumps, he will have none left.

Defending at Notrump

When your side is defending against a notrump contract, your very best source of tricks, when available, is from long cards. This is because at notrump your long cards cannot be trumped. Usually you will be able to defeat a declarer at notrump only if your side can make long cards good.

If you are making the opening lead, look for a long suit—five cards or more. If you have one, this is almost always your best lead unless it was bid by the opponents. If the suit is headed by three honors which make a solid sequence, a broken sequence or an interior sequence, lead the highest card which is truly in sequence. Otherwise lead your fourth-highest card.

Do not be deterred from leading your long suit at a notrump contract by the fact that your suit is headed by a tenace that you would normally not lead from. At notrump the importance of getting started on your longest suit is so great that you must think "damn the torpedoes, full speed ahead."

An alternative to leading your own long suit is to lead a suit which your partner has bid. If you think your partnership has a longer fit in your partner's suit than in yours, lead his suit. Pick the card to lead using the guidelines we have already given.

When you don't have a long suit, and your partner has not bid, you have to make a guess among the suits which no one has bid. You may pick a 4-card suit of your own, but because it is somewhat short, it should be fairly strong and not contain a tenace—a combination which would provide a finesse if your partner were the first to lead the suit. The alternative is to pick a 3-card suit and hope your partner may have five or more cards in that suit. An unbid major suit is generally a better choice than an unbid minor suit. If the opponents hold many cards in a major suit they probably would have bid it, whereas they might not bid a long minor suit.

You are defending against a 3 NOTRUMP contract, no suit having been bid. What is your opening lead? What is your plan?

YOU

♠ K Q J 7 5
♡ A 5 4
◇ 4 3
♣ 7 5 4

Your long spades give you an opportunity to set up some long cards. Since you have a 3-card sequence, start with the king which will probably win—either your partner will have the ace or the declarer will hold it up. If your partner discards high, he must hold the ace—you will continue with a low spade. If he discards low, you will continue with the queen. The declarer may not play his ace until you have played your jack, but your ace of hearts is there as an entry to your long spades.

YOU

♠ 7 3
♡ A 10 6 5 2
◇ 8 5 2
♣ 7 5 4

Your hand is pretty anemic but those hearts may set up. Start with the five of hearts, your fourth highest. The only entry to your hand is the ace of hearts, so you must save it until the third round of hearts is played. Your partner must have a few high cards since you don't. He may even have the king of hearts.

He should keep leading hearts to you until you take your ace, unless he has an excellent suit of his own.

YOU	
♠ K Q 10 3	You have no five-card suit, but your four spades are strong, being headed by a broken sequence. Lead the king of spades, and continue with a low spade if your partner signals high—otherwise, shift to another suit after studying the dummy. That will keep your queen-ten intact for a later finesse.
♡ 5 3 2	
◊ 8 4	
♣ K 7 4 3	

YOU	
♠ K 4 3	This isn't much of a hand. Your only hope is to guess what your partner's long suit might be. Since an unbid major is a better guess than an unbid minor, and since your spades are better than your hearts, try leading the three of spades. Your clubs are longer, but for that very reason the chance of your partner holding five of them is less.
♡ 6 5 2	
◊ K 7 4	
♣ 9 5 4 3	

Cooperating with Your Partner

When your partner starts leading a long suit, you must cooperate by also leading that suit every time you get a chance. Remember what we said about playing the high cards in the short holding first? If you have the short holding, you must use your high cards first. Usually you will save your lowest card to play last, so that you won't take that trick and block the suit. You want your partner to take that trick so that he can continue on with his remaining long cards.

There is always the possibility that your partner has led from a 4-card or 3-card suit, probably because he has no long suit. How can you tell? Suppose he leads a two. If that is his fourth-highest card, he can have no fifth-highest card because there is nothing lower than the two. He must hold (probably) four or (possibly) three cards in that suit. If he leads some other small card, say the four, and you can see the three and the two in your own hand or in the dummy hand, he has led the lowest card he has, so again he has no fifth card in that suit. When your partner leads from a short holding, and you have the long holding, you should arrange for your partner to play his high cards first to unblock the suit for you.

Once in a while your partner starts off in the wrong suit. A look at the dummy and your own hand may tell you that the opponents have too many cards in the suit which your partner led. Generally you should not be frightened off because they have the high cards if your side has at least an 8-card fit. But when you are convinced that your partner has gotten off on the wrong foot, you may do better to switch to another suit. When lucky, you may even hold a 5-card suit of your own.

Your partner has led as indicated against a 3 NOTRUMP contract. No suit has been bid. How do you plan to play your cards?

DUMMY
♡ 8 4

PARTNER   YOU
♡ 3 (led)   ♡ A Q 5

Since you can't see the two of hearts anywhere, your partner may well have five hearts. Win with your ace and continue with your queen, saving your five to play last.

DUMMY
♡ K 7
(K played)

PARTNER   YOU
♡ 5 (led)   ♡ Q J 6

You will find this hard to take, but you must play your queen on the dummy's king in order to save your six to play last. Perhaps your partner holds ♡ 10 9 8 5 4 3.

DUMMY
♡ 7 5

PARTNER   YOU
♡ K (led)   ♡ A 6

Since both you and the dummy are short in hearts, your partner probably has five or six of them. His lead must be from the king-queen-jack or king-queen-ten. Now that you have the idea of unblocking, you will play the ace and return the six.

DUMMY
♡ 4 3

PARTNER   YOU
♡ K (led)   ♡ A J 8 7 5

This time you have the long holding so you will not unblock. Your partner has probably led from king-queen-small. You will signal with the eight, telling your partner to continue, first with his queen, then with his small card. He must unblock for you.

DUMMY
♡ 6 5

PARTNER   YOU
♡ 3 (led)   ♡ A 10 7 2

Your partner led the three and you have the two so he has four hearts at most. You are not the short hand since you have at least as many hearts as he does. Play your ace and return the two. You do not unblock in this case.

DUMMY
♡ Q J 10 9
(Q played)

PARTNER   YOU
♡ 4 (led)   ♡ A 6

At best your partner holds ♡ K 8 7 4 3 and that looks pretty bleak. Play your ace and then look for another suit to lead. (There is no point in having your partner take his king immediately—that only establishes the dummy's jack and ten.)

Defender Summary

Communicate. Learn to make the conventional lead or signal from your own holding. Learn to read what your partner is saying when he makes a conventional lead or signal.

Cooperate. If your partner's play indicates that your side should continue in that same suit, do so unless you have information to the contrary which your partner couldn't know about. If your partner signals that he has no trick in a suit, consider continuing in another suit unless your hand dictates otherwise.

Set the contract. Try to figure out what the declarer is up to and then thwart his plans. If he wants to ruff in the dummy, consider leading a trump. If he has a long suit in the dummy,. set up and cash your own tricks quickly. Play it safe if the dummy has neither ruffing possibilities nor a long suit. Try to pump the declarer by leading your longest suit when that may embarrass him. Work to make long tricks when the contract is in notrump.

Chapter 9 ///////////////////////////////////

PREEMPTIVE BIDS

///

A

Bidding Situations

There are three bidding situations which commonly arise. You will have to handle each of these quite differently.

1. NONCOMPETITIVE BIDDING
   One side has most of the strength.

   - The stronger side does most of the bidding, looking first for a fit and then going on to a game or slam if possible.
   - The weaker side does not bid or bids only once at a low level.

2. COMPETITIVE BIDDING
   The strength is more or less evenly divided between the two sides.

   - Both sides bid, competing to win the contract or to drive the other side a little too high. The bidding seldom goes above the 3-level.

3. PREEMPTIVE BIDDING

One side has most of the strength but the other side has a long suit.

- The weaker side takes advantage of its long suit to make a PREEMPTIVE bid (an early high bid) which will obstruct the strong side's bidding.
- The stronger side tries to find its fit and get to game or slam in spite of the obstruction. Otherwise, the stronger side will look for an opportunity to double and set the weaker side.

We have already said a lot about noncompetitive bidding and a little about competitive bidding. Now we will take a look at preemptive bidding.

B

Considerations for a Preemptive Bid

The Basic Idea Behind Preemptive Bidding

Suppose you were the dealer and held this hand:

♠ A K J 9 7 5 4
♡ 8
◇ 6 2
♣ 8 5 4

You can see that you cannot open the bidding with this hand. You have only 11 points. Besides, an opening hand should have at least 10 HCP so that it does not lean too heavily on distribution. Although this hand has only 8 HCP, it still looks as though you ought to be able to do something with it—just because of the good distribution.

You can imagine that the opponents may have a lot of high cards in hearts, diamonds and clubs since you have none. They are likely to bid a game or even a slam in one of these suits, perhaps in hearts where you are very short. As for spades, you have so many that one of your opponents is likely to have a singleton or even a void. Your ace of spades may take a trick against their contract but the other spades will probably be ruffed.

Suppose you were to open the bidding with 3 SPADES. This is an example of a preemptive bid. Now if the opponents want to bid hearts or any other suit, the lowest bid they can make is at the 4-level. Will they be able to? They may give up on looking for a game or a slam. Instead they may say that nasty word DOUBLE.

How will you make out playing 3 SPADES DOUBLED? Your partner will probably hold at least one spade, so you will have a normal 8-card fit. After three rounds of spades, the opponents are likely to be out of them. Even if your jack of spades loses, you will take six tricks with your seven spades. You could be down three, doubled. But wait—if your partner can supply no trick at all, the opponents could have made a small slam, your side's only trick being the ace of spades. If your partner has a trick or two, they could still make a game, but at your spade contract you will only be down by one or two tricks. The real question is: Will you lose less by SACRIFICING (going down deliberately) than you would if they were allowed to bid their game or slam? When your own suit is long and your hand is otherwise weak, the answer is frequently yes.

Playing Tricks

So far you have used point count exclusively for evaluating your hand. This is the best method when both hands in the partnership have some strength. It provides the means of estimating how the two hands together will perform. But it fails when most or all of the tricks must be taken in your own hand. Then you use a simple alternative—you count the number of tricks (PLAYING TRICKS) which you think your hand will actually take *without* help from your partner. Playing tricks are counted with the assumption that you will be the declarer and your long suit will be the trump suit.

To count playing tricks:

- Count the tricks your high cards will take, assuming that all finesses will fail.
- Count each trump in your hand after the first three as a trick.

How many playing tricks will you assume in the following hands with spades as the trump suit?

♠ A K J 9 7 5 4
♡ 8
◇ 6 2
♣ 8 5 4

The ace and king of spades give you two playing tricks. The jack is a POSSIBLE trick which depends on a finesse, so you will not count it as a playing trick. The remaining spades can be counted on as four playing tricks, because you hope that the opponents will be out of spades after the spades have been played three times. You have six playing tricks.

♠ K Q J 8 5 3 2
♡ K 7 5
◇ 10 9 3
♣ —

The king of spades will lose to the ace (which you must assume to be in an opponent's hand). The remaining spades can be counted as playing tricks. The king of hearts is a possible trick, but it depends on a finesse. So you can count only six playing tricks.

♠ Q J 9 8 6 3 2
♡ K J 8
◇ Q 8
♣ 9

You must assume that the queen and jack of spades will fall under the opponents' ace and king. The third round of spades may be lost to the ten. That leaves you only the remaining four spades as playing tricks in the whole hand. That is obviously pessimistic since you have a number of possible tricks which *may* materialize. But the number of playing tricks is still four.

♠ A Q J 10 9 3
♡ J 10 9 3 2
◇ 5
♣ 7

Here you assume that the ace of spades will win, the queen will lose on the second round, the jack will win on the third round, and the remaining spades will be good after that. That gives you five playing tricks. The hearts may possibly yield a trick also. Compare this with the previous hand. Here fewer HCP give you more playing tricks.

Vulnerability

A preemptive bid frequently ends up as a sacrifice. A major factor in determining whether a sacrifice will be worthwhile is vulnerability. You probably have pretty much ignored vulnerability up to now. But from now on it is going to be a very important factor in many hands.

* *Your* vulnerability determines how much it hurts you to be set.
* *Their* vulnerability determines how much it hurts you if they make a game.

If you overbid when you are vulnerable, you are going to lose a lot more than when you are not. And if you sacrifice against opponents who are not vulnerable, it may not be worth it since they won't make as much for a game when they are not vulnerable. Therefore, when you are vulnerable and the opponents are not, the vulnerability is UNFAVORABLE for you to make a sacrifice. But if you are not vulnerable when the opponents are vulnerable, the vulnerability is FAVORABLE for you to try a sacrifice. In summarizing this, let's use VUL and NOTVUL for *vulnerable* and *not vulnerable,* respectively.

YOU	THEY	VULNERABILITY	YOUR ATTITUDE
VUL	NOTVUL	unfavorable	conservative
VUL	VUL	equal	neutral
NOTVUL	NOTVUL	equal	neutral
NOTVUL	VUL	favorable	aggressive

C

Making a Preemptive Bid

Opening with a Preempt

An opening bid of 3 in a SUIT or 4 in a SUIT (or even 5 in a MINOR SUIT) is a preemptive bid. You make this kind of bid when your hand is so weak that you fear your opponents will be able to make a game or a slam. But you need a long suit with a supply of playing tricks or you may find that you have made too great a sacrifice. (An opening bid of 2 in a SUIT is reserved for special kinds of hands, as you will see later.)

Usually you will base an opening 3-bid, such as 3 SPADES, on the holding of a 7-card spade suit. Similarly you will base an opening bid of 4 SPADES on an 8-card spade suit. Opening preemptive bids are never higher than the game level, so only in a minor suit would you preempt with a 5-bid, for example 5 CLUBS. This is very rare and would normally be based on a 9-card club suit.

Sometimes when you preempt, the number of trumps in your hand will be one more or one less than the usual number. The correct bid comes not from the number of trumps but from the number of playing tricks which you can find in your hand. You must count your playing tricks and then overbid that number by an OVERBID MARGIN, which depends on the vulnerability.

When preempting, overbid the number of your playing tricks by the following overbid margin:

VULNERABILITY	OVERBID MARGIN
Unfavorable	2
Equal	3
Favorable	4

The margin given above will result in a satisfactory sacrifice, if it comes to that, providing your partner comes up with one trick. That is a reasonable expectation—anything less would be unduly pessimistic.

For an opening preemptive bid, from 3 CLUBS up to 5 DIAMONDS, you need:

- Less than an opening hand
- Insufficient strength to defeat a small slam by the opponents, should they bid it
- Enough playing tricks plus the appropriate overbid margin to equal the level of your preempt.

Immediately make the highest bid indicated by this guideline, but not higher than the game level.
Do not bid again unless your partner forces you to.

If you have the strength of an opening hand, you must not preempt—open with the normal bid. If you hold two aces or the equivalent, you are simply too strong to preempt. Open normally if you can, otherwise pass.

Against an opposing contract, assume that all cards in your 7-card (or longer) suit will be ruffed except the ace, should you hold it.

What would you bid with the following hands? Assume you are the dealer, and therefore the first to have a chance to bid.

YOU: THEY:

NOTVUL vs. VUL

♠ Q 2
♡ K J 10 9 7 4 3
◇ 8
♣ 7 5 4

You certainly don't have an opening hand but your long hearts suggest a preempt. You have five playing tricks in hearts. The vulnerability is favorable for preempting so you add an overbid margin of four, making nine. That's enough to open with 3 HEARTS.

VUL vs. NOTVUL

♠ —
♡ J 10 9 8 4 3 2
◇ A K 8 4
♣ Q 2

You have every reason not to preempt on this hand. Firstly, the hand is strong enough to open with, so your bid should be 1 HEART. Your two high diamonds will probably be good against an opposing contract, so a slam bid by the opponents is doomed. The vulnerability is unfavorable for sacrifice: Your six playing tricks plus an overbid margin of two does not add up to the seven needed for a 3-bid. A typical preemptive hand has most of its strength in the long suit, not in the side suits.

VUL vs. NOTVUL

♠ A K Q 10 9 5 3
♡ 7 2
◇ 8 5
♣ 9 8

This hand is not strong enough for an opening bid. Your DEFENSIVE TRICKS (the tricks you can take against an opposing contract) are limited to the ace of spades. Even though the vulnerability is unfavorable, your playing tricks (seven) plus your overbid margin (two) add up to nine. Open with 3 SPADES.

NOTVUL vs. VUL

♠ 8
♡ 10 5 2
◇ K Q J 10 3 2
♣ Q J 2

Your five playing tricks plus an overbid margin of four add up to nine. A bid of 3 DIAMONDS should pay off. Although you only hold six diamonds, they are good ones. The count of playing tricks is what tells you that you can go ahead.

NOTVUL vs. VUL

♠ Q 10 9 8 6 5 4 3
♡ —
◇ K Q 5
♣ 8 7

You won't see this kind of hand very often. You have six playing tricks plus an overbid margin of four, making ten in all. Opening with 1 SPADE is out of the question, but opening with 4 SPADES is fine. Do not make the mistake of bidding only 3 SPADES—you must make your maximum bid at once.

VUL vs. VUL

♠ Q 10 9 8 6 5 4 3
♡ —
◇ K Q 5
♣ 8 7

This is the same hand as before but the vulnerability now is equal. Your overbid margin now is only three, so you must settle for an opening bid of only 3 SPADES. Again your playing tricks plus the overbid margin, which is based on the vulnerability, is your guide.

Responding to an Opening Preempt

When your partner makes a preemptive bid, you become the captain. His preemptive bid has effectively limited his hand. Do not expect your partner to bid again unless you force him to do so. If you bid a new suit over your partner's opening preempt, that would be forcing under the general principle that a new suit by the captain is forcing. But this is a rare action because your partner's hand is really only good for playing in his suit. You will normally raise or pass, even if you have a good suit of your own.

There are two different reasons why you might want to raise your partner's preempt. One is CONSTRUCTIVE, with the idea of making your contract. The other is PREEMPTIVE, with the idea of carrying your partner's preempt to a higher level to further obstruct the opponents. Since your partner is not going to bid again, it is not necessary for him to know which you are doing.

If you hold a hand of opening strength when your partner opens with a preempt, you will usually find that you have just about enough for your partner to make his bid. But if your hand is better than the minimum for an opening bid, you may be able to raise your partner and still have him make the contract. For such a bid to be successful you will need enough playing tricks to make up for your partner's overbid margin, plus one playing trick if you are raising him one level. When counting your playing tricks, include any ruffs which you (as dummy) expect to get. As far as support for your partner is concerned, one card in your partner's suit is enough because you can assume that he holds at least seven.

If you should hold as many as three cards in your partner's suit, and you are not strong enough to raise constructively, it may still be profitable to raise your partner for preemptive purposes. A 10-card fit and a weak hand is always conducive to preempting. Your

---

When raising your partner's opening preempt:

- For a constructive raise to game you need:

  - Better than a minimum opening hand
  - Playing tricks to cover your partner's overbid margin plus a playing trick for each level by which you must raise
  - 1-card support or better

- For a preemptive raise (not above the game level) you need:

  - Two playing tricks for a single raise, or three playing tricks for a double raise
  - 3-card support or better

partner has already counted on you for one playing trick to make his preemptive bid a satisfactory sacrifice. If you can provide a second playing trick, you are in a position to raise your partner one level, but not beyond the game level. (A third playing trick should induce you to raise 3 CLUBS or 3 DIAMONDS to the 5-level.)

Your partner has opened 3 HEARTS and the next opponent has passed. Would you raise or pass with the following hands?

NOTVUL vs.
NOTVUL

♠ K Q 4 3
♡ 9 4
◇ A K 9 8
♣ J 6 2

Your hand only evaluates to opening strength. Besides, your partner has already overbid by three tricks, which you will just make up with your three playing tricks in spades and diamonds. PASS.

NOTVUL vs. VUL

♠ A 10 9
♡ 8
◇ Q J 8
♣ A K J 10 4 3

This is a very respectable 16-point hand. (Do not count any distribution point for shortness in a suit your partner has bid.) Even though your partner has overbid by four tricks, you have good expectations of providing five playing tricks. Bid 4 HEARTS. Do not consider bidding clubs. It is better to play in the suit of the weaker hand.

NOTVUL vs.
NOTVUL

♠ —
♡ K 7 5 4
◇ J 8 5 3 2
♣ 10 7 6 4

This is the kind of hand that makes you say "ugh." The opponents obviously have all the good cards, including lots of spades. Before they find that out, bid 4 HEARTS. Your king of hearts can be counted as a playing trick because your partner should have plenty of high hearts to go with it. That and a ruff or two will keep your sacrifice within bounds.

The Preemptive Raise

> A long-standing tradition in Standard American is that:
>
> * Any single jump is strong.
> * Any double (or greater) jump in a *suit* is preemptive up to the game level.

That means that any bid which is one level higher than it needs to be is a strong bid. But a suit bid which is more than one level higher than necessary to bid that suit is a preemptive bid. Modern players have made some exceptions to this tradition, but you can assume it to hold unless you have agreed with your partner to treat some cases differently.

The most common double jump is the preemptive raise. Whenever you have a 10-card or longer fit with your partner, the opponents will necessarily have a singleton or void in your suit. If you are also short of high cards, the opponents may have a game in another suit with no fear of your suit where they are short. Here is an example:

PARTNER	OPPONENT	YOU
1 HEART	1 SPADE	???
	or PASS	

♠ 5
♡ K 9 7 6 2
◇ Q 7 5 3
♣ J 4 3

You have a 10-card fit and a singleton. Your points come to 11 after revaluation, but only 3 of them are in high cards outside of the trump suit. Head off a possible opponent game by bidding 4 HEARTS. You will probably be ahead whether you can make your contract or not.

A preemptive raise is usually based on partnership strength at the invitational level (3-level) as in this example, but the strength may be a little less when you are not vulnerable and are willing to make a bigger sacrifice.

Preemptive Overcalls

Preempts are also used on the defensive. Here is a typical case. Your right-hand opponent opens the bidding with 1 CLUB when you hold:

NOTVUL vs.
NOTVUL

♠ 8 5 4	Overcall 3 HEARTS, the same as you would
♡ K Q J 10 5 4 2	if you were making an opening preempt.
◇ 10	Your six playing tricks plus the overbid mar-
♣ 7 5	gin of three justify this bid. Your partner will
	recognize it as a preempt because it is a
	double jump. (1 HEART would be a non-
	jump and 2 HEARTS a single jump.)

Now suppose, holding the same hand, your right-hand opponent opens 1 SPADE. You would still like to overcall with a preemptive 3 HEARTS but that is only a single jump. So we make a special exception, the WEAK JUMP OVERCALL:

Any jump overcall in a suit as the first bid by the defenders is a preemptive bid.

NOTE: Some players stick to the older tradition of a STRONG JUMP OVERCALL (a good 6-card suit or longer, and much better than a minimum opening hand) or to the modified tradition of an INTERMEDIATE JUMP OVERCALL (a good 6-card suit or longer and slightly better than a minimum opening hand). This is a matter for you to agree on with your partner. However, the strong jump overcall is markedly inferior to the weak jump overcall and the intermediate jump overcall.

The guideline for a weak jump overcall is the same as for an opening preempt:

For a weak jump overcall you need:

- Less than an opening hand
- Insufficient strength to defeat a small slam by the opponents, should they bid it
- Enough playing tricks plus the appropriate overbid margin to equal the level of your preempt

Immediately make the highest bid indicated by this guideline, but not higher than the game level.

Do not bid again unless your partner forces you to.

One of the advantages of the weak jump overcall is that it allows you to make a preemptive overcall as low as at the 2-level. Suppose that your right-hand opponent has opened with 1 HEART and you hold:

NOTVUL vs.
NOTVUL

♠ A Q J 9 3 2
♡ 6
◇ J 8 7
♣ 10 9 5

You can make a preemptive weak jump overcall of 2 SPADES based on your five playing tricks and an overbid margin of three. A 6-card suit is the minimum length for a preemptive bid, and is the usual length for a preempt at the 2-level. If your jack of diamonds were an ace, you would be too strong to preempt and would bid 1 SPADE.

Your right-hand opponent has opened with 1 DIAMOND. What is your bid when you hold the following hands?

NOTVUL vs.
NOTVUL

♠ J 10 7
♡ 3
◇ 9 8
♣ A K J 10 6 5 4

Virtually all of your strength is in your club suit. You have enough playing tricks for a preemptive overcall of 3 CLUBS, and that is your best bid.

NOTVUL vs. VUL

♠ K J 3
♡ 7 4
♢ K 8
♣ A K 10 8 6 5

Here you have a hand of opening strength so a preempt is not appropriate. Bid 2 CLUBS.

NOTVUL vs. NOTVUL

♠ K Q J 8 4 3
♡ K 9
♢ 4
♣ 8 7 5 4

A preempt of 2 SPADES will give your partner the correct picture of your hand. You have five playing tricks and an overbid margin of three.

Aggressive Count of Playing Tricks

There are times when you can afford to be a little more optimistic in counting the number of playing tricks which you expect to take. One of them is when you are not vulnerable.

> **When NOTVUL, use an aggressive count of playing tricks: Add one extra playing trick whenever you have one or more possible tricks in your hand which may materialize under favorable circumstances.**

This guideline allows you to add one (only one) playing trick to the normal conservative count providing that you are not vulnerable and that you hold some POSSIBLE tricks—those which depend on a finesse for succeeding or depend on some other favorable event. The guideline applies whether you are opening or overcalling with a preemptive bid.

NOTE: If you should be playing for serious amounts of money, or in a tournament which is being scored by International Match Points (called IMPs), you should be rather cautious about relying on possible tricks. But at duplicate bridge (scored by normal matchpoints) or at the usual social bridge game, it pays to follow the aggressive line.

What is the aggressive opening bid in the following cases?

NOTVUL vs. NOTVUL

♠ K 4
♡ A J 10 9 5 4 2
◇ J 8 4
♣ 3

You have five playing tricks in hearts plus a possible trick in spades. Since you are NOTVUL you can assume six playing tricks. Adding in the overbid margin of three, you come up with 3 HEARTS.

NOTVUL vs. NOTVUL

♠ K 5 4
♡ Q 2
◇ 10 9 8 5 4 3 2
♣ 4

Here you have four playing tricks in diamonds. When you also count the king of spades and the overbid margin, you find a total of eight, so you must PASS. Even if the vulnerability were favorable, giving you a total of nine, you would do well to pass—your trump suit should be headed by a queen at the least.

NOTVUL vs. NOTVUL

♠ 10
♡ K 8
◇ K 3
♣ K 10 9 7 6 5 4 2

You have five playing tricks in clubs plus three possible tricks. You can assume six playing tricks plus the usual overbid margin to justify 3 CLUBS. If the vulnerability were favorable, you could bid 4 CLUBS.

NOTVUL vs. VUL

♠ A
♡ K J 8
◇ A 9 8 7 6 5 4 3
♣ 8

Not every hand with a long suit calls for a preempt. Start with 1 DIAMOND. You have 16 points and two aces. Either of these factors alone would rule out a preemptive bid.

Preempting after Strong Opponent Bidding

Now that you know how to make preemptive bids, you may overdo it when the opponents open with a strong bid, such as 1 NOTRUMP. The normal overbid margin assumes that your partner will provide one trick, but this is unlikely to be true when the opponents have bid strongly. Therefore you must reduce your overbid margin by one trick when you overcall against strong opponent bidding. Since there is little chance for your side to bid in this situation except to make a preempt, any suit overcall is a preempt, even if no jump at all is involved. You will always have a good six-card suit and almost always a singleton or void to go with it.

Judging the Results

If you are playing rubber bridge, a preemptive bid should not result in a loss of more than 500 points. There will be a few unfortunate exceptions, especially if you are bidding aggressively, but they should not occur very often. And of course if you find out that the opponents couldn't have made a game anyway, you have probably sacrificed when you shouldn't have. All players have to accept an occasional bad result—the better player you become, the less often it will happen.

If you play duplicate, you can compare your results with those of others who have played the same hand. This will tell you immediately whether you have judged well or too conservatively or too aggressively.

Chapter 10 //

COMPETITIVE BIDS

//

A
Considerations for a Competitive Bid

Competitive versus Preemptive Bidding

When you make a preemptive bid, you are afraid that the opponents will bid a game or slam and that you have too little defense against their contract to prevent them from making it. You have a long suit which will give you a certain number of tricks if you can play at your own contract, but you realize that it will be almost useless against their contract. The amount of sacrifice that you are willing to take is considerable (about 500 points) because you are fighting against a probable game by the opponents which will be worth about that much to them if they succeed in their contract.

Competitive bidding usually starts with an opening bid by one side and an overcall by the other side. Unless one side is unable to continue bidding, the competition is on. Most often the strength is split more or less evenly between the two sides so that neither side can make a game. Usually either side can succeed in a 2-level contract if they can find a fit, but it is unclear whether a 3-level contract will succeed or not. So the battle is to push the opponents to the 3-level where possibly they will be set, or to outbid the opponents at a level where your contract will succeed.

A hand suitable for a preempt will have a long suit of at least six cards and will not have two DEFENSIVE TRICKS (tricks which can be taken against an opposing contract). A hand suitable for an ordinary competitive overcall may have only a 5-card suit. If it has a longer suit, it will normally have at least two defensive tricks, otherwise it would probably be more suitable for a preemptive bid.

Competitive versus Noncompetitive Bidding

When your side opens the bidding, you and your partner may bid several suits looking for a fit. If no fit is found you may settle into notrump or simply play in a subnormal trump fit. Even if you end up in a contract which you can't make, the opponents seldom know it and so they will not double you. Their strength is usually divided between their two hands, and if neither one has bid, neither one knows what the strength of the other is.

Now imagine that the opponents open the bidding in some suit and you are about to make an overcall. Finding a fit is not so easy because the opponents have already laid claim to one of the suits. Besides that, their bidding is going to take away some of the bidding space which you would otherwise have for finding a fit. Moving into notrump is probably not going to be successful unless your side has the opponents' suit well stopped. And if you blunder into a suit where you have a poor fit with your partner, you are likely to be doubled. The opener may be strong enough to double you himself, or the responder may make this unpleasant move after mentally adding up his own strength with that revealed by his partner. For this reason, some hands which would be good enough to open the bidding must be passed if the opponents have already opened the bidding.

Duplicate versus Other Forms of Bridge

When you play duplicate bridge, your results are measured against the results of every other pair who plays the same hand as you do. You receive 1 matchpoint for each of these pairs you beat, by however little, and ½ matchpoint for each of these pairs you tie. By and large, whenever a bid or a play gives you a better than 50-50 chance of scoring more points, you will try it without regard to how much you may lose if you fail.

When you play at other forms of bridge, you should look upon the score you receive as if it were money. (Perhaps you do play for money, in which case this is literally true.) There is no point in taking a risk to make a few points (a little money) when failure may involve the loss of a lot of points (a lot of money). On the other hand, you can afford to take a bigger risk than a duplicate player would when the potential gain is large and the potential loss is small.

In competitive bidding, the duplicate player is more aggressive because he cannot allow the opponents to make even a partscore if he can force them to take less. At other forms of bridge, a slightly more conservative attitude can be taken when the opponents can only make a partscore. This is simply because there are fewer points involved in making a partscore than there are when a game is at stake.

Sacrificing

If the opponents are outbidding you in a competitive situation, you may consider a small sacrifice to prevent them from making a partscore. The opponents will make the same partscore, whether they are vulnerable or not. It is only *your* vulnerability which matters when you consider a sacrifice against a partscore.

If you are doubled and set by one trick when you are not vulnerable, you will lose 100 points. This is less than most partscores are worth. (In rubber bridge the mere advantage of having a partscore makes it worth somewhere between 100 and 200 points—the exact value is not known.) But if you are doubled and set by one trick when you are vulnerable, you will lose 200 points. At rubber bridge this is a maximum sacrifice to prevent a partscore. At duplicate bridge a 200-point loss is a very bad sacrifice when the opponents can only make a partscore.

When fighting for a partscore:

- If you are NOTVUL, be aggressive—accept going down one trick in order to outbid the opponents.
- If you are VUL, be conservative—give them the partscore rather than be set.

B
The Overcall

Considerations in Making an Overcall in a Suit

When you overcall in a suit, you must worry about entering the bidding and then not finding a fit. Therefore your overcall will always be based on a good suit, at least five cards long. A GOOD SUIT contains any two of the following:

A   K   Q   J-10

The opponents will seldom double you unless they hold some length and strength in your suit. But the more you hold in your trump suit the less they can hold. Thus your best hope to find a fit and to escape a double is to have a good suit with some length to it.

If you should have two 5-card (or longer) suits, it is only necessary for one of them to qualify as a good suit. Bid the longer first, or of equally long suits, bid the higher-ranking one first.

Your partner will almost always have a fit for one of your suits, so there is safety in having two possibilities.

Even if your side bids no further and the opponents outbid you, your overcall may do some good. It will suggest a good lead to your partner. This is another reason why you need a good suit for an overcall. If it is your partner who overcalls, you will almost always lead your partner's suit at your first opportunity.

Your overcall may obstruct the opponents, taking some of their bidding space away. Suppose your right-hand opponent opens with 1 CLUB and you overcall with 1 SPADE. If your left-hand opponent had intended to respond 1 DIAMOND or 1 HEART, he can no longer do so.

If your partner raises you, you may relax. You have a fit. Your partner will seldom make any other bid if he can raise you.

If your partner responds to your overcall with a notrump bid, he has a real interest in notrump—a balanced hand and a stopper in the opponents' suit (or suits). There is no room for a flaky notrump on the defense. If your partner does not have a decent bid, he must pass.

If your partner bids a new suit after you have overcalled, beware! He most probably has no fit for your suit. If you do not have a fit for his suit, you have no place to go. Your partner's new-suit bid is not forcing (because you are on the defense), and it will usually be six cards long. You will normally pass with no fit, or with a fit but not enough strength to raise. A new suit after an overcall is not particularly encouraging—it may be simply an attempt to get out of a bad fit in the hope of getting into a better one.

Guidelines for Overcalling

Overcalling is one of the most difficult decisions in bridge. You are always taking some risk and you have to decide whether there is something to be gained to make the risk worthwhile. There are no exact guidelines possible in an area which involves so much judgment. However, the risk will usually be reasonable if you hold a good suit of at least five cards and if you do not overbid your playing tricks by more than three tricks.

Point count holding is rather flexible when you are overcalling. Unlike an opening bid, an overcall does not promise some specific number of points. Instead we can attach a nominal point count to an overcall—the count which your partner will assume that you hold, whether you actually do or not.

- When you can overcall by bidding 1 in your SUIT, you need:
  - A good 5-card suit (or longer)
  - 11 points (nominal)

- When you can overcall only by bidding 2 in your SUIT, you need:
  - A good 5-card suit (or longer)
  - 14 points (nominal)

- Do not overbid your playing tricks by more than three in any case.

In counting your playing tricks, use the aggressive count when you are not vulnerable or when you will be overcalling at the 1-level. The aggressive count allows you to count an additional playing trick whenever you hold one or more POSSIBLE tricks.

There is one warning to heed to avoid taking an unwanted sacrifice. At rubber bridge or progressive bridge, opponents will double an overcall of 2 CLUBS or 2 DIAMONDS rather readily. If they are wrong, and you make your contract, the double will not give you enough score for game. They cannot be so free with the double against any higher bid because if you make your contract you also make a game. Therefore, when overcalling with 2 CLUBS or with 2 DIAMONDS you should have either a good 6-card suit or an extra good 5-card suit. This does not apply to duplicate bridge, because the fight for a partscore is more important than the risk of an occasional set.

You will seldom have to go to the 3-level in order to overcall.

But perhaps one of the opponents has opened the bidding with 3 CLUBS. If you don't want to be shut out of the bidding, you will have to bid at the 3-level. You never preempt after the opponents have preempted, so the question is whether you have a constructive bid which can make.

At the 3-level or above, a good 6-card suit (or possibly an extra-good 5-card suit) is absolutely mandatory. Your strength will run 15 points and up. The risk of bidding at a high level is considerable. You may decide to pass for safety's sake, only to find out later that a bid would have succeeded. Or you may elect to bid only to be set. The best experts are often put to a guess after an opposing preempt.

Would you overcall in the following cases? What would your bid be? All of these hands contain at least the nominal point count for the bid you might consider, so base your conclusion on suit quality and playing tricks.

VUL vs. VUL

RHO opens 1 HEART

♠ K J 10 5 4
♡ 8
◇ A J 5 2
♣ K Q 7

You have a good spade suit and 16 points. You also have five playing tricks which is plenty for an overcall of 1 SPADE.

VUL vs. VUL

RHO opens 1 DIAMOND

♠ K Q 9 8 7
♡ K 6 5
◇ K 10 8
♣ 7 6

Here you have three playing tricks plus a possible trick in each of the red suits. Since you are planning to bid at the 1-level, you may assume four playing tricks. Your good suit and your 12 points support a bid of 1 SPADE.

VUL vs. VUL

RHO opens 1 DIAMOND

♠ K J 7
♡ Q J 9 5 4

Your heart suit lacks the 10 to be a good suit, and you have only two playing tricks. You

◇ K 9 8
♣ Q J

might allow your excess of points to compensate for the slightly defective suit, but points cannot compensate for a lack of playing tricks. You must PASS.

NOTVUL vs. NOTVUL
RHO opens 1 CLUB

♠ A K Q J 8
♡ 10 8 3
◇ 10 7 6
♣ 9 5

This 11-point hand looks like a preempt, but you cannot preempt with a 5-card suit. However, your good suit and your five playing tricks cry for a bid of 1 SPADE. You will be suggesting a good suit for your partner to lead if the opponents take the contract. And you deny to the opponents the bids of 1 DIAMOND and 1 HEART. If your partner is able to raise you, you will have the effect of a preempt in that the opponents must go to the 3-level to outbid you. Bid 1 SPADE.

NOTVUL vs. NOTVUL
RHO opens 1 CLUB

♠ A K Q J 8 3
♡ 10 8 3
◇ 10 7 6
♣ 9

This is the same hand as before, but with an extra spade and therefore six playing tricks. Now your suit is long enough for a preemptive bid. Your overbid margin is three for this vulnerability, so an overcall of 3 SPADES is not too aggressive. You have less than an opening hand and what strength you do have is all in your trump suit.

NOTVUL vs. NOTVUL
RHO opens 1 HEART

♠ J 5 4
♡ 8
◇ K Q J 9 2
♣ A J 8 7

Your good diamond suit and your five playing tricks let you bid 2 DIAMONDS. You are not vulnerable and and your singleton heart (their suit) is a good asset. Your 14 points will provide some strength if your partner raises you to 3 DIAMONDS.

VUL vs. VUL
RHO opens 1 SPADE

♠ A 8
♡ K J 10 7 5 4
◇ A 9 4 2
♣ 3

Your good hearts and six playing tricks make a bid of 2 HEARTS quite sound. Your partnership could even end up in game if your partner can take care of some of your diamond losers. If your suit had been a minor, your prospects for game would be reduced considerably.

NOTVUL vs. VUL
RHO opens 3 DIAMONDS

♠ A K 9 8 7 5
♡ A Q J 3
◇ 2
♣ 10 9

The opponents are trying to do you in, and they may succeed if your LHO has most of the remaining points. But you have safety in your good 6-card suit. In spades you have five playing tricks and in hearts you have two plus an additional possibility. Your 16 points and your vulnerability also favor an overcall of 3 SPADES. If your partner has some help, you may even be able to make a game.

NOTVUL vs. NOTVUL
RHO opens 1 DIAMOND

♠ J 10 7 4 3
♡ A K 6 5 2
◇ Q 2
♣ 8

You have two possible trump suits, one of which is good. You have two playing tricks in hearts, two more in whichever suit becomes trump, and the possibility of some long tricks in the other suit which becomes the side suit. Queens and jacks in the opponents' suits are of no value, but even not counting the queen of diamonds, you have 11 points. Bid 1 SPADE (the higher ranking of equal-length suits). If your partner does not support spades, you will later bid 2 HEARTS if you get the chance. This also gives you an escape if your spade bid is doubled.

Aggressive Overcalls

Most of your overcalls will be based on a hand which has at least as many points as the nominal count for the bid. But on occasion you will find that you have the playing tricks but not the point count necessary. The modern trend is to be aggressive in these cases, especially at duplicate bridge. But unless you have a good partner who agrees that an overcall may be light on points, you may get your side into trouble. Your bid may be sound and go undoubled, but your partner, expecting more strength from you, may bid too high and "go for a number" (be set badly) when doubled at a higher level.

An aggressive overcall should always be based on a good reason. The reason may be that you hold an extra long or an extra good suit. Or it may be that your bid has obstructive value. And when you can bid spades, you have the advantage of having the highest ranking suit and can outbid the opponents more easily.

You should never be short more than one or two points for an aggressive overcall. Most aggressive overcalls occur at the 1-level, or when not vulnerable at the 2-level. Here are some examples.

What would your bid be in the following circumstances?

NOTVUL vs. VUL
RHO opens 1 CLUB

♠ A K 9 5 4	This 10-point hand does have a good suit and four playing tricks, so that 1 SPADE is within the normal bounds. The spade suit is obstructive, you are bidding at the 1-level, and you are not vulnerable—all good reasons to bid.
♡ Q 8 3	
◇ 10 8	
♣ 9 7 6	

NOTVUL vs. NOTVUL
RHO opens 1 SPADE

♠ 9	With five playing tricks plus two possible tricks, and with a fine club suit, this hand is better than the point count of 13 would suggest by itself. You can bid 2 CLUBS.
♡ K 3	
◇ 10 9 8 6	
♣ A K J 10 5 3	

NOTVUL vs. VUL
RHO opens 1 DIAMOND

♠ 9 8
♡ A 8 7
◇ 7 5
♣ A K 10 9 5 4

This hand has only 12 points but it has six playing tricks. Also, the extra good club suit is filled out with the ten and the nine, which are intermediate cards. Since you are not vulnerable, you can take the risk of a 2 CLUB bid. Notice how this obstructs the opponents, preventing them from bidding 1 HEART or 1 SPADE or 1 NOTRUMP.

NOTVUL vs. NOTVUL
RHO opens 1 DIAMOND

♠ 4
♡ K Q J 10 7 5
◇ 9 8
♣ J 7 5 4

With a six-card suit you must always ask yourself if the hand qualifies for a preempt. Your lack of defensive tricks makes the answer yes. With five playing tricks and an overbid margin of three, you must bid 2 HEARTS, a weak jump overcall.

VUL vs. NOTVUL
RHO opens 1 SPADE

♠ K 2
♡ Q 8 4
◇ K J 10 4 2
♣ K J 4

This hand is a 14-point trap. You have three playing tricks in the good diamond suit, but only possible tricks in the other suits. This doesn't add up to the four playing tricks needed, especially considering that you are vulnerable. PASS. Points that don't make playing tricks are better for defeating the opponents than for overcalling.

Responding to an Overcall

When you are responding to an overcall, you are the DEFENSIVE RESPONDER. Unless the overcall was a preempt, your bidding will proceed pretty much as if your partner had opened the bidding. But there are some differences:

- Your partner supposedly has only 11 points for a 1-level overcall and 14 points for a 2-level overcall (nonjump).
- You can count on your partner to have at least five cards in his suit, even if it is a minor.
- You are using full-value bidding as a defender—no defensive bids are forcing (except certain special cases described later).
- The opponents' bidding has revealed where their strength lies, allowing you to go to game and to invite game *in a suit* with 1 point less.

This leads to the following guideline:

When raising an overcall (not a preempt) you need:

- **3-card support**
- **7 points (maybe a good 6) to raise to the 2-level**
- **A partnership total of 22 points to raise to the 3-level**
- **A partnership total of 25 points to raise to the 4-level**

Revaluate your hand when counting your points, but do not count any points for queens or jacks in the opponents' suits.

Assume that your partner holds the nominal count for his overcall.

Notice that the partnership totals are one point less than for offensive bidding in a suit. If you are able to raise, you must immediately go to the maximum level permitted by the guideline. This is what "full-value bidding" means—bid what you think you can make.

What would you bid in the following situations? The bidding has been:

LHO	PARTNER	RHO	YOU
1 DIAMOND	1 HEART	PASS	???

NOTVUL vs.
NOTVUL

♠ Q 7 3 2
♡ J 5 3
◊ 9
♣ K J 10 9 5

You have support for hearts and 10 points (since your singleton revaluates to 2 points). Because you are on the defensive, you must not even think of bidding clubs. Latch on to your fit in hearts with 2 HEARTS. Partnership points are only 21.

NOTVUL vs. NOTVUL

♠ K 10 8
♡ 8 7 5 3
◊ J 2
♣ K 8 4 3

Ignoring the jack of diamonds and taking an extra point for the 9-card fit in hearts, you have just 7 points. That is enough to bid 2 HEARTS.

NOTVUL vs. VUL

♠ K 5 2
♡ Q 4 3 2
◊ 8 5
♣ A J 9 8

With 11 points you can see a partnership total of at least 22. Bid 3 HEARTS.

VUL vs. VUL

♠ 9
♡ A 10 5 2
◊ A 8 4 3
♣ K 10 4 3

This doesn't happen very often. You have 14 points which, added to your partner's 11, come to 25. You must bid 4 HEARTS.

What would you bid in each of the following situations?

LHO	PARTNER	RHO	YOU
1 SPADE	2 HEARTS	PASS	???

VUL vs. VUL

♠ 9 7
♡ K 4 3
◇ K Q 9 8
♣ 10 8 5 4

Your 8 points plus your partner's assumed 14 put your partnership just up to the 22 mark. Bid 3 HEARTS.

LHO	PARTNER	RHO	YOU
1 SPADE	2 HEARTS	2 SPADES	???

VUL vs. NOTVUL

♠ 10
♡ 9 7 4
◇ A 9 8 7 5
♣ Q 6 3 2

Your original 8 points have gone up to 9 now that your partner has bid hearts. Your heart support is minimum but acceptable. Bid 3 HEARTS. Your side might have game if your partner has a little extra.

LHO	PARTNER	RHO	YOU
		1 HEART	PASS
2 HEARTS	2 SPADES	3 HEARTS	???

VUL vs. NOTVUL

♠ 10 9 5
♡ K 10 4 3
◇ K J 5 4
♣ 9 8

The opponents are already up to the 3-level so there is no need to overdo. Your heart holding suggests that they may have a hard time making their contract. They may have overbid at 3 HEARTS, intending to sacrifice. They are not vulnerable and can afford to do that. You are vulnerable, and your defensive possibilities against 3 HEARTS suggest that you should PASS.

LHO	PARTNER	RHO	YOU
		1 CLUB	1 DIAMOND
1 HEART	2 DIAMONDS	2 HEARTS	???

NOTVUL vs. VUL

♠ A 8 5
♡ 7 5
◇ A Q J 9 5
♣ 10 9 7

You have 12 points and your partner has promised 7, making a minimum of 19 for the partnership. You cannot make 3 DIAMONDS unless your partner has some extra points. But you probably will not be set more than one trick and you are not vulnerable. Bid the 3 DIAMONDS. You would not do this when vulnerable.

Other Responses to an Overcall

Once in a while your partner will overcall in a suit which you can't support. You may have only a small doubleton in his suit, or a singleton, or possibly even a void. If you are not doubled, don't panic. ("No double, no trouble.") You should not introduce a new suit as a defensive response unless you feel that it will probably provide a better trump fit than the misfit in the suit your partner has already bid. You must be prepared for your partner to have possibly only one or two cards in your suit. Therefore you will normally consider only a good 6-card suit, although if you can bid at the 1-level you might consider a good 5-card suit. To bid your suit, your hand should be only a little weaker than what you would overcall on if your partner hadn't bid. In marginal cases let your vulnerability decide.

On a few occasions, usually when you cannot raise your partner's suit, you may find that a notrump bid is appropriate. You will need a balanced hand with the opponents' suit well stopped. Unlike suit bidding, where you could work with a reduced partnership total, you will need the full total for notrump. If anything, the opponents' bidding has made notrump more difficult, not less.

When responding in notrump on the defensive, you need:

- 20 partnership points to bid 1 NOTRUMP
- 23 partnership points to bid 2 NOTRUMP
- 26 partnership points to bid 3 NOTRUMP

You must have a balanced hand and the opponents' suit(s) stopped.

Notice that a 1 NOTRUMP bid represents real notrump values. There is no place for a flaky notrump bid on the defensive. Here is a typical example:

LHO	PARTNER	RHO	YOU
1 CLUB	1 SPADE	PASS	???

♠ 8 5
♡ K 5 4
♢ Q 8 7 4
♣ K J 10 3

You have 9 points so the partnership total comes to 20. Your hand is balanced and you have the opponents' suit stopped. You cannot raise your partner's spades, so 1 NOTRUMP is in order.

What would you bid in the following situations?

LHO	PARTNER	RHO	YOU
1 DIAMOND	1 HEART	PASS	???

NOTVUL vs. NOTVUL

♠ K Q 9 7 5 4
♡ 8
♢ 7 6 3 2
♣ A 9

It looks as though spades can be no worse than hearts as a trump fit. You would have overcalled 1 SPADE even if your partner had not bid. So go ahead with 1 SPADE now.

VUL vs. NOTVUL

♠ A 8 3
♡ J 4
◇ K J 5 4
♣ 10 9 8 4

You have a partnership total of 20 points, just enough to bid 1 NOTRUMP. You have diamonds stopped and even your clubs aren't too bad—the 10, 9 and 8 are intermediate cards, not really low ones.

VUL vs. NOTVUL

♠ Q 10 8
♡ K 5
◇ A 4 3
♣ K 10 7 5 4

Your 12 HCP plus your partner's assumed 11 points come to 23. Bid 2 NOTRUMP and hope that your partner has additional points to continue bidding with.

Captaincy

On the defense as well as on the offense, a limit bid elects the other partner as captain. So far we haven't seen any forcing power for a defender before he becomes captain. As captain he has full forcing power—his new suits are forcing (except when signing off after 1 NOTRUMP) and his jumps are forcing to game. However, a defensive captain seldom gets to use his forcing power because usually there is not enough strength in the partnership to go on to game. The principal exception occurs when the overcall is in notrump. The defensive bidding then proceeds as if over an opening notrump, but with an eye on the suit which the opponents have bid.

A defensive preempt makes the other partner the captain, but the chances of making a game are very slim after the opponents have opened the bidding. For this reason a defensive captain remains with no forcing power if he was elected by his partner's preempt. If the captain bids a new suit, he is inviting a raise from his partner, but he knows that a pass is more likely.

When both sides are bidding, it is difficult for both the offense and the defense to distinguish a competitive bid from a game invitation.

LHO	PARTNER	RHO	YOU
1 HEART	1 SPADE	2 HEARTS	2 SPADES
3 HEARTS	3 SPADES	???	???

You have to assume that your partner (the captain) has bid 3 SPADES to compete and outbid the opponents. If you are vulnerable, he should not have overbid by more than a point, so you may consider his bid as a weak game invitation. But if you are not vulnerable, he may have overbid as a sacrifice. This is no game invitation and you should PASS—your partner would jump to 4 SPADES if he thought your side had a chance at game, even if he had to assume an extra point in your hand. Your right-hand opponent has to give the same line of thought to his partner's 3 HEART bid.

C
The Double

The Takeout Double

Sometimes, when your partner has not yet bid, you'd like to know what his best suit is. Look at this hand.

RHO opens 1 CLUB

♠ K Q 7 5
♡ K J 9 4
◇ A 9 3 2
♣ 4

You would like to compete in any suit but clubs. But which one? Of course you would prefer a major. But any suit would do if you knew you had a fit with your partner. Is there some way to ask your partner to pick one of the unbid suits? Yes, there is.

For the first time you are going to use a CONVENTION—a bid which has been given an artificial meaning. But if a bid is used for an artificial purpose, it can no longer be used with its natural meaning.

When your partner has not already bid, you rarely can double the opponents successfully, just because you do not know how much help your partner can give you in setting the opponents. Since the double would not be useful in its natural meaning in that case, we use it as a TAKEOUT DOUBLE—a conventional use which demands that your partner take your side out of the double (which you really didn't mean anyway) into his best suit. With the hand given above, if you DOUBLE you are asking your partner to pick one of the unbid suits: spades or hearts or diamonds.

A takeout double says to your partner:

• I have the strength to bid.
• I can support *any* unbid suit, especially the majors.
• I want you, partner, to name the suit.
• But I have no desire whatsoever to play in their suit doubled.

Obviously it is necessary to know for sure whether a double is a takeout double or is a PENALTY DOUBLE (made with the expectation of setting the opponents and collecting the penalty score).

A double is for takeout if:

• **The doubler's partner has not bid (a pass is not a bid)**
  and
• **The doubled bid is below the game level**
  and
• **The doubled bid is a suit bid or the flaky 1 NOTRUMP RESPONSE.**

All other doubles are for penalty.

Notice that the double of a *normal* notrump bid is for penalties. When the opponents' bidding reaches the game level, you are more likely to be able to set them than to compete against them, so then a double is for penalties. And once your partner has bid, you already know what he has so there is no need for a takeout double—all doubles are then for penalty.

NOTE: Only the most unsophisticated bridge player would fail to recognize a takeout double. Of course it would be entirely improper to make any difference in one's voice or manner when saying DOUBLE, whether it is for penalty or for takeout. Be sure that *you* know which is which.

When you make a takeout double, your partner will name the suit in which your side will play. That will make you the dummy, so you can revaluate your hand accordingly.

For a takeout double you need:

- 13 points
- At least 3-card support in *all* unbid suits.

Revaluate your hand as the dummy hand: Take 1 additional point for a singleton and 2 additional points for a void.

Since you are especially looking for a fit in a major suit, you can consider your hand to be a point stronger if you have four cards in each unbid major suit and a point weaker if you have only three cards in each unbid major suit.

Are the following situations suitable for you to make a take-out double?

LHO	PARTNER	RHO	YOU
		1 DIAMOND	???

♠ K 9 5 3
♡ Q J 9 4
◇ 8 4
♣ A K 8

You have 13 points and 3-card support for all the unbid suits. You are particularly pleased to have four cards in each of the majors, making your hand worth about 14 points. DOUBLE and let your partner choose between spades, hearts and clubs.

LHO	PARTNER	RHO	YOU
		1 CLUB	???

♠ K Q 8
♡ Q 8 5 4
◇ A Q 9 8
♣ J 8

Not counting the jack of clubs (jacks and queens in the opponents' suits are worthless), you have 13 points and 3-card support for all unbid suits. You would like an additional spade, but three will do. DOUBLE.

LHO	PARTNER	RHO	YOU
		1 HEART	???

♠ K Q J
♡ K 4 3 2
◇ A J 9 6
♣ 10 8

You cannot make a takeout double because you have only two clubs and thus you are quite unprepared for a club response by your partner. You will simply have to PASS in spite of your 14 points.

LHO	PARTNER	RHO	YOU
1 CLUB	PASS	1 HEART	???

♠ K 9 8 5
♡ A 8 3

There are still two unbid suits left. You have 13 points, counting an extra point for the singleton club. You will be pleased whether

◇ K 10 9 7 5   your partner picks spades or diamonds.
♣ 9   DOUBLE.

LHO	PARTNER	RHO	YOU
1 DIAMOND	PASS	1 NOTRUMP	???

♠ K J 10 3
♡ Q J 7 5
◇ 8 4
♣ A K 8

You can double the flaky 1 NOTRUMP RESPONSE and the meaning is for your partner to pick one of the three unbid suits. Notice that your partner will have to bid at the 2-level, no matter which suit he chooses. But your hand has solid support for all three suits.

Takeout Double by the Opener

Sometimes you will make a takeout double when you are the opener. If the opponents compete but your partner only passes, you can force him to choose between raising your 5-card suit or bidding one of the unbid suits by doubling the opponents' bid. Here is an example.

LHO	PARTNER	RHO	YOU
			1 DIAMOND
1 SPADE	PASS	PASS	???

♠ 4 3
♡ K 9 8
◇ A Q 10 8 7
♣ A K 5

Your partner may have a rather poor hand, but your hand is quite good. You don't want the opponents to get the contract for only 1 SPADE. Since your partner has not bid, and since you support both the unbid suits, you can DOUBLE for takeout. Your partner will either raise your diamonds on the assumption that you have five of them, or he will bid hearts or clubs.

Recognizing your Partner's Takeout Double

When your partner doubles and you have not already bid, it is probably a takeout double. If the bid being doubled is not a normal notrump bid and is below the game level, that confirms that your partner has made a takeout double.

In each case, tell whether the double is for takeout or for penalty.

LHO	PARTNER	RHO	YOU	
1 DIAMOND	DOUBLE	PASS	???	You have not bid. The double is for takeout.
1 CLUB	DOUBLE	2 CLUBS	???	Takeout. You may pass since an opponent has intervened.
3 CLUBS	DOUBLE	PASS	???	Takeout. Same meaning after a preempt.
4 SPADES	DOUBLE	PASS	???	Penalty. The bidding has reached game level. PASS!
1 DIAMOND 2 CLUBS	1 HEART DOUBLE	PASS PASS	PASS ???	You have not bid. The double is for takeout. Bid spades or raise hearts.
1 CLUB 2 DIAMONDS	PASS DOUBLE	1 DIAMOND PASS	PASS ???	You have not bid. The double is for takeout.

1 CLUB	DOUBLE	2 CLUBS	PASS	The takeout double is being repeated. You could pass before, but now you must bid. Partner is strong.
PASS	DOUBLE	PASS	???	

1 NOTRUMP	DOUBLE	PASS	???	The opponents have bid a normal notrump. Therefore the double is for penalty.

		1 HEART	PASS	You have not bid. Their 1 NOTRUMP is flaky. The double is for takeout.
1 NOTRUMP	DOUBLE	PASS	???	

PASS	1 HEART	1 SPADE	PASS	You have not bid. The double is for takeout. Bid a minor or raise hearts.
PASS	DOUBLE	PASS	???	

1 HEART	1 SPADE	2 HEARTS	2 SPADES	You have bid. The double is for penalty. PASS!
3 HEARTS	DOUBLE	PASS	???	

		1 HEART	DOUBLE	Your double is equivalent to a bid. Partner's double is for penalty.
2 HEARTS	DOUBLE	PASS	???	

PASS	1 HEART	DOUBLE	???	*Their* takeout double against your side.

NOTE: Experts consider that a double of a *preemptive* bid of 4 HEARTS is for takeout. A game in spades is still a possibility.

Responding to a Takeout Double

A takeout double is forcing—you must bid unless your right-hand opponent intervenes with a bid. Your partner wanted to bid one of the unbid suits but didn't know which one might produce the best fit. So he has asked you to name the suit which you think is best. You will ordinarily bid your longest suit, but in case of a tie you will prefer a major. A major suit makes it much easier to compete against the opponents, so much so that you will usually prefer a 4-card (or longer) major to a minor which is one card longer. This is one of the few cases in bridge bidding where you will pick a shorter suit over a longer one.

Occasionally your partner will make a takeout double after he has already bid a suit himself. In that case you have the additional option of responding by raising his suit (which you can assume to be at least five cards long). You may have to raise with less than 3-card support when any other bid looks worse.

Of course you will hate to respond to a takeout double with a 3-card suit, but you must do so when you have nothing longer in the unbid suits. Look at this horror:

LHO	PARTNER	RHO	YOU
1 CLUB	DOUBLE	PASS	???

♠ 4 3 2
♡ 4 3 2
♢ 4 3 2
♣ 5 4 3 2

You have only three cards in each of the unbid suits, and you have no points at all. But your partner has asked you to name a suit. The least of the evils, when you have only 3-card suits to choose from, is to pick the cheapest bid you can make. Bid 1 DIAMOND. That leaves the maximum room for someone else to bid and take you off the hook. Bid confidently and perhaps someone will.

Beginners sometimes panic and pass opposite a takeout double when they have few or no points. The opponents then romp through their doubled contract for a very big score. *To pass because you have nothing is to commit suicide.* You must do what your partner asked you to do—name a suit (unless an opponent intervenes with a bid).

When responding to a takeout double:

- **Respond in your longest unbid suit—but prefer a 4-card (or better) major over a minor which is one card longer.**
- **In case of tie, prefer a major—but if you have only 3-card suits to choose from, pick the cheapest.**
- **You have the option of raising any suit your partner has bid.**

Your strength will affect the level of your response to a takeout double. You will be the declarer and you can revaluate your hand on that basis. You should assume 3-card support for your minor suit or 4-card support for your major suit (even though only 3-card support is guaranteed.) A 9-card fit is worth an extra point, a 10-card fit is worth 2 extra points, and so on. With a 6-card (or longer) suit in your hand, also take an extra point for a singleton and two extra for a void.

Notice once again that invitational and game-going bids in a *suit* are made with one point less for defensive bidding than for offensive bidding.

When responding to a suit to a takeout double you need:

- 0 points to respond when your RHO passes
- 6 points to respond when your RHO makes a nonjump bid
- Partnership total of 22 to make a jump response (nonforcing)
- Partnership total of 25 to jump to the 4-level

Revaluate your hand as the declarer, assuming 4-card support for your major or 3-card support for your minor.

How would you respond to a takeout double in the following cases? The bidding has been:

LHO	PARTNER	RHO	YOU
1 DIAMOND	DOUBLE	PASS	???

♠ K 8 9 4
♡ Q 3 2
♢ 8 7 4
♣ 9 7 3

Your hand is anything but exciting, but you do hold spades. Bid 1 SPADE.

♠ Q J 8 3
♡ 8 7
♢ J 2
♣ A 9 8 5 4

You have 8 points, not counting the jack of diamonds. Spades is a better choice than clubs so bid 1 SPADE.

♠ K 9 7 4
♡ K J 7 5 4
♢ 5 4 3
♣ 10

You have an original count of 9 points. After your partner's takeout double, you can take an extra point for the probable 9-card fit in hearts. You must jump to 2 HEARTS since the partnership total has more than reached the 22 mark. (You would have bid 1 HEART even with no high cards at all.)

♠ J 8 3 ♡ 5 4 3 ◇ Q 8 ♣ J 8 7 5 4	Bid 2 CLUBS. Your partner asked for a suit and clubs is it. Your partner is short in diamonds and so are you, so the opponents will probably continue bidding in diamonds.
♠ 10 8 4 ♡ J 9 4 ◇ A 7 5 4 2 ♣ 8 5	This kind of situation makes you wonder why the takeout double was ever invented. It really does work well most of the time. But no bid works all of the time. Bid 1 HEART and hope for the best.
♠ K Q 8 7 3 ♡ 9 4 ◇ Q 3 ♣ K 10 7 6	This hand revaluates to 10 points, not counting the queen of diamonds, and taking an extra point for the assumed 9-card spade fit. That makes 23 partnership points so give a jump—bid 2 SPADES.

Would you bid or pass after the following bidding?

LHO	PARTNER	RHO	YOU
1 HEART	DOUBLE	2 HEARTS	???

♠ K 9 8 4 ♡ 9 7 5 3 ◇ J 10 8 ♣ 8 3	Since your right-hand opponent has intervened with a bid, you may pass with a poor hand. Although you see a fit in spades, your hand is not worth a bid.
♠ K J 4 3 ♡ 8 7 5 4 ◇ Q 8 7 ♣ 10 9	Your 6 points are just enough to warrant a bid. Bid 1 SPADE and get into the competition.

Notrump Responses to a Takeout Double

Your partner is really looking for a suit bid from you when he makes a takeout double, but sometimes a notrump bid is your best response. This happens when you have some points but no major suit to bid. If you have the opponents' suit well stopped and have a balanced hand, then consider notrump. The guideline is the same as the one you saw before.

When responding in notrump on the defensive, you need:

- 20 partnership points to bid 1 NOTRUMP
- 23 partnership points to bid 2 NOTRUMP
- 26 partnership points to bid 3 NOTRUMP

You must have a balanced hand and the opponents' suit(s) stopped.

Notice that a 1 NOTRUMP bid represents real values. There is no place for a flaky notrump bid on the defensive. For example:

RHO	PARTNER	LHO	YOU
1 CLUB	DOUBLE	PASS	???

♠ K 8 5
♡ J 4 3
◇ Q 9 3
♣ K 10 7 6

You can see that 1 NOTRUMP is a better bid than 1 DIAMOND. You have 9 HCP. The partnership total is 22 (almost enough for 2 NOTRUMP.)

♠ K 10 7 5
♡ 9 8
◇ J 5 3 2
♣ A 3 2

You could respond 1 NOTRUMP but you should prefer to bid your major. Your best bid is 1 SPADE.

Further Bidding after a Takeout Double

If you make a takeout double and get a nonjump response in a suit from your partner, you will normally stop bidding at this point. Your partner has not promised any strength whatsoever unless he bid after an intervening opponent bid. However, he will usually have a little something (assume 4 points, or 6 after an intervening opponent bid). If you think that your side could have a game, or if you need to outbid the opponents, you may then bid again.

Other responses from your partner are more encouraging. Use the partnership total and common sense to decide how to proceed.

The Penalty Double

When you double the opponents for penalty, you score higher if you are able to set them. But on the other hand, they will score higher if they make their contract. Odd tricks, bid and made, count double toward game if the contract has been doubled and count quadruple toward game if the contract has been redoubled. Except at duplicate bridge, this puts a damper on doubling. However, you must not be frightened off entirely. The risk must be taken when the prospects of setting the opponents are good.

You should consider making a penalty double against the opponents when your side is stronger (you think your side has more than half of the 40 HCP) and yet the opponents are outbidding you for a partscore. This action works best when your side does not have a fit. The theory is that when one side does not have a fit the other side is not likely to have one either. And conversely, when you have a fit the other side may also have one. With a fit, they may have enough strength in distribution to make up for the lack of HCP.

A penalty double against a suit should be accompanied by a decent holding in the opponents' bid suit. If they have only bid at the 1-level, you will generally need at least five good cards in their suit, and even then you may not succeed in setting them. At higher levels, you will usually have four cards in their suit.

When you make a penalty double against an opposing notrump bid and you will be on lead, consider whether you have a good lead to make. This usually means leading from a 5-card (or longer) suit or leading from a strong sequence of honors. With no good lead, refrain from doubling.

It is very difficult for you to set an opposing notrump bid when it is bid on your left. Your left-hand opponent, who has the strength, is in a position to top your high cards with a higher one of his own. Remember that he plays after you do. You must always downgrade the value of a high card when it is very likely that there is a higher card in the hand on your left.

When the opponents have bid up to game with normal constructive bidding, they can seldom be doubled successfully unless they are very poor bidders or you have a big surprise for them—usually an unexpectedly long holding in the trump suit. On the other hand, when the opponents reach any level through preemptive bidding, you will frequently double them when you cannot outbid them. The unknown factor in these cases is usually how much strength the preempter's partner holds.

When you want to make a penalty double, you must be aware of whether a double in that situation is for penalty or for takeout. If your system says that it is for takeout, you simply can't make a penalty double however badly you might like to do so. According to the guideline given previously, a penalty double can be used after your partner has bid or after the opponents' bidding has reached the game level. In addition, the double of an opponent's opening notrump bid is for penalty because the double of a normal notrump is always for penalty.

After your partner makes a penalty double, you may find yourself worrying that your hand is not good enough to support your partner's double. Remember that he has already taken into consideration how bad your hand may be. Only if your hand is quite different from what your partner may expect from your previous bidding (or lack of bidding) should you take his double out into some bid of your own.

Once in a blue moon, when your partner makes a takeout double, you may find that you have a massive holding in the opponent's suit. In that case you may pass, converting his double into a penalty double. However, he had no intention that you should do this, and he is in no way to blame if the opponents make their bid.

Lastly, do not expect every penalty double to succeed. Sometimes the opponents will make their contract even though you thought they wouldn't. But if all your penalty doubles succeed, you are not doubling often enough.

D
Choosing the Defensive Bid

Bidding versus Passing

When the opponents open the bidding, the usual choices for a defensive bid are:

PASS	You have nothing.
Overcall in a suit	You have a good suit.
Takeout double	You support all unbid suits.
1 NOTRUMP overcall	You have an opening 1 NOTRUMP hand and a stopper in the opponents' suit.
PASS	You have strength but none of the above apply.

PASS is probably the hardest thing to say. A common error in defensive bidding is to bid with insufficient values. But it is even easier to insist on bidding with adequate values but with no good bid to make. Remember that your values are better used to set the opponents with when you have no sound defensive bid of your own to make.

Vulnerability is an important factor when you overcall in a suit above the 1-level. It is a lesser factor when you overcall at the 1-level or you make a takeout double or you overcall in notrump. In these cases, when your hand is marginal, you may decide to bid or to pass based on the current vulnerability.

The Overcall versus the Takeout Double

In summary:

- You overcall when you want to play in *your* best suit. You double when you want to play in *partner's* best suit.

- You overcall when you have a good suit to name. You double when you want your partner to name the suit.
- A good 5-card (or longer) suit suggests a suit overcall. No 5-card suit suggests a takeout double.

A takeout double gives you some of the security of an opening bid. Although the opponents have already bid, you can be fairly sure of finding some kind of a fit—often a normal fit. A suit overcall is a gamble which usually pays off if it is sound—either you find a fit and/or the opponents continue bidding rather than making a penalty double. Playing tricks plus points make a sound suit overcall.

The Constructive Overcall versus the Preemptive Overcall

A jump overcall is a preemptive bid. It is made when you have little defense against a contract by the opponents but you have a long suit which provides you with some playing tricks at your own contract. You overbid your playing tricks by a margin of two, three or four depending on whether the vulnerability is unfavorable, equal or favorable.

A nonjump overcall is partly competitive, based on playing tricks, and partly constructive, based on high cards. At duplicate the emphasis tends toward the competitive; at other forms of bridge the emphasis tends toward the constructive. You will not overbid your playing tricks by more than three tricks, although you may evaluate them aggressively when you are not vulnerable or you intend to bid at the 1-level. Sound overcalls will be based on at least the nominal count for the bid, but aggressive overcalls may have a point or two less.

Aggressiveness

Good bidding is accurate bidding. Only in competitive situations is there some room for personal style. This is because it is not clear how much aggressiveness pays off. But this is true only within a very small range. Aggressiveness results in more and larger losses along with whatever gains can be accomplished. For this reason it is more successful at duplicate bridge where the size of a loss is less important. Aggressiveness tends to be successful also at social bridge where the opponents may be more timid or may not be able to cope against competition. Don't overdo it. And always consider what your partner expects of your bids. If you bid aggressively with a partner who expects conservative bids, any bad result is strictly your fault.

Choose your bid.

LHO	PARTNER	RHO	YOU
		1 HEART	???

VUL vs. NOTVUL

♠ A Q 6 5
♡ 7
◇ A 9 5 2
♣ J 6 5 4

Your distribution suggests a takeout double. You have support for all the unbid suits, especially for the unbid major (spades), where it counts the most. As dummy, you can count an extra point for your singleton, bringing your count up to 14. DOUBLE.

VUL vs. NOTVUL

♠ A Q 8 5 2
♡ 4
◇ Q 10 3
♣ K 7 6 2

You have support for the unbid suits, but you particularly want to play in spades. With a 5-card major, your first thought should be to overcall. You have three playing tricks plus several possible tricks, which is adequate. You have 13 points which is more than adequate. Bid 1 SPADE.

NOTVUL vs. NOTVUL

♠ K 9 7 3
♡ K 8 6 5
◇ 9
♣ A K 6 4

This happens all the time. You have a hand which could make a takeout double after a diamond bid, but has to be passed after a heart bid.

NOTVUL vs. NOTVUL

♠ A Q 7 4
♡ 2
◇ K 8 3
♣ A J 10 9 4

An overcall of 2 CLUBS would not be terrible, but it gives up the chance to find a fit in spades. A double is preferable in this case. That would not be true if you only had three spades.

VUL vs. VUL

♠ A 9 3
♡ A K
◇ K J 3 2
♣ Q 8 3 2

1 NOTRUMP describes this hand best. A double may get you into a 4–3 fit in spades, or into a minor fit when you could be in notrump. Besides, after a notrump bid, your partner will know all about your hand and will be able to judge whether a game is possible.

NOTVUL vs. NOTVUL

♠ A Q
♡ 9 8 4
◇ Q J 8 3
♣ K J 10 9

You can't double because you only have two spades, an unbid suit. No matter that they are good ones. This is maddening, but you must PASS. Otherwise you may end up in a 6-card fit in spades, giving your partner a different kind of fit.

NOTVUL vs. VUL

♠ A Q J 9 6 5 4
♡ —
◇ A 9 8
♣ 5 3 2

This is too strong for a preempt. Bid 1 SPADE. You will try to bid spades a second time, even if your partner passes.

NOTVUL vs. VUL

♠ A Q J 10 8
♡ 9
◇ Q 9 3
♣ 9 8 5 3

This calls for 1 SPADE overcall. It doesn't do much to obstruct the opponents, but you want a spade lead from your partner if the opponents take the contract. And your side might possibly have a fit in spades, leading to a partscore or a satisfactory sacrifice. This is a fairly aggressive bid but should be safe enough with most partners at this vulnerability.

VUL vs VUL

♠ 9
♡ 5 3
◇ K Q J 10 6 5 3
♣ K 8 5

This hand qualifies for a preemptive bid. With six playing tricks plus another possibility, jump right in with a bid of 3 DIAMONDS. If the vulnerability were favorable, you could even bid a level higher.

NOTVUL vs VUL

♠ A J 10 9 8 5
♡ J 2
◇ Q 9
♣ J 4 2

This is a pretty poor hand except for the spades. Queens and jacks at the head of a side suit are not really worth their full count value. But you have four playing tricks, and at this vulnerability you can make a weak jump overcall of 2 SPADES. A bid of only 1 SPADE would suggest a better hand.

Updated Summary of Forcing Principles

FULL FORCING POWER	LIMITED FORCING POWER	NO FORCING POWER
New suit ROUND FORCING except simple takeout (nonjump, nonreverse) after 1 NOTRUMP	New suit reverse ROUND FORCING	(Conventional bids remain forcing)
Single jump GAME FORCING	Single jump in new suit GAME FORCING	
Phase 1	Phase 1	Phase 1

Full power

OPENER → (box)

after 2-over-1

RESPONDER → No power / if he passes → (box)

DEFENDERS

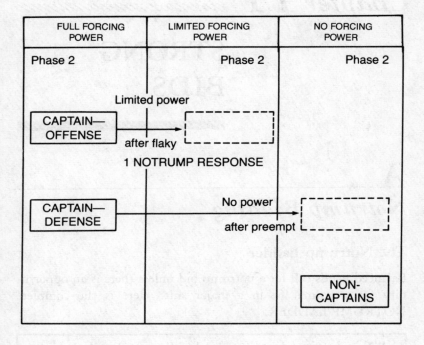

FULL FORCING POWER	LIMITED FORCING POWER	NO FORCING POWER
Phase 2	Phase 2	Phase 2

Chapter 11

STRONG BIDS

A

Notrump Bidding

The Notrump Ladder

Balanced hands call for a notrump bid unless there is an opportunity for a normal fit in a major suit. Here is the complete NOTRUMP LADDER:

> When you are opening the bidding with a balanced hand:
>
> - 13,14,15 Open in a suit, later make a nonjump notrump bid unless an opportunity in the majors presents itself.
> - 16,17,18 Open with 1 NOTRUMP.
> - 19,20 Open in a suit, later make a jump in notrump unless an opportunity in the majors presents itself.
> - 21,22,23 Open with 2 NOTRUMP.
> - 24,25,26 Open with 3 NOTRUMP.

Notice that there is a 2-point gap between an opening 1 NOTRUMP and an opening 2 NOTRUMP. Within this gap you must open in a suit, and any response from your partner places your partnership at the game level or beyond. If your partner's response is minimum, your next bid will usually be a jump bid in notrump. However, if he responds in a major and you have 4-card support for it, you should jump directly to game in that suit. Any lesser raise would not be forcing, so you must bid the full value of your hand.

The opening 2 NOTRUMP and 3 NOTRUMP bids show a very strong hand, but they are not forcing bids. Your partner may pass if he sees no point in going further.

NOTE: We used to use a range of 22,23,24 for an opening 2 NOTRUMP, but few players still do. This is a matter for you and your partner to agree on, but you should do better with the modern aggressive range of 21,22,23.

How would you handle the following hands as the opening bidder? If you decide to open with a suit, what will your rebid (your second bid) be after each of the possible nonjump responses which your partner might make?

♠ A K 3 ♡ K Q ◇ Q J 8 4 ♣ A Q 10 7	Your 21 points is just enough to open 2 NOTRUMP with this balanced hand. If your partner is able to respond at all, you will go on to game at least.
♠ A 8 5 ♡ K J 4 ◇ K Q 8 4 3 ♣ A Q	This 20-point hand is just below a 2 NOTRUMP bid, so open with 1 DIAMOND. If your partner responds with 1 HEART or 1 SPADE, you may only have a 7-card fit, so rebid 2 NOTRUMP. If your partner responds with 1 NOTRUMP or 2 CLUBS or 2 DIAMONDS you will make a rebid of 3 NOTRUMP.

♠ A K 8 5 4 ♡ K 4 3 ◇ A 7 ♣ A K 5	With 22 points and a balanced hand, open with a bid of 2 NOTRUMP.
♠ K 2 ♡ A Q 10 7 4 ◇ A J 8 ♣ A 9 8	Open this 19-point hand with 1 HEART. If your partner responds 1 SPADE, jump to 2 NOTRUMP. If he responds 1 NOTRUMP or 2 CLUBS or 2 DIAMONDS, jump to 3 NOTRUMP. If he responds 2 HEARTS, jump to 4 HEARTS.
♠ A J 9 ♡ A K 3 ◇ A J 10 8 ♣ A K 5	This may happen once a year, if you play a lot. But just to show you what an opening 3 NOTRUMP hand looks like, here is a 24-pointer.

Notrump Ladder for the Responder

When your partner opens with a notrump bid and you also have a balanced hand, you will usually decide that notrump is the best place to play the hand. The only question is: At what level?

At notrump:

- 26 partnership points equal the game level.
- 33 partnership points equal the small-slam level.
- 37 partnership points equal the grand-slam level.

When you are only 1 or 2 partnership points short of a given level, there is hope that your partner's notrump hand will be enough over minimum strength to make up the shortage which you see. This leads to the following notrump ladder when responding in notrump to your partner's opening notrump bid.

When you are responding to an opening notrump bid
and you wish to play in notrump because of your
balanced hand:

PARTNERSHIP POINTS AT LEAST	YOUR BID	
Below 24	PASS	Game out of the question
24	2 NOTRUMP	Inviting game
26	3 NOTRUMP	Game
31	4 NOTRUMP	Inviting small slam
33	6 NOTRUMP	Small slam
35	5 NOTRUMP	Insisting on small slam, inviting grand slam
37	7 NOTRUMP	Grand slam

The last two cases rarely occur so you may ignore them until you
are familiar with the others.

NOTE: Just in case you have already heard of the Blackwood
convention, note that 4 NOTRUMP is never Blackwood in the
above cases.

If your partner opens with 2 NOTRUMP, there is no bidding
space left for you to invite game—you must either pass or go on to
game. Because of this we have the rule: Any bid at all in reponse to
an opening 2 NOTRUMP is forcing to game. After 1 NOTRUMP
you would make an invitational response with partnership points
totaling 24 or 25. But after 2 NOTRUMP, since there is no room
for an invitational response, you must go for game with 25 and
hold back with only 24.

If your partner opens with 2 NOTRUMP:

- Assume that 25 partnership points will be enough for game.
- Any response that you make is forcing to game.
- With less than 25 partnership points you must pass.

How will you respond to an opening 1 NOTRUMP with the following hands? Assume that the opponents pass.

♠ A K 8 ♡ K 8 ◊ Q 4 3 2 ♣ J 7 5 3	Your 13 points and your partner's promised 16 come to 29. You are well past the game level but not close enough to slam for a slam invitation. Bid 3 NOTRUMP.
♠ A 10 5 ♡ K 7 6 ◊ K Q 5 2 ♣ A J 4	You can see 33 partnership points so don't hedge, bid 6 NOTRUMP.
♠ 10 8 3 ♡ A K 4 ◊ A 9 8 ♣ A 9 5 3	Now you can count 31 partnership points. Since your partner could have 2 extra points, bid 4 NOTRUMP. If your partner has even 1 extra point over his promised 16, he should go on to 6 NOTRUMP, otherwise he should pass. You may end up in a small slam with only 32 points, but your chances of making it are still fair. Bidding can't be absolutely accurate.

How will you respond to an opening 2 NOTRUMP?

♠ 10 7 4 ♡ Q 3 2 ◊ 9 7 6 5 ♣ Q 8 5	Before your partner has bid, you will think that this is a terrible hand. But when your partner opens with 2 NOTRUMP, any high card becomes very valuable. Your partner's 21 plus your 4 equals 25. There is no way to

invite game so away you go with a bid of 3 NOTRUMP.

♠ A 8 7
♡ K 5
♢ J 10 5 4 2
♣ Q 10 6

Your 11 plus your partner's 21 equals 32. Make a 4 NOTRUMP bid, inviting your partner to go on to a small slam.

♠ 10 7 5
♡ J 8 3 2
♢ J 4
♣ 7 5 4 3

Sometimes you do have to PASS. Your partner's bid is not forcing and the partnership points do not suggest a game.

How will you respond to an opening 3 NOTRUMP?

♠ 5 4 2
♡ K 7 4
♢ Q J 8 5 4
♣ 9 5

When your partner has so many points, you are not likely to have a lot, but every little bit counts. Your 7 points plus your partner's 24 add up to a near-slam 31. Bid 4 NOTRUMP. With less you would pass.

Responding with a Suit-Oriented Hand

When your partner opens with 1 NOTRUMP, you may want to play in a suit, especially if your hand is unbalanced. For example, if your suit is spades and you have at least five of them, you may bid 2 SPADES, to sign off in spades, or 3 SPADES, for a strong hand of at least game strength.

When your partner opens with 2 NOTRUMP, any bid you make is forcing to game. With 25 partnership points and a 5-card major, simply bid the major. But if your suit is a minor, you should prefer to play in notrump unless your hand is unbalanced. Even then you may have to compromise and play in notrump when that seems to be the only possibility for making a game.

When you respond with a suit to your partner's notrump bid, assume that your partner will give you 3-card support and revaluate your hand accordingly. You are only guaranteed 2-card support, but 3-card support is more likely and that assumption gives a better evaluation.

How do you respond to an opening 2 NOTRUMP in the following cases?

♠ 9 7 ♡ K 10 8 5 4 ◇ Q 8 7 2 ♣ J 4	You have 7 points to add to your partner's 21. You have no problem in responding 3 HEARTS. If your partner has at least three hearts, he will raise you to 4 HEARTS. If he rebids 3 NOTRUMP you will PASS.
♠ Q 9 8 5 4 ♡ J 8 7 ◇ 6 ♣ 10 6 5 3	You only have 5 points, but your partner is loaded with at least 21 points. It will be better to play in your spades than at notrump. Bid 3 SPADES and hope it turns out well.
♠ 9 8 7 5 4 3 ♡ — ◇ K 9 8 4 ♣ 6 5 3	Your original count is 6, but assuming a 9-card fit, you can add 1 point for the fit and 2 points additional for the void. You can bid 3 SPADES, and even if your partner responds 3 NOTRUMP you will rebid 4 SPADES. A more sophisticated bidder would bid 4 SPADES in the first place. The jump to game shows a long suit and points which are mostly in distribution. The jump is preemptive and is intended to keep the opponents out of the bidding.

The Stayman Convention

The Stayman convention, named for the expert Sam Stayman who promoted it, was invented to help you find a major-suit fit after your partner has opened in notrump. Everyone who plays duplicate bridge should use this convention. In social bridge you may decide to get along without it, and besides you may find out that your partner doesn't know how to use it anyway.

First of all, you must agree with your partner whether or not you will use Stayman. Your opponents are also entitled to know. It is so commonly used that from now on we will assume you are using it too.

STAYMAN OVER AN OPENING 1 NOTRUMP

If you open the bidding with 1 NOTRUMP and your partnership is playing Stayman, then a response of 2 CLUBS by your partner is an artificial bid which has nothing to do with clubs. It asks you whether you hold a 4-card or 5-card major suit. To answer "no" you make the artificial rebid of 2 DIAMONDS. To answer "yes" you simply bid 2 of your major. If you should have two 4-card majors, bid the hearts—the cheaper of two 4-card suits is the general rule.

A responder, to use Stayman, must have at least an invitational hand (partnership points of at least 24) and at least one 4-card major suit. If the responder in the following examples were not playing Stayman, he would immediately reply to the opening 1 NOTRUMP with a raise in notrump. But the Stayman convention allows him to investigate the possibility of a major-suit normal fit before settling on notrump.

♠ A K 3			♠ J 10 8 5
♡ K 4			♡ A 9 3
◇ Q 10 8 4			◇ J 9
♣ A 9 7 5			♣ Q 10 8 4
I have 16,17,18 and a balanced hand.	1 NOTRUMP	2 CLUBS	Do you have a 4-card or 5-card major?
No.	2 DIAMONDS	2 NOTRUMP	OK. I have only enough for an invitation.
And I hold a minimum.	PASS		

♠ A K 3 2			♠ J 10 8 5
♡ K 4			♡ A 9 8
◇ Q 10 8			◇ J 9
♣ A 9 7 5			♣ Q 10 8 4
	1 NOTRUMP	2 CLUBS	Do you have a 4-card or 5-card major?

Yes, spades.	2 SPADES	3 SPADES	Good, we can play in spades. Can we make a game?
Sorry, I can't go on.	PASS		

♠ A K 3 2		♠ J 10 8 5
♡ K 4 3 2		♡ A 9 8
♢ Q 10		♢ J 9
♣ A 9 7		♣ A 10 8 4

	1 NOTRUMP	2 CLUBS	Do you have a 4-card or 5-card major?
Yes, hearts.	2 HEARTS	3 NOTRUMP	Wrong suit, but I have enough for game in notrump.
If you don't have hearts, you must have spades.	4 SPADES	PASS	Right you are.

You have opened with 1 notrump and your partner has responded with 2 clubs. How do you rebid?

♠ K 8 3 ♡ Q 10 5 ♢ A K 10 8 ♣ A J 4 3	You have no 4-card major so bid 2 DIAMONDS. Your partner has invited game and you are going to accept as soon as you see where it is to be played.
♠ A 9 7 4 ♡ A 10 5 2 ♢ Q 2 ♣ A K 8	You could bid either 2 HEARTS or 2 SPADES. But you should follow the general rule of bidding the lower ranking of two 4-card suits.
♠ K Q 8 ♡ A Q 9 8 4 ♢ 4 3 ♣ A Q 5	You will bid 2 HEARTS. If your partner now bids 2 NOTRUMP, you will want to go on to game with your maximum hand. Now bid 3 HEARTS so that your partner will know that you have five of them and that you want to play in 3 NOTRUMP or 4 HEARTS.

Notice that after a notrump opening, either partner may bid a 5-card suit. But 4-card holdings are shown only as part of a Stayman sequence.

SUMMARY OF STAYMAN

When your partner opens with 1 NOTRUMP and you hold a 4-card major, if you are going to bid at all, start with Stayman to look for a major fit. Otherwise, if you hold a 5-card major, you will generally bid it. However, if your hand is too strong to bid two in your major (which says "drop dead") and too weak to bid three in your major (which is game forcing) then you will have to use Stayman for lack of anything better.

When responding to 1 NOTRUMP with a Stayman response:

>2 CLUBS asks the opener, "Do you have a 4-card or 5-card major?"

You need at least:

- 24 partnership points (invitational level)
- At least one 4-card major suit

The opener then rebids:

- 2 DIAMONDS (negative reply)
  or
- 2 HEARTS or 2 SPADES

The responder then rebids naturally.

In each of the following pair of hands, how would the bidding go when the partnership is not using Stayman? How would it go with Stayman?

OPENER	RESPONDER	
♠ K Q 9 3	♠ A 7 6 4	Without Stayman:
♡ Q J 5	♡ K 10 8 7	1 NOTRUMP 2 NOTRUMP
◊ Q 2	◊ J 9 8	3 NOTRUMP
♣ A K 5 4	♣ 8 7	With Stayman:
		1 NOTRUMP 2 CLUBS
		2 SPADES 3 SPADES
		4 SPADES

OPENER	RESPONDER	
♠ K Q 9 3	♠ A 7 6	Without Stayman:
♡ Q J 5	♡ K 10 8 7	1 NOTRUMP 2 NOTRUMP
◊ Q 2	◊ J 9 8 4	3 NOTRUMP
♣ A K 5 4	♣ 8 7	With Stayman:
		1 NOTRUMP 2 CLUBS
		2 SPADES 2 NOTRUMP
		3 NOTRUMP

OPENER	RESPONDER	
♠ K Q 9 3	♠ A 7 6	With or without Stayman:
♡ Q J 5	♡ K 10 8	1 NOTRUMP 2 NOTRUMP
◊ Q 2	◊ J 9 8 4	3 NOTRUMP
♣ A K 5 4	♣ 8 7 3	The responder does not use Stayman because he has no 4-card major.

OPENER	RESPONDER	
♠ A J 4	♠ K Q 9 7 5	With or without Stayman:
♡ A K 8 5	♡ 9 7 6	1 NOTRUMP 3 SPADES
◊ K Q J 2	◊ A 6 5 4	4 SPADES
♣ 9 8	♣ 7	With *game* strength the responder jumps in his 5-card major.

OPENER	RESPONDER	
♠ A J 4	♠ K Q 9 7 5	Without Stayman:
♡ A K 8 5	♡ Q 7 6	1 NOTRUMP 2 SPADES
◊ K Q J 2	◊ 9 6 5	PASS
♣ 9 8	♣ 7 3	2 SPADES is an underbid.
		3 SPADES is an overbid.
		2 NOTRUMP may work out badly as here.

With Stayman:

1 NOTRUMP	2 CLUBS
2 HEARTS	2 SPADES
4 SPADES	

Since the responder bids only 5-card suits, the opener knows there is an 8-card fit in spades.

♠ A J 4	♠ K Q 9 7
♡ A K 8 5	♡ Q J 7 6
◇ K Q J 2	◇ 8 6 5 4
♣ 9 8	♣ 7

Without Stayman:

1 NOTRUMP	?!*&!?

The responder will probably pass, but he might try 2 NOTRUMP with bad results in this particular case due to the club shortage.

With Stayman:

1 NOTRUMP	2 CLUBS
2 HEARTS	3 HEARTS
4 HEARTS	

STAYMAN OVER AN OPENING 2 NOTRUMP

After an opening 2 NOTRUMP, a 3 CLUB response is Stayman and the opener can deny possession of a 4-card or 5-card major suit by bidding 3 DIAMONDS. As usual, you will need to see 25 partnership points before responding to 2 NOTRUMP.

When your partnership is using Stayman, how would you respond to an opening bid of 2 NOTRUMP?

♠ 10 9 8 5
♡ J 7 4 3
◇ 2
♣ Q 8 4 2

Your hand will be worth 5 points if you can find a fit in a major, but only 3 at notrump. Try 3 CLUBS. If your partner rebids with 3 DIAMONDS, rebid with 3 NOTRUMP. If your partner is short in the majors, he is likely to have the diamonds covered and may have a fit with your clubs to bring in the game.

♠ K 8 6 5
♡ Q 10 8 5 4
◊ 4 3 2
♣ 7

Bid 3 CLUBS. If your partner bids 3 SPADES or 3 HEARTS (!) you will have found your major game. If he bids 3 DIAMONDS, you can then bid 3 HEARTS showing that you have five of them and thus only need 3-card support.

SUMMARY OF SUIT-ORIENTED RESPONSES TO AN OPENING NOTRUMP BID

Now we can give a general guideline for responding to an opening 1 NOTRUMP with a suit-oriented hand when your partnership is using Stayman.

When you are responding to an opening 1 NOTRUMP and you wish to find a fit in a suit:		
PARTNERSHIP POINTS	YOUR BID	
below 24	2 DIAMONDS, 2 HEARTS, 2 SPADES	signoff, 5-card or longer suit
24,25	2 CLUBS	Stayman, with 4- or 5-card major
26 up	3 in a SUIT	with 5-card or longer suit (usually a major)
	or	
26 up	2 CLUBS	Stayman, with 4-card major

Remember that after an opening notrump bid, neither partner introduces a 4-card suit into the bidding except as part of a Stayman sequence. Therefore, if you have both a 4-card major and a 5-card major, start with Stayman. The same would apply with a 4-card major and a long minor.

Most partnerships agree that when 1 NOTRUMP is followed by Stayman, the bidding will proceed at least to 2 NOTRUMP or 3 of a MAJOR.

After a 2 NOTRUMP opening:

When you are responding to an opening 2 NOTRUMP and you wish to find a fit in a suit:		
PARTNERSHIP POINTS	YOUR BID	
below 25	PASS	no other signoff available
25 up	3 CLUBS	Stayman, holding a 4-card major
	or	
25 up	3 DIAMONDS, 3 HEARTS, 3 SPADES	5-card or longer suit

Stayman can be used after an opening 3 NOTRUMP (although some partnerships prefer not to). If no major fit is found, the partnership will end up in 4 NOTRUMP at the least, so the Stayman bidder must be prepared for this level.

Stayman is regularly used after an opening notrump bid. Today, most partnerships also use Stayman when their side begins the defense with a (normal) notrump overcall. This is a good practice to adopt.

B
Big Limited Bids

When your partner opens with a bid of 1 in a SUIT, you will sometimes find yourself with 13 or more points—enough for game or even a slam if a suitable fit can be found. There are several bids which will allow you to show your strength immediately. However, each of them has certain restrictions so sometimes none of them will apply. In that case you can always bid a new suit, forcing your partner to continue, but your second bid will be very important. You must keep the bidding going with forcing bids until game is reached or until you give up because of a misfit between the two hands.

Responding with a Jump Raise

You know that when you are the responder and make a jump response, you are forcing the partnership to game. Therefore it is logical that in a sequence such as:

PARTNER	YOU
1 HEART	3 HEARTS

your jump to 3 HEARTS must be based on 13 points (after revaluation) to bring the partnership points up to 26. Since all suit raises represent a 4-point range, a jump raise is based on 13, 14, 15, 16 points. The partnership points will run from 26 to 29, just short of the near-slam level.

Whenever you raise your partner's suit *immediately* with a jump, you must have extra-long support for his suit. This allows you to show in one bid both your strength and your extra supporting trump. When your partner knows about that extra trump, he can be more optimistic in thinking about slam possibilities.

When responding to your partner's opening bid of 1 in a SUIT with a jump raise, you need:

- 4-card (or longer) support for a major suit
- 5-card (or longer) support for a minor suit
- 13, 14, 15, 16 points after revaluation

Do not raise a minor if you can bid a major at the 1-level.

Would you make a single raise, a jump raise or some other bid in the following situations?

PARTNER	YOU
1 HEART	???

♠ K 2 ♡ 9 7 5 3 ◇ A K J 8 ♣ K 8 5	You have 4-card support for your partner and can see partnership points totaling 28 after you take an extra point for the 9-card heart fit. Bid 3 HEARTS.
♠ J 7 5 4 ♡ A 8 5 3 ◇ J 10 7 4 ♣ 4	When your partner opens in hearts, you revaluate, taking an extra point for the 9-card fit and also an extra point for the singleton. That only comes to 9 points, 22 partnership points, so bid 2 HEARTS.
♠ A 7 ♡ A K 4 ◇ Q J 8 7 5 4 ♣ 8 5	You have 15 points with no extras to gain through revaluation. The 28 partnership points certainly spell game in hearts. You cannot make an immediate jump raise with only 3-card support and you are much too strong for a single raise. Bid 2 DIAMONDS for now and bid 4 HEARTS later.
♠ K 9 ♡ A 10 7 4 ◇ Q 8 4 ♣ J 8 4 3	You have 11 points after revaluation. That is too much for 2 HEARTS and not enough for a jump to 3 HEARTS. Temporize for now with 2 CLUBS. That at least shows your strength. Raise hearts later.
♠ 6 3 ♡ K Q 8 6 4 ◇ A 5 4 ♣ A 9 7	After taking 2 extra points for the 10-card fit, you have 16 points for a maximum 3 HEART bid. Points in the partnership total 29. With 30 or more, you would want to take even stronger action.

PARTNER	YOU
1 CLUB	???

♠ A 10
♡ 9 8 3
◇ K Q J
♣ A 10 8 7 5

You have at least an 8-card club fit. Your 15 points bring the partnership total to at least 28. Bid 3 CLUBS. The unstopped hearts prevent a notrump bid at this time. But if your partner bids hearts you can then bid notrump.

♠ K 8 4 3
♡ 3 2
◇ K Q
♣ K Q 7 5 4

You have an original 14 points and a good fit for a contract in clubs. But you would much rather be in spades if you can find a fit there. Bid 1 SPADE. You can raise clubs later if appropriate.

PARTNER	YOU
1 CLUB	1 HEART
1 NOTRUMP	???

♠ 9
♡ A K 9 7 5 4
◇ K J 9
♣ Q 5 2

You can't raise either of your partner's bids, but his notrump bid shows at least two hearts. Bid 3 HEARTS. Since you are now the captain, your jump is forcing to game. It tells your partner that you see at least 26 partnership points and, because you made a limit bid, that your range is 13, 14, 15, 16.

Responding with a Jump in Notrump

Just as you must have 13 points to respond with a jump raise, you must also have 13 points to respond with a jump into notrump. A jump by the responder is game-forcing, so you need to see 26 partnership points.

PARTNER	YOU
1 DIAMOND	2 NOTRUMP

Since notrump bids are based on a 3-point range, you will have exactly 13, 14, 15 points. And of course you will have a balanced hand.

When responding to your partner's opening bid of 1 in a SUIT with a jump into notrump, you need:

- A balanced hand
- A stopper in any suit not bid by your partner
- 13, 14, 15 points to respond 2 NOTRUMP
- 16, 17, 18 points to respond 3 NOTRUMP

Do not respond in notrump if you can bid a major suit at the 1-level or if you can raise your partner's major suit.

What would you bid in the following situations?

PARTNER	YOU
1 HEART	???

♠ K J 10
♡ 8 6
◇ A 10 7 5
♣ K Q J 8

You have a balanced hand with 14 points. All suits are stopped except hearts—your partner's length in hearts assures you that the opponents won't have a long heart fit to use against you. Bid 2 NOTRUMP.

♠ Q J 10 8
♡ K 2
◇ K J 8 5
♣ K 8 7

You have a balanced hand with 13 points, but you should bid your spades first, 1 SPADE. You will probably end up in game in notrump or in spades, or possibly in hearts if your partner has six of them.

♠ A 2
♡ J 9 7 6
◇ A K 8
♣ J 10 9 5

Again you have 13 points and a balanced hand, but you have good support for your partner's major. Bid 3 HEARTS.

♠ 9 5 4
♡ K 3
◇ A K 7 5
♣ A Q 8 7

This balanced hand has 16 points, equal to an opening 1 NOTRUMP hand. There are enough advantages to *open* in notrump with an unstopped suit that you should do so. But for later bidding, it is not the best thing to do. Bid 2 CLUBS. If your partner bids spades or notrump (showing that he has spades stopped), the way is cleared to play in notrump.

♠ K Q 4
♡ A Q
◇ Q J 9 4
♣ Q 7 5 2

Again a hand that could open 1 NOTRUMP. This time you have all suits stopped. You are up in the range for responding 3 NOTRUMP, which is what you bid.

Responding with a Preference Bid

You have already seen the case where your partner has bid two suits, asking you to pick one of them.

PARTNER	YOU
1 HEART	1 SPADE
2 CLUBS	???

With a minimum hand, you PASS or make the simple preference bid of 2 HEARTS. In either case you are only showing which suit you prefer without promising any real support.

When you hold a hand which is good enough to bring the partnership total up to the game level, you do not want to show preference with a minimum action. If you see at least an 8-card fit in hearts, jump to 3 HEARTS. With an 8-card fit in clubs, consider first 3 NOTRUMP, then 4 CLUBS. But if there is no good fit in either suit, you might still bid 3 NOTRUMP or bid 3 SPADES if your hand is suitable.

One other possibility, when three suits have already been bid, is to bid the fourth suit, 2 DIAMONDS. Bidding the fourth suit at the 2-level or 3-level promises at least invitational values and is forcing for one round. This will give you a second chance to go to game after you to hear more from your partner. But be careful—since you have no fit, and are unlikely to find one in the fourth suit, perhaps you should not be aiming at the game level.

NOTE: Many players today use a fourth-suit bid as a forcing bid of at least invitational strength, without necessarily having either length or high cards in that suit. There should be advance partnership agreement before doing this.

When your hand is neither minimum nor game-going, you will have to avoid both the minimum bids and the jumps bids. After the bidding sequence shown above, you could bid 2 NOTRUMP or the fourth suit. You could even rebid your spades with six of them.

When making a preference bid, you need to be able to judge the fit. If your partner opens in a major and then bids another suit, you should initially assume a distribution of 5–4. If he opens in a minor and then bids a major, you have to allow for a distribution of 3–4. If he opens in diamonds and then bids clubs, you can assume 4–4. If he opens in clubs and then bids diamonds, the reverse indicates at least 5–4.

If your partner bids one suit twice and then, not having found support in that suit, bids a second suit, you can assume six cards in the first suit and four in the second. The same is true if he bids his first suit, then his second, then his first again, but his hand is probably stronger.

When a second suit is bid a second time, this shows at least five cards in the second suit, not necessarily six.

When you bid your second suit a second time, you are showing at least five cards in each suit.

If your partner bids in this way, you should assume that his distribution is 5–5 although it may be 6–5 or 6–6 or even 7–5 or 7–6.

What is the profitable distribution in your partner's hand in
the suits he has bid? How would you bid to show preference?

PARTNER	YOU	YOU
1 SPADE	2 CLUBS	♠ K 4 3
2 HEARTS	???	♡ J 9 8
		◊ 9
		♣ A K 10 7 5 3

(Distribution probably 5–4.) You see an 8-card fit in spades and
wish to be in game. Jump to 3 SPADES. You don't need 4-card
support for a jump preference if there is an 8-card fit.

1 SPADE	2 CLUBS	♠ J 5
2 HEARTS	???	♡ Q J 9 8
		◊ A 7
		♣ A Q 7 5 4

(Distribution probably 5–4.) With an 8-card fit in hearts and with
partnership strength at the game level, bid 4 HEARTS. A bid of 3
HEARTS would be only invitational.

1 SPADE	2 CLUBS	♠ A 8
2 DIAMONDS	3 CLUBS	♡ 9 8 5
3 SPADES	???	◊ K 4
		♣ K Q J 5 3 2

(Distribution probably 6–4.) At first you avoided a preference bid
in favor of bidding your good club suit again—but only because
your hand is strong. Now you see a spade fit and bid 4 SPADES.

1 DIAMOND	1 SPADE	♠ K Q 8 7
2 CLUBS	3 NOTRUMP	♡ A 8 6
4 CLUBS	???	◊ K 10
		♣ Q 8 5 4

(Distribution at least 5–5.) After your partner bid 2 CLUBS, you
went into notrump rather than play in a minor. But now that your
partner insists, with a strongly unbalanced hand, bid 5 CLUBS.
You have at least a 9-card fit and at least 28 partnership points.

C
Big Unlimited Bids

Responding with a Jump Shift

When you respond to your partner's opening suit bid with a new suit of your own, you have made a forcing bid. There is no need to jump when you bid your new suit in order to create a forcing situation. Therefore an immediate jump shift as your first response is used in a very restricted case. This bid is often abused by beginners who use it when it does not apply. You must fit the conditions of the bid before you use it, and that does not happen very often. If fact, you could put off reading about this without harming your bridge bidding by any noticeable amount.

A jump shift must be exactly one level higher than necessary, for example:

PARTNER	YOU		PARTNER	YOU
1 HEART	2 SPADES	or	1 HEART	3 CLUBS

Firstly, you must have a good idea where the contract will be played because you have taken up so much bidding space with your jump. You must either have one strong 6-card or longer suit of your own (not a two-suited hand), or you must have good support for your partner, or your hand must be suitable for play at notrump. Otherwise you should keep the bidding low until a fit is found. Secondly, you must be close to slam. Partnership points totaling at least 30 are necessary, which means that you must hold at least 17 points.

When you are making a second or later response, a jump shift no longer has the slam implications of an immediate jump shift. It becomes just like all the other jumps you might make as the responder—game forcing and based on partnership points at the game level.

When responding to an opening 1 in a SUIT with a jump shift, you need:

- A good place to play—

    - One extra-good 6-card suit (or longer)

        or

    - Support for your partner of better than minimum length

        or

    - A hand suitable for notrump with the unbid suits stopped

- Slam potential—partnership points at least 30

With support for your partner, revaluate your hand; otherwise, devaluate it.

If you pass before your partner opens the bidding, you are a PASSED RESPONDER. In that case none of your bids are forcing, since you must have less than an opening hand. A jump shift by you is still strong, but not forcing. The partnership points will be slightly below the game level unless you picked up extra points through revaluation. Since a jump shift is not forcing after you have passed, you will only jump shift into a good suit, usually 6 cards long, in case your partner has to pass.

Are these hands suitable for a jump shift after your partner has opened with 1 HEART?

♠ K Q J 9 7 5 4
♡ 5
◇ A K
♣ Q J 8

This hand has 16 HCP plus 2 distribution points for the seven spades—don't count points for shortage in a suit your partner has bid. You are quite sure of playing in spades, so 2 SPADES is your bid.

♠ A 2
♡ A J 8 7
◇ K Q 8 7 5
♣ K 8

Here you have a good fit for your partner and have 19 points counting an extra point for the 9-card heart fit. That is too much for a 3 HEART bid so you start with 3 DIAMONDS. The partnership total of 32 strongly suggests that a slam may be possible.

♠ A Q 4
♡ A 5
◇ Q 9 8 7
♣ K Q J 4

Your 18 points plus your partner's 13 make 31. You could bid 3 NOTRUMP, but you are so close to slam that beginning with a bid of 3 CLUBS is better. The jump shift is more suggestive of slam possibilities.

♠ A Q 8 7 5
♡ Q 2
◇ A K Q 10 8
♣ 8

Is your partnership going to play this hand in spades? Or diamonds? Or hearts? Go slow until you find out. Bid 1 SPADE.

Making a Jump Shift after You Open the Bidding

When you open the bidding with 1 in a SUIT, you have normally only one forcing bid—the jump shift. Of course if you become the captain or if your partner responds with a 2-over-1 shift, then you have additional forcing bids: your new suits become round forcing and all your jumps become game forcing.

A jump shift by the opener is game forcing and shows partnership strength at least at the game level. It is useful when you want your partner to choose between two of your suits without taking a chance that he will pass. Here is an example:

YOU	PARTNER
1 HEART	1 SPADE
???	

♠ 9 3
♡ A K J 10 8
◇ K Q J 8 3
♣ A

You have 18 HCP and your distribution will add more points if you can find a fit. Even if your partner has a minimum 6 points, a game is almost certain. Bid 3 DIAMONDS.

The Jump Takeout after a Notrump Bid

When you make a notrump bid, your partner becomes the captain. When he feels that the partnership should not play in notrump, he will take out into a suit, and may do so by jumping. This is a jump takeout (not a jump shift, which would be a shift out of your suit into his suit).

After a normal notrump bid, the captain gains full forcing power even if he is a passed responder. Then *any* jump bid by the captain is forcing to game. After the flaky 1 NOTRUMP RESPONSE, however, the captain has only limited forcing power because of the uncertain nature of the notrump bid. In that case, the captain creates a game force by jumping in a new suit, but he only makes a nonforcing invitation if he jumps in a suit which has been bid before.

What do you bid in the following cases?

PARTNER	YOU
PASS	1 NOTRUMP
3 HEARTS	???

♠ A Q 8 7
♡ J 6 3
♢ A Q 8 4
♣ K 10

Although your partner couldn't open the bidding, he now states that he has the 10 points necessary to bring your 16 up to the game level. His jump takeout is forcing. Bid 4 HEARTS.

PARTNER	YOU
1 SPADE	1 NOTRUMP
3 HEARTS	???

♠ 8
♡ 9 8 5 3
♢ A 8 7 5
♣ Q J 7 4

You only have 7 HCP. Your singleton spade is not worth any points since your partner bid that suit. Nevertheless, your partner's bid is forcing to game so bid 4 HEARTS. It is up to him to be prepared for the poor hand which your flaky 1 NOTRUMP may represent. Fortunately you have four hearts.

PARTNER	YOU
1 SPADE	1 NOTRUMP
3 SPADES	???

♠ 8
♡ 9 8 5 3
◇ A 8 7 5
♣ Q J 7 4

This is the same hand with the same 7 HCP, but now you have 1-card support instead of the 4-card support you had before. This illustrates why your partner's rebid in his spade suit is invitational but not forcing. You are at the low end of the range for your bid and so you should PASS.

D

Slam Bidding

Notrump versus Trump Slams

You can tell when you should bid a slam in notrump simply by counting points. The guideline, which you have already used, is:

At notrump;

- **33 partnership points equal the small-slam level.**
- **37 partnership points equal the grand-slam level.**

Once your partner has limited his hand with a notrump bid, you can proceed to a notrump slam by immediately bidding it, or by inviting the slam with the natural bids of 4 NOTRUMP or 5 NOTRUMP.

It is more difficult to decide whether or not you have a slam when the contract is to be in a trump suit. You can use roughly the same point count as for a notrump slam, but point count is not enough. When you count points for a trump contract, you may be counting quite a lot of distribution and therefore fewer high cards. That may leave enough high cards for the opponents to defeat you—if they hold the right ones.

For a slam at a trump contract, your fit with your partner is critical—not only your fit in the trump suit but also your fit in the side suits. In the trump suit an 8-card fit may do, but a 9-card fit greatly improves your chances. That gives you more ruffing power and makes it much less likely that some opponent will hold four trumps. Your partnership must hold enough high trump cards so that you will not lose two trump tricks, and not even one at a grand slam.

In the side suits, a 5-card suit in one hand, supported by a few cards of the same suit in the other hand, may allow you to make your slam with ease. If your hand is unbalanced, you want your partner's strength to be outside of your short suit. In the same sense, you want your own strength to be outside of any short suit which your partner may hold.

The better the fit and the more unbalanced the hands, the more likely that your partnership can make a slam with a point or more below the notrump guideline figures. Thus when the partnership total runs into the 30's, you can begin to think about a slam. However, without indications of a good fit, you should have the full count before committing your partnership to a slam.

When you bid a small slam and fail to make your contract, you have given up what surely could have been a successful game contract. But the extra bonus for the small slam is large enough that you should gamble on bidding it whenever you have a 50–50 chance of succeeding. On the other hand, giving up a small slam to try for a grand slam does not pay off as heavily. You should only bid a grand slam when the chances are 2 to 1 in your favor. Therefore, most of your slam bids are going to be small slam bids. It doesn't pay to bid a grand slam unless the indications are strong that you will make it.

Do the following pairs of hands make a good enough fit with each other to make a small slam bid?

♠ A K 9 8 5
♡ 8
◇ K Q 8 5 4
♣ A 8

♠ Q J 3 2
♡ 9 7 6 4
◇ A 6 2
♣ K 7

These hands are a perfect fit: a 9-card trump fit, an 8-card side suit fit, high cards concentrated in three suits with a singleton in the fourth. Even with only 30 partnership points, a small slam can be bid in spades or even in diamonds.

♠ A Q 9 5 3 2
♡ A K 3
◇ K 8
♣ K 4

♠ K 8
♡ 9 5
◇ A Q 9 6 5
♣ Q J 10 7

Here is a moderately good fit with 33 partnership points. If one opponent holds 4 spades, a small slam may be defeated, but it should be bid anyway. The high hearts opposite the small hearts are key factors for success.

♠ J 10 8 7 5
♡ A K Q 4
◇ A 9 7
♣ 4

♠ Q 9 4 3 2
♡ J 3
◇ K Q 8 4
♣ A K

These two hands have plenty of points for a small slam, but the lack of the ace and king of spades will be fatal to any slam.

♠ K Q J 10 7
♡ K J
◇ K Q 8 4 3
♣ A

♠ A 8 5
♡ Q 9
◇ J 10 7 6
♣ K Q 5 2

Here again there are enough points for a small slam, but the ace of hearts and the ace of diamonds are missing. The partnership needs a way of detecting this fatal flaw.

The Blackwood Convention

After you see that your side has the strength and the fit to try for a slam in a suit, then and only then should you begin to worry about how many aces the opponents may hold. Two aces in their hands will set your small slam bid immediately, and even one ace will set your grand slam bid. To guard against this occurrence, you use the Blackwood convention, named for the famous Easley Blackwood who invented it. This convention is used by all players (although some sophisticated partnerships use variations on it).

When it is clear that your slam contract will be in a *suit,* you may use the artificial Blackwood bid of

4 NOTRUMP.

It asks your partner how many aces he has. From his answer and a look at the number of aces in your own hand you can determine how many aces the opponents hold. Then you will stop short of slam if you find that the opponents have too many aces, or go ahead if they do not.

The replies to a Blackwood 4 NOTRUMP are also artificial and go up the line of available bids:

When replying to a Blackwood 4 NOTRUMP, bid:

- **5 CLUBS** when holding no ace or all the aces
- **5 DIAMONDS** when holding 1 ace
- **5 HEARTS** when holding 2 aces
- **5 SPADES** when holding 3 aces

The reply in clubs may seem to be ambiguous, but in reality it never is. You will either have some aces yourself so that you know that your partner's reply represents no aces, or you will have none and your partner is showing that he has all four.

If your partner's reply shows you that your side has *all* the aces, and if you are interested in a grand slam, you may ask about the number of kings that your partner holds by following your 4 NOTRUMP bid with a bid of 5 NOTRUMP. The replies follow the same scheme except that there is no double meaning for a club reply.

When replying to a Blackwood 5 NOTRUMP, bid

- 6 CLUBS when holding no king
- 6 DIAMONDS when holding 1 king
- 6 HEARTS when holding 2 kings
- 6 SPADES when holding 3 kings
- 6 NOTRUMP when holding 4 kings

Blackwood is intended for use when your contract will be in a suit. When your contract may be in notrump, a 4 NOTRUMP bid has its natural meaning.

- 4 NOTRUMP is Blackwood, asking about aces, when your side has never bid notrump, or after bidding notrump your side has later agreed on a trump suit.
- Only the Blackwood 4 NOTRUMP bidder may bid a Blackwood 5 NOTRUMP, asking about kings and promising all four aces within the partnership.

Would you use Blackwood in the following situations? If your answer is yes, and if your partner replies with 5 HEARTS, what will your next bid be?

YOU	PARTNER
1 SPADE	3 SPADES
???	

♠ A K Q 9 5
♡ K Q 8 3
◇ 8
♣ K J 9

You have 20 points and your partner has at least 13. Your 9-card spade fit plus the three top spade honors means that you won't lose any tricks in spades. But you need to know if your partner has at least two aces. Bid 4 NOTRUMP and find out. If he replies 5 HEARTS (2 aces), bid 6 SPADES. But if he shows fewer aces, bid 5 SPADES. Your partner must pass, accepting your decision whichever it is.

YOU	PARTNER
1 CLUB	1 HEART
3 HEARTS	4 CLUBS
???	

♠ K 9 2
♡ A Q 10 8
◇ 9
♣ K Q J 10 6

After your partner bid hearts, you counted 24 partnership points and invited game in hearts. Any rebid by your partner except 4 HEARTS is a slam invitation. You see a fit in both hearts and clubs and you have more points than you needed for your previous bidding so you accept the slam invitation. Bid 4 NOTRUMP to investigate aces. If your partner replies 5 HEARTS (2 aces) you will bid 6 HEARTS. If he shows fewer aces, you will sign off at 5 HEARTS.

YOU	PARTNER
1 HEART	2 NOTRUMP
???	

♠ K 5
♡ K Q J 9 3
◇ A 9 8
♣ A Q 3

You have 20 points and were just short of opening 2 NOTRUMP. Now your partner's bid tells you there are 33 partnership points so you jump to 6 NOTRUMP. Since your partner has already bid notrump, a bid of 4 NOTRUMP would not be Blackwood, but a natural raise in notrump and only an invitation to a slam.

NOTE: Warning! Some players, even some very experienced players, treat all 4 NOTRUMP bids as Blackwood. This is not the expert way. However, if you have any doubts about your partner's bidding habits, do not use 4 NOTRUMP as a natural bid.

YOU	PARTNER
1 HEART	3 DIAMONDS
???	

♠ K J 3
♡ A Q J 5 4 3
◇ K 9 3
♣ A

Your partner has promised at least 17 points, and so you see enough points for a grand slam. But you don't know yet whether you should be playing in hearts or diamonds. It would be premature to go into Blackwood. Bid 3 HEARTS. Your partner's game force guarantees that he will not pass before game is reached. If he responds 4 DIAMONDS or 4 HEARTS as expected, that sets the trump suit and you can then bid a Blackwood 4 NOTRUMP.

YOU	PARTNER
	1 NOTRUMP
3 HEARTS	4 HEARTS
???	

♠ 7
♡ A K J 8 5 3
◇ 8
♣ K Q 9 4 3

Although your partner started with notrump, you have since agreed on hearts as the trump suit, so now 4 NOTRUMP will be Blackwood. You have a 9-card fit in hearts and at least a 7-card fit in clubs. Your 20 revaluated points plus 16 makes 36. 4 NOTRUMP is your present bid. If your partner replies with 5 HEARTS, you will continue with 6 HEARTS. If he replies with 5 SPADES you will bid 7 HEARTS. Your wild distribution is a strong reason for optimism.

YOU	PARTNER
	2 NOTRUMP
3 SPADES	3 NOTRUMP
???	

♠ A K Q J 3
♡ 9 8 5
◇ 4 3
♣ 6 4 2

Your partner apparently has only two spades. But 11 points plus your partner's promised 21 still come to 32. If you know that your partner will not be confused, bid 4 NOTRUMP—this is a natural slam invitation, not Blackwood. Your partner should either pass or bid 6 NOTRUMP. But if you can't count on your partner, then it would be *your* mistake to bid 4 NOTRUMP—if your partner plays well, take a chance on 6 NOTRUMP, otherwise PASS. Without the 4 NOTRUMP natural slam invitation, you have to guess. With the invitation, your partner makes the final decision.

HINT: Learn that a 5-HEART reply means 2 aces. After that, the other replies come easily.

WHEN NOT TO USE BLACKWOOD

There are some occasions when you should not use Blackwood even though you have the strength and the fit for a slam in a suit. Other slam methods are called for. Look at these cases where you opened 1 SPADE and your partner responded 3 SPADES:

♠ A K Q J 8
♡ —
◇ K Q 8 2
♣ K Q 10 7

If the use of Blackwood tells you that your partner has one ace, you have not learned what you need to know. The ace of diamonds or the ace of clubs will give you a good small slam bid. But the ace of hearts will not help you. This is all because of your void.

♠ A K Q J 8
♡ 5 4
◊ K Q
♣ A J 10 8

If you learn from the use of Blackwood that your partner has one ace, you worry which ace it is. If it is the ace of diamonds, the opponents may hold the ace and king of hearts and take the first two tricks. Your problem is a suit (hearts) where you may lose the first two tricks.

A further problem may arise when your suit is a minor and your own hand is somewhat short on aces. Consider this case when you have opened 1 CLUB and your partner has responded 3 CLUBS.

♠ K J 10
♡ K Q 4
◊ 8
♣ A K J 10 8 7

If the reply to your Blackwood bid is 5 DIAMONDS (one ace), you want to stop at 5 CLUBS but it is already too late.

Do not use Blackwood when you have:

- A void
- A suit where you can lose the first two tricks
- A minor trump suit, and your partner's reply could prove embarrassing

---

Cue Bidding of Controls

When your partnership has proceeded in the bidding to the point of having already found the trump suit, a high-level bid in one of the other suits is a CUE BID, showing the ace of that suit. (A cue bid cues your partner in to some feature of your hand without suggesting that the bid suit become trumps.)

You will only start cue bidding your aces when you have an interest in going to slam. A cue bid is only an invitation to a slam, and the bidding may stop below the slam level when appropriate.

You will usually see 31 or 32 partnership points to make a slam invitation, but there might be a point less for a trump-suit slam with an excellent fit.

A cue bid to show an ace is always at the level of 4 CLUBS or above with one exception: 3 SPADES may be used to show the ace of spades when the trump suit is hearts. (If you had to use 4 SPADES, the bidding couldn't stop at 4 HEARTS.)

The first cue bid must be in a hitherto unbid suit, or in a suit which the opponents have already bid. If your partner makes the first cue bid to show an ace, he is inviting you to cue bid also. But if you are not interested in a slam, you will simply rebid the agreed trump suit. After the first cue bid, additional cue bids may be in any suit except the trump suit which your partnership has agreed on. You cannot ever cue bid in an agreed trump suit, even though you might like to use this means to show that you hold the ace of trumps.

Both of you, when you possess several aces which you could show, should make your cheapest cue bid first. Sometimes you may cue bid a void just as if it were an ace. Either an ace or a void gives your side FIRST ROUND CONTROL of the suit—the opponents cannot take the first trick in that suit in either case.

NOTE: "Cheapest first" is not always the best, but it takes expert judgment to know when to do otherwise.

A second cue bid in any one suit shows SECOND ROUND CONTROL of that suit—either the king or a singleton or even a void. Any of these will stop the opponents from taking the second trick in that suit.

There are two occasions when you might want to begin cue bidding. One is when you have only enough strength to invite a slam, but not enough to insist on it. The other occasion for cue bidding is when Blackwood will not work properly, for instance, when you have a void. Even after cue bidding has begun, Blackwood can still be used when there will be no problem in doing so. Aces which have been shown by cue bidding are still counted when replying to Blackwood, but voids are never counted as aces (nor singletons as kings).

Although cue bidding of controls is a standard procedure which everyone should understand, the fact remains that many social players do not. You always have to take into consideration who your partner is when you make bids which are the least bit advanced.

You have opened the bidding with 1 HEART and your partner has responded with 3 HEARTS. Are you interested in slam? What is your next bid?

♠ K Q 5
♡ A K J 10 8 5
◇ 9 4
♣ A Q

Your original 20 points have gone up to 21, making a partnership total of 34. You cannot use Blackwood because of your two immediate losers in diamonds. You must learn specifically whether your partner has the ace of diamonds. Bid 4 CLUBS. If your partner replies 4 DIAMONDS, you can go ahead with Blackwood because your concern about diamonds has been removed.

♠ K 10 3
♡ A K Q 9 5 4
◇ —
♣ K J 10 8

You need the ace of clubs or the ace of spades, not the ace of diamonds, to get to a slam. You cannot use Blackwood successfully because of your void. So bid 4 DIAMONDS, showing first-round control of that suit. If your partner bids 4 HEARTS you will pass, but if he bids 4 SPADES or 5 CLUBS you will bid 6 HEARTS. He could even bid 5 DIAMONDS, showing the king of diamonds which is useless to you in this case—you will sign off at 5 HEARTS.

♠ A K
♡ A Q J 10 8
◇ 6
♣ Q J 8 7 4

You can count 32 partnership points so there might be a slam here. You need the ace of clubs, but not necessarily the ace of diamonds, because of your two top losers in

clubs. You can cue bid 3 SPADES and hope
your partner accepts the invitation with a cue
bid of 4 CLUBS. You can see why 3 SPADES
is used for a cue bid—4 SPADES would be
above the 4 HEART game level and you may
need to stop at game.

The Direct Slam Try

When your trump suit is hearts or spades, a bid of 5 HEARTS or 5
SPADES is a slam invitation unless it was necessary for outbidding
the opponents or some similar reason. You can use this approach to
a slam when your only problem is that you are missing too many of
the high cards in the trump suit.

YOU   PARTNER
1 SPADE   3 SPADES
???

♠ J 10 8 5 4 Your only problem is in the trump suit. It is
♡ A K J   almost impossible for your partner not to
◇ A K J 4   have at least one high card in spades, but you
♣ A   need at least two for a slam. Bid 5 SPADES
      to tell him you need help in the form of
      several high trump cards.

E
Strong Opening Hands

Some hands are too strong to be opened with a bid of 1 in a SUIT. There are two ways of handling these hands, both of which can be considered to be standard. One is used almost universally in social bridge while the other is used almost universally by serious players, especially in tournaments. Since everyone plays social bridge at some time or other, let's start there.

Strong Two Bids

When you and your partner agree to play strong two bids, very strong hands which are not suitable for a notrump bid are opened by a bid of 2 in a SUIT.

When opening the bidding with 2 in a SUIT, you need:

- **22 points and a 6-card suit (or longer)**
  or
- **24 points and a 5-card suit**

Are these hands suitable for opening with a two bid, assuming your partnership is using "strong twos"? What is your bid?

♠ A K J 7 5   This hand totals 24 points and should be
♡ K 2   opened with 2 SPADES.
♢ K Q J 3 2
♣ A

♠ 7   With 22 points and a 6-card suit you can
♡ A K Q 10 8 5 open with 2 HEARTS.
♢ A Q J
♣ K J 4

♠ K Q 5
♡ A Q J
◇ A Q J 10
♣ A J 3

You hold 24 points, but since your hand is balanced you should open with 3 NOTRUMP.

Responding to a Strong Two Bid

When your partner opens the bidding with a strong two bid, you may well have enough points to bring the partnership total up into the near-slam zone (30 points) or even into the slam zone (33 points or more). To warn your partner when your hand is not that strong, you must invariably respond to an opening strong two bid with the artificial NEGATIVE response of 2 NOTRUMP. This does not express or deny any interest in playing in notrump. Your next bid will begin to describe the true nature of your hand.

When you hold 8 points or more opposite your partner's minimum of 22, so that the partnership total reaches at least 30, you will begin immediately to bid your hand naturally. You may bid any suit, or if interested in notrump, you may bid 3 NOTRUMP. Any bid except the artificial 2 NOTRUMP is a slam invitation and you will frequently end up in a slam contract.

When responding to a strong two bid:
- With less than 8 points (30 partnership points), your first bid is automatically the artificial negative 2 NOTRUMP.
- With more, make any other appropriate bid and look for a slam opportunity.

When your partner opens the bidding with a strong two bid, his bid is forcing to game. If you have a terrible hand, you may partly inform your partner of your plight by a first response of 2 NOTRUMP (or if your right-hand opponent intervenes with a bid, you may pass with the same meaning). But in spite of your miserable holding you will never let the bidding die until game is reached—after all, your partner may well have more than enough points for game in his own hand and all he needs from you is some help in finding the best fit.

There is one exception to the rule that neither partner can pass before game is reached, and the exception applies to just this one case: The two-bidder gets a negative 2 NOTRUMP reply and then rebids his original suit. For example:

PARTNER	YOU
2 HEARTS	2 NOTRUMP
3 HEARTS	???

Your partner has six hearts or more and 22 or 23 points. You may pass with a terrible hand that cannot bring the partnership total up to at least 25. If your partner had wanted to rebid hearts without having you pass before game is reached, he would have bid 4 HEARTS.

- A strong two bid is forcing to game.
- The responder may pass before game is reached only if he first responds 2 NOTRUMP, and the opener then rebids the original suit.

NOTE: Some partnerships do not permit passing below the game level in any circumstances other than after an intervening bid by an opponent.

How will you respond after your partner opens the bidding with 2 HEARTS?

♠ K J 5 4 3
♡ J 8
◇ A 9 5 3
♣ 8 7

You have 10 points opposite at least 22. That makes 32 partnership points and you are pleasantly thinking of a slam if you can find a fit. Bid 2 SPADES and see how things develop from there.

♠ Q 3
♡ 9 7 5 4
◇ J 9 8
♣ A 9 7 6

Your 8 points, including 1 for the 9-card fit, is enough for a positive response. Bid 3 HEARTS. With a lesser hand you would start with 2 NOTRUMP and raise hearts later.

♠ A 10 4
♡ 7 5
◇ K 5 4 2
♣ Q 8 7 6

With 9 points opposite at least 22 you can count on at least 31 points in the partnership. Your hand is balanced and you have a little something in each of the unbid suits. Bid 3 NOTRUMP, inviting slam. (You can't bid only 2 NOTRUMP because that is the artifical negative bid and you have no reason to be negative.)

♠ 5 4 3 2
♡ 7
◇ J 9 4 3
♣ 7 6 5 2

They don't come much worse than this. Bid 2 NOTRUMP and hope your partner rebids in another suit. But only if he rebids 3 HEARTS will you pass. In any other case you will brave it out until game is reached, with reasonable expectancy of making it. Your partner could even have a grand slam holding:

♠ A
♡ A K Q J 5
◇ A K Q 6 2
♣ A K

F
Strong Defensive Hands

The Strong Takeout Double

Once in a great while your partner makes a takeout double and then, surprisingly, ignores the suit in which you responded, bidding his own suit instead. He has just used the takeout double in its alternate use. He is saying, "Forget the usual message carried by a takeout double. This is a POWERHOUSE DOUBLE. I have a big hand with a strong suit. I am not interested in your suit."

OPPONENT	PARTNER	OPPONENT	YOU
1 CLUB	DOUBLE	PASS	1 SPADE
PASS	2 HEARTS !!		

Your partner's hand may look something like this:

♠ 7
♡ A Q J 9 8 4
◇ A J 4 3
♣ A 8

18 points is too much for him to make a simple overcall of 1 SPADE, because you might pass when game could be made. At first you will think that your partner has made an ordinary takeout double, but his second bid changes the message.

When your partner makes a takeout double first and then bids his own suit, he has at least 17 points and a good 5-card suit. He probably does not support your suit, although he may support the unbid suit. When your partner makes a takeout double first and then bids notrump, this is also a powerhouse double. He was too strong to overcall immediately with 1 NOTRUMP (which would be 16, 17, 18)—he had more than 18 points.

NOTE: A jump overcall in notrump is reserved for a special use, the "unusual notrump," which you will learn about later.

> When making a strong takeout double with a hand too
> strong to overcall immediately in your suit, you need:
>
> • At least 17 points
> • A good suit of at least 5 cards
>
> When making a strong takeout double with a hand too
> strong to overcall immediately in notrump, you need:
>
> • At least 19 points
> • A balanced hand with the opponents' suit(s)
>   stopped

When you overcall in a suit with 16 or even 17 points, you can show your strength by bidding your suit a second time or by bidding a second suit if you have one. With 17 points, optionally, and with 18 points, surely, you must double first and then overcall.

Defensive Cue Bid in an Opponent's Suit

A bid in an opponent's suit is a cue bid, which provides an artificial way of showing a strong hand. You use a defensive cue bid when other available bids are not strong enough for the hand which you hold. It is normally the only forcing bid available to the defense outside of the takeout double.

A strength-showing cue bid in an opponent's suit may be based on either game or invitational values. When made as the first bid by the defense, it shows a hand as strong, or almost as strong, as an opening strong two bid. The strength-showing cue bid is forcing for only one round, but if the cue bidder follows it with a bid in a new suit, that bid is again forcing for one round.

NOTE: The strength-showing cue bid occurs before agreeing on a trump suit, whereas the control-showing cue bid (showing an ace or void) occurs after agreeing on a trump suit. This distinguishes the two.

OPPONENT	YOU
1 CLUB	???

♠ A K J 8 5 3
♡ K Q 10 5
◇ A Q J
♣ —

You had in mind opening with 2 SPADES but your RHO, who is the dealer, opened first with 1 CLUB. Bid 2 CLUBS to announce your big hand and to force your partner to bid (although he may pass if your LHO intervenes with a bid).

OPPONENT	PARTNER	OPPONENT	YOU
1 CLUB	DOUBLE	PASS	???

♠ K Q 9 8
♡ Q 10 8 5
◇ K Q 8
♣ 8 3

With your partner's 13 you can count 25 partnership points. You don't want to bid 1 HEART or 1 SPADE which your partner would probably pass. Neither do you want to jump to 2 HEARTS or 2 SPADES because that is only invitational. Besides, you only have 4-card suits, leaving you in doubt as to which one will best fit your partner's hand. Bid 2 CLUBS and see which suit he bids. It is typical to use this cue bid when you are strong but not sure where the hand should be played.

You may be wondering what to do when the opponents have bid your suit before you could bid it. Often you simply pass, waiting to give them trouble and perhaps to make a penalty double if they persist in the suit to a high enough level. However, when your right-hand opponent opens with 1 CLUB or 1 DIAMOND, he may have done it on a 3-card suit and you could hold much better cards in that suit than he does. In that case you can pass and then bid your suit later—you can't be cue bidding to show strength if you have already passed, so your bid is natural.

NOTE: A few partnerships go contrary to the above, deciding that 2 CLUBS over an opening 1 CLUB, or 2 DIAMONDS over an opening 1 DIAMOND, is a natural bid.

A second alternative, when you have a preemptive holding in the opener's minor suit, is to make a jump cue bid. For example, you can jump to 3 CLUBS over an opening 1 CLUB on your right—a jump cue bid is natural (unless your partnership has made some other agreement).

NOTE: A strength-showing cue bid is sometimes used by the offense, but then it is a game-forcing bid. It is most useful to the opener or to a passed responder because another forcing bid may not be available. It implies good support for partner's suit. For some partnerships it also implies first- or second-round control of the opponents' suit.

Chapter 12 ////////////////////////////

SYSTEMS
AND
CONVENTIONS

//

A
Class A Conventions

A very large number of conventions are used by various partnerships. However, only a few of these are in standard use. The American Contract Bridge League has designated the most usual ones as being Class A conventions. Your opponents do not have to let you know whether their partnership has decided to use these conventions—you are supposed to be able to recognize when they might be using one. For example:

OPPONENT	PARTNER	OPPONENT	YOU
1 NOTRUMP	PASS	2 CLUBS	???

You recognize that the 2 CLUBS is probably Stayman, but perhaps the opponents do not use Stayman. Whenever it is your turn to bid or play, you may ask the *partner* of the bidder what their agreement is on that particular bid. (We don't allow the bidder to explain his own bid.)

Common Conventions

Some of the Class A conventions are a normal part of Standard American. You can assume that your partner will know and use Blackwood, the takeout double, and a cue bid in your opponents' suit. However, in social bridge there are many players whose knowledge of the game is so elementary that they do not recognize a natural 4 NOTRUMP, are not sure when a double is for takeout and think that perhaps a cue bid in the opponents' suit is actually natural. You will not find this true of experienced players.

The Stayman convention is considered to be standard today, but many social players have not caught up with the times and do not use it. You must ask your partner, before you start to play, whether you are going to use Stayman or not.

Strong opening two bids ("strong twos") have been in use the longest and work very well when you have a strong hand. However, you don't have a hand good enough for a strong two bid very often. For that reason, an alternative approach has been developed which makes better use of the available bidding space.

The Strong Artificial 2 CLUB Bid

Serious bridge players almost universally have abandoned the strong two bid. Instead, all hands which would have otherwise been opened with a strong two are now opened with an artificial bid of 2 CLUBS. The opener shows what his real suit is on his second bid unless he chooses to raise his partner or to bid notrump. You will have to agree with your partner on whether you will use this approach or the strong-two approach.

The negative response to this 2 CLUB bid is an artificial 2 DIAMONDS (instead of the negative 2 NOTRUMP which is used only with strong twos). For a positive response, 2 NOTRUMP is available to show a balanced hand, and 2 HEARTS, 2 SPADES, 3 CLUBS and 3 DIAMONDS are available to show a suit.

When opening the bidding with a strong artificial 2 CLUBS, you need:

- 22 points and a 6-card *major* suit (or longer)

or

- 24 points and a 5-card suit

or

- 24 points and a balanced notrump hand

When responding to an opening strong artificial 2 CLUBS:

- With less than 8 points (30 partnership points), your first bid is automatically the artificial negative 2 DIAMONDS.
- With more, make any other appropriate bid and look for a slam opportunity.

If you open the bidding with 3 NOTRUMP, you don't leave any room for exploring a slam or a major fit. A simple but reasonable approach with a hand of that strength (24,25,26) is to open 2 CLUBS and bid notrump as your next bid unless an opportunity in the majors presents itself. The sequence

YOU	PARTNER
2 CLUBS	2 DIAMONDS
2 NOTRUMP	???

is treated just as if you had opened 2 NOTRUMP but with the higher point count range. Your partner may then use 3 CLUBS as Stayman (assumng that you are using Stayman).

NOTE: The more sophisticated approach, which is widely used, has the following ranges:

- 21,22—Open 2 NOTRUMP.
- 23,24—Open 2 CLUBS and rebid a nonjump notrump.
- 25,26—Open 2 CLUBS and rebid with a jump to 3 NOTRUMP.

Other arrangements are also used, but this one avoids the awkward opening 3 NOTRUMP, which is used by experts only for a convention.

An opening 2 CLUB bid is forcing to game except when a negative response is followed by a rebid of 2 NOTRUMP:

YOU	PARTNER
2 CLUBS	2 DIAMONDS (artificial negative)
2 NOTRUMP	???

Your partner may pass. However, to make a game he only needs a point or two—anything which will take a trick—so he almost never passes. It is also reasonable to allow the responder to pass after the sequence

YOU	PARTNER
2 CLUBS	2 DIAMONDS (artificial negative)
2 HEARTS	2 NOTRUMP (holding two hearts)
3 HEARTS	

(where the negative response is followed by a notrump response while the opener merely rebids his suit), but there is no standard on this matter.

Obviously you must agree with your partner on whether you will use strong twos or the strong artificial 2 CLUBS. Strong twos are satisfactory at rubber bridge because it is important to be able to handle big hands well and make those big scores. At duplicate it is important to be able to handle the most common hands well even if the uncommon hands become more difficult to handle. The strong artificial two bid is the favorite with veteran duplicate players because it opens up another opportunity which we will now discuss.

The Weak Two Bids

When the strong artificial 2 CLUB bid is used to show all big hands, the other opening 2-bids (2 DIAMONDS, 2 HEARTS, 2 SPADES) are used as preemptive bids. They become like the opening 3-bids but on a smaller scale. The suit is normally a good 6-card suit (not shorter) and the number of playing tricks needed is scaled down to the level of the bid. The guideline for opening preempts becomes modified only to include the three additional bids.

For an opening preemptive suit bid, from 2 DIA-MONDS up to 5 DIAMONDS, you need:

- Less than an opening hand
- Insufficient strength to defeat a small slam by the opponents, should they bid it
- Enough playing tricks plus the appropriate overbid margin to equal the level of your preempt

Immediately make the highest bid indicated by this guideline, but not higher than the game level.

Do not bid again unless your partner forces you to.

NOTE: The American Contract Bridge League has ruled that in their games a weak two bid must contain at least 5 HCP and at least a 5-card suit. Bidding on so little is only for highly aggressive experts.

Playing weak twos, how would you open the following hands?

NOTVUL vs. NOTVUL

♠ K Q J 8 5 4
♡ Q 8
◇ J 6 5
♣ 7 4

You have five playing tricks with an overbid margin of three, which makes eight— enough to bid at the two level. Open 2 SPADES. A good trump suit, such as here, is typical of a weak two bid.

VUL vs. NOTVUL

♠ 5
♡ A Q J 10 8 3
◇ K J 3
♣ 9 7 4

You are strong enough to open 1 HEART so do so.

VUL vs. NOTVUL

♠ 6 2
♡ 5
◇ A K 10 9 4 3 2
♣ J 7 6

You have six playing tricks and an overbid margin of two. In spite of your 7-card diamond suit, the vulnerability limits you to bidding 2 DIAMONDS.

NOTVUL vs. VUL

♠ A K Q J 9 8
♡ A Q
◇ A J 10 8
♣ 8

You have 23 points and a 6-card major suit. Open 2 CLUBS. You plan to bid spades next to show what your real suit is.

VUL vs. VUL

♠ J 8 7
♡ J 5 4
◇ 8
♣ K Q J 8 5 4

It is easy to get mixed up on this kind of hand and bid 2 CLUBS, which of course is not a weak two. But you won't do it twice. The lowest preempt in clubs is 3 CLUBS and unfortunately you don't have enough playing tricks for that level, so PASS.

RESPONDING TO A WEAK TWO BID

The responses to a weak two bid follow the same pattern as for any other opening preempt, but you will need 2-card support to make a constructive raise since your partner usually will have a 6-card suit. There is one special response, for instance:

YOU	PARTNER
2 SPADES	2 NOTRUMP
???	

Your partners' response of 2 NOTRUMP is forcing and asks how good your hand is. With a poor hand you simply rebid your suit, in this case 3 SPADES. With a good hand, closer to an opening bid, you respond in any side suit where you have a high card (a so-called FEATURE).

DEFENDING AGAINST A WEAK TWO BID

Sauce for the goose is sauce for the gander, and you will sometimes find yourself trying to combat an opponent's opening weak two bid. The general guideline in bidding against a preempt is that you should have an opening hand plus an extra point for each level (above the 1-level) at which you must start. If you can bid at the 2-level, 14 points and a good 5-card suit will do. At the 3-level, 15 points and either a 6-card or a very good 5-card suit will suffice. If you are considering a takeout double, the same guideline for points applies. The minimum level at which your partner can respond determines the number of points you should have. You may bid 2 NOTRUMP on the same hand you would have opened 1 NOTRUMP with, providing you have a stopper in the opponent's suit. Your bids won't always succeed, but you must fight back if your hand gives you anything to work with.

Other Class A Conventions

The other Class A conventions are very useful in certain special cases which do not occur very often. For this reason, many social players have never even heard of them. But experienced players should know about them and have them ready for time in need, providing they have an experienced partner. (The description of these remaining Class A conventions has been somewhat simplified to suit present needs.)

Lightner Slam Double. Doubling a slam contract will seldom bring you many points because good players investigate carefully before bidding a slam. However, there are times when you see that you can set the slam provided that your partner, who will be on lead, makes an unusual opening lead.

The late Ted Lightner introduced the idea that the double of a slam contract should ask your partner to try and find the unusual lead which you are looking for. For example, you might hold a void and can get a quick ruff if your partner finds the right suit to lead. An unusual lead would never be the trump suit, and it would not be a suit which either of you have bid, because those would be the usual leads. If your partner has a long suit elsewhere, he should suspect that it corresponds to a void in your hand. If not, he must pick out the unusual suit as best he can. It is often a side suit bid by the opponents.

SOS Redouble. Sometimes, when an opponent doubles your bid or your partner's bid, you know that your partnership should be in some other contract—any other contract has a chance to be better. For example:

YOU	OPPONENT	PARTNER	OPPONENT
1 CLUB	DOUBLE	PASS	PASS

You have opened with a 3-card club suit and it looks as though you are going to be zonked. To raise a cry for help, you can REDOU-BLE, asking your partner to take you out of the redouble into his best suit. The basic principle is that a REDOUBLE after two passes is for takeout. (But some partnerships use the redouble for SOS even if it is not after two passes.)

Grand Slam Force. When your partnership has agreed on a trump suit, a bid of 5 NOTRUMP (not as part of a Blackwood sequence) asks your partner to choose between a small slam and a grand slam in your agreed suit. It is used when the only thing missing from your hand for a slam is one or two of the three top trump cards (the ace, king and queen). If your partner has two of these cards, he immediately bids a grand slam. If he only has one of them, he may bid six in the agreed trump suit, but if available he will bid six in any lower-ranking suit. If he has none of the missing honors, he must bid six of the agreed trump suit. (You have also seen that a bid of 5 NOTRUMP is used as part of notrump bidding to ask your partner to choose between bidding 6 NOTRUMP and 7 NOTRUMP.)

Unusual Notrump. This bid is notorious for causing disaster. It sounds like an ordinary notrump, but the unusual circumstances under which it is used is supposed to tip you off. Suppose your partner suddenly makes a *defensive jump* to 2 NOTRUMP.

OPPONENT	PARTNER	OPPONENT	YOU
1 HEART	2 NOTRUMP	PASS	???

Your partner is showing that he holds at least five cards in each of the two minor suits, clubs and diamonds. You are required to take the unusual notrump bid out into one of your partner's suits unless an opponent intervenes with a bid. The unusual notrump hand normally has no strength outside of the two long suits, so it is really preeemptive in nature, not strong. However, it is also used for very strong hands, the strength being shown by making a second bid. Ordinary opening strength (13 to 16) is best handled by overcalling normally in one of the suits.

Some partnerships agree that the unusual notrump will show the two lower unbid suits instead of the two minor suits. Needless to say, the unusual notrump bid is strictly to be avoided unless you have a solid understanding with your partner about when it is to be used and what is to mean.

The simplest agreement is that a notrump bid is unusual, and shows the two minor suits, only in two cases. Firstly, a jump overcall in notrump directly after the opening bid, as in the example above, is unusual. (A real notrump hand in that situation is shown by a nonjump notrump overcall, or for a bigger hand, by a takeout double followed by notrump.) Secondly, any notrump bid is unusual when the opponents have already bid a normal notrump.

If the opponents make a notrump bid which sounds suspicious, you can always ask the partner of the bidder whether the bid is a natural or an unusual notrump. But don't be surprised if he isn't sure!

Gerber. The Gerber convention was invented by the late John Gerber as an alternate way of asking for aces and kings. When a 4 NOTRUMP bid would be natural, not Blackwood, the Gerber convention can be used to ask for aces and kings. The Gerber

---

4 CLUBS is Gerber only when it immediately follows:

- **An opening bid of 1 NOTRUMP or 2 NOTRUMP**
  or
- **A strong artificial 2 CLUBS followed by 2 DIAMONDS followed by 2 NOTRUMP**

The replies are:

- **4 DIAMONDS showing no ace or all the aces**
- **4 HEARTS showing 1 ace**
- **4 SPADES showing 2 aces**
- **4 NOTRUMP showing 3 aces**

5 CLUBS following a Gerber 4 CLUBS asks for kings, the replies being:

- **5 DIAMONDS showing no king**
- **5 HEARTS showing 1 king**
- **5 SPADES showing 2 kings**
- **5 NOTRUMP showing 3 kings**
- **6 CLUBS showing 4 kings**

convention uses a jump to 4 CLUBS to ask for aces and then 5 CLUBS to ask for kings. This convention is so seldom needed and so error-prone (because it gets confused with a real club bid) that you may do best not to use it at all.

The main case when Gerber is useful is when your partner opens with a notrump bid and you have a long suit in which you see a slam. Because you are going to play in a suit, you may need to ask about aces, but 4 NOTRUMP would be a raise of your partner's bid, not Blackwood. If your partnership is using Gerber, you have a way of asking for aces.

The trouble with using this guideline, which is fairly standard, is that you have no way of stopping in 5 CLUBS if that is your suit. If you do not find enough aces for a slam, you may have to play in 4 NOTRUMP instead.

Some partnerships make a broader use of Gerber than that of the guideline given above. For instance, after any bid of 1 NOTRUMP or 2 NOTRUMP by one partner, a jump to 4 CLUBS by the other becomes Gerber. (After 3 NOTRUMP a jump to 5 CLUBS becomes Gerber for aces, with the responses adjusted accordingly.) This sophistication will only bring about an unnecessary catastrophe until you reach the expert level. Agree with your partner not to use Gerber or to use it in the simplest way possible.

B
Beyond Class A

Conventions Not in Class A

There is no reason for you to use conventions which are not in Class A until you become quite experienced. However it may be useful for you to understand a few of these which other partnerships may use.

Your opponents must always let you know if they are using any convention which is not Class A. In a formal duplicate game, each pair has a CONVENTION CARD on which is indicated the conventions they use. In addition, if one of the partners makes a conventional bid which is not in Class A, the other partner must immediately say "alert." He is not allowed to give any further explanation spontaneously, but an opponent may ask for a full explanation any time it is that opponent's turn to bid or play. In a social game, where procedures are normally relaxed, it is good sportsmanship to make some remark when your partner makes a conventional bid (even if it is in Class A) if you think the opponents won't recognize it.

Transfers. A transfer is an artificial bid which requests your partner to bid the suit that you are really interested in. The purpose of such a bid is to transfer the declarership from yourself to your partner when that may be of benefit. The most common transfers, called JACOBY TRANSFERS, are used as a response to an opening notrump bid—a nonjump diamond or heart response to an opening notrump shows five cards in the next higher ranking suit and requires the partner to bid that suit. It is more advantageous for the notrump bidder to play the hand than to be the dummy and have his good hand revealed.

Distributional Conventions. There are many conventions designed to show a two-suited hand—the unusual notrump is in this category. There are also a number of conventions which show a singleton or void.

Doubles for Takeout. There are several conventions which use a double for takeout in circumstances where Standard American would use the double for penalty. Although these conventions reduce the ability to make a penalty double, they are widely used by serious players. But then overcalls by the opponents can become bolder, because they are not so easily doubled for penalty. This is one reason why experts playing against experts will overcall on slightly lesser hands than our guidelines suggest.

Doubles for Lead. You have already seen the Lightner double against a slam contract. Somewhat similarly, a double of a 3 NOTRUMP bid, when your partner will be on lead, asks him not to shy off from leading a suit which your side has bid. If your side has not bid any suit, then it asks him to lead the first suit bid by the dummy. This double is used when you expect the requested lead to set the contract. A double of an artificial bid, such as a Stayman club bid, asks your partner to lead that suit. Good players often use a double in these circumstances without prior agreement on the assumption that the bid will be properly understood.

Other Systems

Some experts base their system on Standard American, to which they add many variations and conventions. Eastern Scientific is such a system. There are also some other systems which are different enough to be in a class by themselves. Many of these systems use ideas from the bridge giant, Alvin Roth, whose own system is not widely used.

Two-Over-1 Game Force. There is a group of somewhat similar systems in which a 2-over-1 shift is forcing to game and therefore is based on game-going values. The trend in this direction is strong and even Standard American has drifted toward a stronger 2-over-1 bid. The principle is to keep the bidding low with strong hands, leaving more room to exchange information about the best game or slam. Many other bids are adjusted to conform with this principle.

Systems in the category of 2-over-1 game force are Aces Scientific, as promoted by Bobby Goldman, and West Coast Scientific, first conceived by Dick Walsh and promoted by Max Hardy. The Kaplan-Sheinwold system (designed by the noted player and theoretician Edgar Kaplan in conjunction with his equally noted partner Alfred Sheinwold) is rather similar, the 2-over-1 being strong enough to promise another bid without being 100 percent game forcing.

Big Club. The big-club systems are even more different from Standard American. The Italian systems generally fall in this category. In the United States, the most common of such systems is Precision, as developed by the Chinese-American C. C. Wei. In these systems all strong hands (16 HCP in Precision) are opened with an artificial 1 CLUB bid unless they qualify for an opening 2 NOTRUMP. There are quite a few other artificial bids which are peculiar to big-club systems.

The big-club systems and the Kaplan-Sheinwold system use an opening 1 NOTRUMP for a hand in the 13–15 point range, or even in the 12–14 point range. The attempt is to make it difficult for you to bid, and you must be much more aggressive in overcalling a WEAK NOTRUMP than you would be after the usual strong notrump opening.

C
Standard American

Summary of Standard American Variations

When you sit down to play with a new partner, you need to find out what variations on Standard American you will be using. In a formal tournament you will work out a convention card together. But in a social setting, a brief word or two with your partner will suffice. The key points to settle are as follows:

SUGGESTED ALTERNATIVE FOR A SOCIAL GAME	OTHER ALTERNATIVES
5-card majors	4-card majors
Strong twos	Weak twos and strong artificial 2 CLUBS
Weak jump overcalls	Intermediate (or strong) jump overcalls
Opening 1 NOTRUMP 16–18	15–17
Opening 2 NOTRUMP 21–23	20–22 (if 1 NOTRUMP is 15–17)
Stayman on offense and on defense	Stayman on offense only, or no Stayman

If you wish to play any other conventions except Blackwood and takeout doubles, which are always used, you must check with your partner first. If you know a convention which you haven't agreed on using, don't use it and don't assume that your partner is using it. However, in a duplicate tournament game, you can assume that all Class A conventions are to be used unless you agree otherwise. Weak twos and the strong artificial 2 CLUBS are also normal.

If you have time, whether for a social game or for a tournament game, you should check to see if your partner considers that 4 NOTRUMP is always Blackwood. You might also check on when your partner considers a double to be for takeout—this also serves to find out how familiar your partner is with takeout doubles.

Occasionally you will find a social player who uses LIMIT JUMPS: if the responder makes a jump raise, or if he makes a jump rebid in his own suit, these are a full-value bids (similar to the same bids when made by the opener). This variation is widely used by sophisticated players and is finding its way slowly into social bridge.

Chapter 13 //////////////////////////

POINTERS FOR THE DECLARER

///////////////////////////////

A
Managing the Suit

Playing for the Drop

Suppose that you, as declarer, find the spades lie as follows:

YOU	DUMMY
♠ A 8 6 5 4	♠ K J 3

You might play the ace (in case the queen is a singleton) and then finesse the jack. Or then again, you might play the ace and king first, hoping for the queen to drop under one of them. Which is likely to make the most tricks? You can decide by using a guideline which works for most cases of this kind.

- Imagine that the outstanding cards are divided as evenly as possible between the two opponents.
- Imagine that the honor which you want to drop is in the hand with the most cards.
- If you could drop the missing honor under these circumstances, play for the drop, instead of finessing.

In the example above, there are five outstanding cards. If they were to split 3–2 with the queen in the 3-card holding, then the queen would not drop when you lead out the ace and the king. Thus the guideline says that finessing is slightly better for this case.

On the other hand, if you hold a 9-card fit,

♠ A 8 6 5 4 2   ♠ K J 3

then there are four outstanding cards. If they were to split 2–2 you could drop the queen by playing the ace and the king. In this case, playing for the drop is better than finessing. There is an old saying which runs "eight ever, nine never," meaning that it is better to finesse for a missing *queen* when you hold an 8-card fit, but not when you hold a 9-card fit.

In those cases where the guideline says that playing for the drop is better, it is only slightly better. Therefore if you have any information which leads you to believe that the missing honor may be favorably placed for a finesse, take the finesse. Perhaps one opponent has bid strongly, making it more likely that he holds the missing honor. Or perhaps one opponent has preempted, making it less likely that he holds any high card outside of his long suit.

Saving the Tenace

Suppose that the spade holdings between you and the dummy were:

YOU   DUMMY

♠ K Q 5 2   ♠ A 10 4 3

In this case the jack is missing and the guideline says that it is best to play for the drop. But notice how the ace-ten forms a tenace around the missing jack. You must play the king and the queen first, saving the tenace. If as you play these two cards your right-hand opponent SHOWS OUT (cannot follow suit because he is out of spades), then you know that the jack is favorably placed to finesse against it. But you can only make the finesse if you have saved your tenace.

When there are alternate ways to play a suit, try to start in such a way as to save any available tenace.

In the following cases, how would you play the cards?

YOU	DUMMY	
♠ K 8 7 6 4	♠ A J 3 2	Play for the drop, starting with the king. But if your RHO shows out on the first round, finesse the jack.
♠ K Q 10 4	♠ A 3 2	Play for the drop, starting with the king and then the ace. This saves the tenace in your own hand and puts the lead in the dummy in case you need to take the finesse.
♠ A K Q 10	♠ 4 2	Take the finesse, but first play the ace just in case the jack is a singleton.
♠ A J 6 5	♠ K 10 4 3	Taking a finesse against the queen is correct. You have a two-way finesse, in that you can lead from either hand toward the tenace in the other hand. Start with the ace or

the king, saving the tenace which you think is most likely to succeed.

The Ruffing Finesse

Suppose that hearts are trump and the spades are as follows:

YOU	DUMMY
♠ —	♠ K Q J 3

You can lead the king of spades, and if the second hand plays the ace you can ruff it in your hand, establishing the queen and jack. If the second hand plays low, do not ruff—instead, discard a loser from your hand. The king wins if the second hand holds the ace. And even if it turns out that the fourth hand has the ace and wins the trick, you have eliminated a loser. You almost can't lose when you take a RUFFING FINESSE such as this.

Hearts are trumps and you have a few of them available to ruff with. Can you make a ruffing finesse in spades with the following hands?

YOU	DUMMY	
♠ 3	♠ Q J 10 9	Play the queen, forcing out one of the missing honors. Later lead the jack for a ruffing finesse.
♠ 2	♠ A Q J	If you think that your LHO holds the king, take the normal finesse. Otherwise play the ace and then take the ruffing finesse against your RHO.

B
Managing the Hand

Creating a Ruff

When your hand and the dummy's hand contain the same number of cards in a side suit, you cannot make a ruff in the dummy by straightforward means. But there is still hope.

YOU	DUMMY	
♠ A K Q 5 4	♠ 8 7 6 3 2	Your contract is 4 SPADES.
♡ A K	♡ 7	The opening lead is the ♡Q.
◇ Q 6	◇ A 2	
♣ 10 8 7 2	♣ J 9 5 4 3	

You do not want to ruff the king of hearts and you do not seem to have a ruff in diamonds. However, if you play the ace and king of hearts, discarding a diamond from the dummy, you have made a ruffing possibility for yourself. You made an equal-length holding of diamonds in the dummy (same length as in your hand) into a short holding by discarding.

Dummy Reversal

When you, as declarer, find that the dummy has more trumps than you have in your own hand, you simply treat your hand the way you would normally treat the dummy's hand, hence the name DUMMY REVERSAL. Since the dummy has the long hand, you count the losers in the dummy's hand and try to ruff them in your own hand. Extra tricks can be taken only when the ruff is made with the short holding in trumps.

YOU (DECLARER)	DUMMY	
♠ A 8 7 4	♠ 6 3	Your contract is 5 CLUBS.
♡ A 2	♡ 9 5 4	The opening lead is the ♡ K.
◇ 9 8 6	◇ A K	
♣ A Q 7 2	♣ K 9 6 5 4 3	

Since the dummy is the long hand, you count the dummy's losers: one in spades and two in hearts. You can eliminate a heart loser by ruffing in your own hand.

In the following case, both hands have four trumps and you could choose either one to be the "long" hand.

YOU	DUMMY	
♠ 8 7 5 2	♠ A 6 4 3	Your contract is 4 HEARTS.
♡ Q 9 3 2	♡ A K 8 7	The opening lead is the ◇ K
◇ 7	◇ 8 5 2	followed by the lead of the ◇ A.
♣ A K J 6	♣ Q 8	

Because of the obvious ruffing possibilities in your own hand, you treat the dummy hand as the long hand. You count the dummy for two losers in spades and three more in diamonds. However you plan to ruff two of the diamonds and to discard two of the spades on the extra winners in the club suit. If all goes well, you will lose a spade and a diamond, making an overtrick.

Once in a while you will be able to ruff the long hand down to where it has fewer trumps than the short hand. In that case you have virtually converted the long hand into the short hand. This unusual case of deliberately ruffing in the long hand is best understood by looking at an example.

YOU	DUMMY	
♠ A 9 7 5 3	♠ K Q J	Your contract is 4 SPADES.
♡ A	♡ J 6 5 4	The opening lead is the ♡K.
◇ 5 4 3	◇ A 8 6	
♣ A 9 6 2	♣ K 7 5	

Your own hand is the natural long hand, and counting losers from that hand you see two in diamonds and probably two in clubs. Making your contract seems to depend on a favorable split in clubs, which is not too likely. But if you notice that you can ruff three hearts in your hand, making your spades shorter than the dummy's spades, you will rethink. Treating the dummy's hand as the long hand and counting losers from that hand, you see three heart losers, all of which you can ruff, and just three diamond and club losers, which you can afford.

Since the spades in the dummy are high enough to draw trump with, you can use the three highest trumps in your own hand to ruff with. After winning with the ace of hearts, you can enter the dummy by means of the king of clubs, ruff a heart with the seven of spades, reenter the dummy by means of the ace of diamonds, and ruff another heart with the nine of spades. You only need the three high spades to ruff with, so you now can use one of the low spades to get to the dummy again for the last heart ruff with the ace of spades. Your last spade in the dummy will now get you to the dummy to finish drawing trumps with as long as they split 3–2.

The Cross Ruff

The clue that starts you thinking about ruffing possibilities is a short holding in a side suit. When there are two short side suits, one in each hand, then a new possibility opens up, which some-times pays off.

YOU	DUMMY	
♠ A K 10 5	♠ Q J 9 2	Your contract is 4 SPADES.
♡ 9	♡ A 7 5 4 3	The opening lead is the ◇K.
◇ A 8 5 4 3	◇ 6	
♣ 9 7 4	♣ J 8 6	

Considering your own hand to be the long hand, you see a lot of losers in diamonds and clubs, and you wonder just how many of the diamond losers you can ruff. As you ruff each diamond loser, you have to get back to your own hand to ruff another. If you do that by leading a trump, you are using up the trumps you need for ruffing. The only other way is to return to your hand by ruffing a heart, and that is the answer to this hand.

Suppose you win the opening lead with the ace of diamonds, ruff a diamond, win with the ace of hearts, ruff a heart. Now you can keep on CROSSRUFFING, ruffing diamonds and hearts alternately, back and forth between the hands. After the first diamond and heart have been ruffed, you will be ruffing with high spades so that you can't be overruffed by the opponents. You will have used up all of your spades, so you can't ever draw trumps. How will you make out?

Counting the losers in your own hand with crossruffing in mind, you see that you have no spade losers (all of them will be used to ruff hearts with), no heart loser (your nine will be covered by the dummy's ace), no diamond losers (they will all be ruffed), and the three clubs will eventually lose.

Crossruffing is usually less dramatic than in the last hand, where all of your trumps were used for ruffing.

YOU	DUMMY	Your contract is 4 SPADES.
♠ A K Q 7 2	♠ J 10 9	The opening lead is the ♡K
♡ 6	♡ J 9 4 3	followed by the lead of the
◇ A K 4 3 2	◇ 6	♡A.
♣ 8 5	♣ A 10 9 7 2	

Here you count five losers but you hope to ruff your three small diamonds and make your contract. Again your problem is to get back to your own hand to continue the diamond ruffs, and again you must do it by ruffing hearts. You will use three spades from each hand for ruffs and be left with the ace and the king.

Before you start a crossruff, you should take any side tricks first—the ace of clubs in this example. The reason is that while you are ruffing hearts and diamonds, one of the opponents may not be able to follow suit and may take advantage of this to discard clubs.

Then when you finally get around to playing your ace of clubs, the opponent may be in a position to ruff it. The same applies to the ace and king of diamonds—you must TAKE (win with) them first before crossruffing.

After you lose the opening lead, trump the second lead, lead a club to the ace, and then lead the six of diamonds so that you can take your ace and king. Now go into your crossruff while the opponents sigh and make the best of it. They know that if they had led a spade on the opening lead, or even on their second lead, your crossruff would have been cut short.

Trump Management in Difficult Situations

In many hands you won't have complete control of the trumps. Here are some cases where you can skirt catastrophe.

YOU	DUMMY	Your contract is 4 HEARTS.
♠ K Q J 7 4	♠ 3 2	The opening lead is the ♣9, to
♡ A K Q 3	♡ J 6 4	which you play the king. The
◇ A K 4 2	◇ 8 7 5	third hand covers with the ace.
♣ —	♣ K Q J 8 6	

You are short of trumps and cannot ruff the opening trick for fear of being unable to draw trumps. However, when you are faced with making a ruff in the long hand, you often will have the alternative of discarding a loser for better results. In this case you can discard a diamond loser. Now the opponents cannot repeat their pumping action because your high clubs will win any club continuation.

YOU	DUMMY	Your contract is 4 HEARTS.
♠ 8 6	♠ 7 4 3	The opponents begin by leading
♡ A Q 7 5	♡ K J 10	three high spades.
◇ 9 8 5 3	◇ A K J	
♣ A Q 5	♣ K 8 4 2	

Again you do not want to ruff in the long hand, but you can discard a losing diamond. If the opponents should continue with another high spade, you could ruff in the short hand and discard another diamond—but they should not help you out by giving you a ruff and a sluff.

In the next hand, you have opened the bidding with 1 DIA-MOND, everybody passes and the dummy hand goes down on the table.

YOU	DUMMY	
♠ A 8 6 5	♠ 9 7 3 2	Your contract is 1 DIAMOND.
♡ A J 4 2	♡ 8	The opening lead is the ♠K.
◊ Q 3 2	◊ 9 6 4	← TRUMPS !@#?!
♣ A 4	♣ K 8 5 3 2	

Ouch! This doesn't happen very often, but when it does it usually means that the opponents should have bid but didn't. So don't panic—going down one will be a good score compared to what they would have made if they had bid.

Because the opponents have so many diamonds you cannot draw trumps. Neither can you make long cards good—they would only be trumped by all those diamonds which the opponents hold. What you need to do is to ruff with as many of your trumps as you can, using trumps from either hand, since they probably won't be any good otherwise.

Begin by winning the opening trick, then lead the ace of hearts and a low heart for a ruff. Get back to your hand with the ace of clubs and ruff again. Now lead the king of clubs, and if all has gone well you have taken six tricks. Now you can try leading another club and ruffing it—you may as well ruff with your queen since it won't do you any good later.

Now here is one more case where you can't draw trumps.

YOU	DUMMY	
♠ A K Q J 5	♠ 8 7 5	Your contract is 4 SPADES.
♡ A 5	♡ 9 7	The opening lead is the ♡K.
◊ 8 7 4 3	◊ A 9 2	
♣ 7 5	♣ A K Q J 4	

You confidently plan to discard two or three of your four losers on the long clubs and set out to draw trump. But when you lead the ace of spades, your left-hand opponent cannot follow suit! That means that your right-hand opponent has five of them! If you lead spades five times, he will win at the fifth time and merrily play hearts. In this case you can safely play spades four times and then start playing clubs. Sooner or later your right-hand opponent will be out of clubs and will be able to trump, but you have a trump left to stop the opponents' hearts and get the lead back to complete your contract.

What you have done is pump the opponent. He had to ruff one of your clubs or let you win the trick, and that got rid of his last trump while you held on to yours. The moral is that when only one opponent has trumps left, sometimes it is better to let him ruff than to try and draw his trumps. This is especially true when his trumps are higher than the ones you have left in your hand.

Inferences from the Bidding

If you pay attention to the bidding, you can often pick up some vital information:

You are playing at 4 SPADES after your right-hand opponent opened the bidding with 1 NOTRUMP.

> If your right-hand opponent has about 16 HCP and your side has about 24 HCP, then your left-hand opponent has just about 0 HCP. A finesse will work against your right-hand oponent, but not against your left-hand opponent.

You are playing at 4 SPADES after your left-hand opponent has opened the bidding with 3 DIAMONDS. His opening lead is the ♣5.

> Your left-hand opponent has seven diamonds (possibly plus or minus one). That means that he has few cards in the other

suits. A typical distribution is 7-3-2-1 and the club lead may be a singleton. He has very few high cards outside of diamonds, so if there is any high card in the other suits which your side does not have, it is probably held by your right-hand opponent.

You are playing at 4 HEARTS after your left-hand opponent overcalled in spades and your right-hand opponent raised the spades.

If you want to ruff some spades in the dummy, you don't have to worry much about being overruffed in the first three rounds—the chances are slight that the spade raise represents less than three spades.

You are playing at 4 HEARTS DOUBLED. The opponents were silent until your left-hand opponent came in with his double.

Your left-hand opponent must have most of the outstanding high cards to double without any indication that his partner has strength. He probably also has more than his fair share of the outstanding trumps, including any honors you are missing. So plan accordingly.

Perhaps hearts is his best suit and that is why he couldn't bid before.

Chapter 14 /////////////////////////////////

POINTERS
FOR THE
DEFENDERS

/////////////////////////////////

A
Signals

Signaling Attitude

When your partner breaks a suit, especially on the opening lead, he wants to know whether he should continue leading that suit or should shift to another suit. Sometimes you as the third hand will have to play a high card in order to win the trick or to force the fourth hand to play a higher card. But the rest of the time you will be free to discard one of your small cards. To the extent possible you use your discard to signal to your partner your attitude toward the suit which he has led.

At any time when you cannot follow suit, and therefore must discard from some other suit, you can use the attitude signal. A high discard asks your partner to lead the suit in which you discarded.

When your partner breaks a suit, or when you cannot follow suit, the attitude signal applies:

- Discard as high a card as you can afford if you want your partner to lead the suit in which you discarded.
- Discard your lowest card if you have no reason for your partner to lead the suit in which you discarded.

When your partner breaks a suit, there are two principal reasons for wanting your partner to continue the suit. One is because you have a doubleton and want to get a ruff. This is most effective when your partner has led a king, showing that he has the ace-king or the king-queen. The other reason is that you have a high card of equal value to an honor led by your partner. For example, if he leads the king and you hold the ace or the queen, you would make a high discard. If he leads the queen and you hold the ten you would also make a high discard since he has probably led from the queen-jack, which gives your ten equal value with the queen. When your partner gets the lead back he will normally continue the suit, having seen your high discard.

You must be sure to distinguish between when you are discarding and when you are not. Suppose you hold:

♠ K Q J 10 2

If your partner leads the ace of spades you must discard something. You want your partner to continue with spades so you signal with the *king,* the highest card you can afford. Thus the discard of an honor normally shows that you also hold the next lower honor but not the next higher one. If your partner leads a small card and the dummy plays the ace, again you signal with the king. But if both your partner and the dummy play small cards, you are not discarding—you are playing "third hand high" to force the fourth hand to play the ace. In that case you follow suit with the *ten,* the lowest of equals when you are not discarding.

When you break a new suit and your partner is able to discard, look very carefully for his attitude signal. However, since signals are not always reliable, look also at the dummy and at your own hand to see if there is any strong evidence for not trusting the signal. But always assume a true signal unless you find a good reason to doubt it. The same applies when your partner does not follow suit. Look at this as a signal in the suit where he has made his discard and try to evaluate it.

Apart from signals, you can often get a general idea of how many high cards your partner holds. If the opponents have reached a contract of 3 NOTRUMP they probably hold about 26 HCP, leaving about 14 HCP for your side. It is then an easy matter to subtract your own HCP from 14 to estimate your partner's holding. If the opponents are in 4 HEARTS or 4 SPADES, some of their count is probably in distribution, so your side probably has about 16 HCP. Again you can estimate your partner's holding and plan accordingly.

Signaling Count

When the declarer breaks a new suit, it is usually a suit which is favorable to him, not to you. Then there is no use for the attitude signal—your attitude is usually negative. But your partner can benefit from the COUNT SIGNAL, which tells him how many cards you hold in that suit. With that information, a look at his own hand and at the dummy will tell him how many cards the declarer holds in the suit.

When the declarer leads a suit and you are discarding, the count signal applies.

- If you currently hold an odd number of cards, discard the lowest card which you hold.
- If you currently hold an even number of cards, discard as high a small card as you can afford.

Usually the count signal gives more information to your partner than to the declarer, but when you get sophisticated enough to recognize an exception you may want to consider giving a false signal. Woe betide you if you lead your partner astray.

The declarer has led the ace of spades. How do you signal your count with the following holdings?

♠ 8 2	Discard the eight—the high discard signals an even length.
♠ 3 2	Discard the three. Your partner may think this is a low discard until later you discard the two.
♠ 9 5 3	Discard the three—your lowest card signals an odd length. When you make a second discard from spades you will then have an even length and will choose the nine.
♠ 9 7 3 2	The nine is a pretty high card and you can't be sure that you won't need it later. So discard the seven. You shouldn't waste a card on signaling which might take a trick later.
♠ K 7 3 2	Discard the seven—this does not signal that you hold the king, but that you hold an even length.

Here is a case where the count signal is essential.

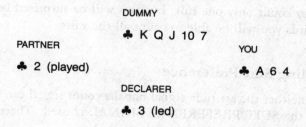

```
                    DUMMY
                 ♣ K Q J 10 7
     PARTNER
                                      YOU
    ♣ 2 (played)
                                    ♣ A 6 4
                   DECLARER
                   ♣ 3 (led)
```

You are defending against a notrump contract and at this point in time you see that there is no entry into the dummy except in clubs. If you play your ace just as the declarer plays his last club, he will have no more clubs to get to the dummy with. If the declarer has two clubs, you want to play your ace on the second round, but if he has three, you want to wait until the third round. Your partner's play of the two suggests that he holds an odd number, probably three. That leaves the declarer with two and so you do not play your ace until the second round. Of course your partner might only have one club, and then your careful calculation is all for nought.

If your partner had played a high club, you would expect him to have an even number of clubs. If he has two, the declarer has three and you will hold up your ace until the third round. Again it is possible that you have misjudged your partner's holding, but you have done the best you can.

With a good partner who gives count signals, you will come to depend on it. You have certainly experienced a situation like this: You have just two cards left in your hand, say a good club and a good diamond. The declarer leads a good card from another suit. You must discard something, but which card? If the declarer's last card is a club, you must keep your club, and likewise for diamonds. If your partner has previously signaled his length in clubs or diamonds, and you paid attention to it, you can figure out what the declarer holds now.

Counting the number of cards which each player has in each suit is the mark of the advanced player. It is difficult at first to think about count, but you too can learn once you feel ready to tackle the job. The bidding and your partner's signals are your clues. At first you may count only one suit, but you will be surprised how soon afterwards you will be able to count all the suits.

Signaling Suit Preference

When neither the attitude signal nor the count signal can possibly apply, the SUIT PREFERENCE SIGNAL is used. There is only one clear-cut case for the use of this signal.

Against a contract of 4 SPADES you hold:

♠ 8 5 4
♡ A K 8 3
◇ A 8 5
♣ 4 3 2

You make the opening lead of the king of hearts and your partner discards the nine. You continue with the ace and he discards the four. He obviously has a doubleton and wants to get a ruff. You plan to lead a heart, but you would like your partner to return diamonds, not clubs.

> When leading a card for your partner to ruff, the suit preference signal always applies.
>
> • Lead your lowest card if you wish your partner to return the lower of the other two side suits.
> • Lead the highest card you can afford if you wish your partner to return the higher of the other two side suits.

You lead the eight of hearts and a good partner will come back with a diamond. Now you can lead another heart for another ruff, setting the contract by two tricks.

You may see other cases where the other two signals cannot or should not apply and decide to use the suit preference signal. But your partner may not see it that way and you will be into an argument as to whether you did right or not. Probably it is best to stick to the given case for the suit preference signal unless you have a secure partnership which is ready to explore new possibilities.

Signaling in the Trump Suit

Suppose the declarer leads the ace of the trump suit and you hold two small trumps. Trumps are too valuable for ruffing to squander your higher trump so you discard your lower one. However, if you hold three small trumps, you are normally free to discard either of your two smaller ones. To signal to your partner that you hold three trumps and not two, you can discard the second highest. Later you discard your lowest trump, and this high-low sequence of discards promises that you hold a third trump. You can use this high-low sequence, often called an ECHO, not only when you are discarding trumps but also when you are leading from small trumps and when you are ruffing.

Some partnerships agree to use the trump signal only when there is a possibility for a future ruff. In that case the high-low echo in trumps means that one or more additional trumps are held and the other partner should try to figure out what suit to lead to bring about the ruff. This is probably the best use of the trump signal for you, if you use it at all.

NOTE: Some partnerships agree to use the trump signal strictly to indicate the length of the trump suit without considering the ruffing possibilities. They use the trump echo when holding three trumps but not when holding two or four. This use works best for experts, for whom count is more meaningful than it is for you.

B
Leads

Interpreting a Fourth-Highest Lead

When your partner breaks a suit with a low card and you believe it to be a fourth-highest lead, you want to take advantage of this situation. At notrump, when your partner makes the opening lead, he will frequently start with such a lead.

You have already learned to look for the cards below your partner's low lead. If you can locate all of them, he has only four cards in that suit, or possibly only three. If there is only one of the lower cards which you cannot locate, perhaps he holds it and therefore started with five cards, but perhaps not. If there are two lower cards missing, probably he holds at least one of them and did start with five or even six.

There is still another conclusion you can reach if the lead was truly the fourth highest in the suit.

DUMMY

♠ K 9 4

PARTNER

♠ 7 (led)

YOU

♠ A 10 2

Against a notrump contract your partner makes the opening lead of the seven of spades. You would like to keep your ace to put on the dummy's king later, so your first inclination is to play your ten. But wait! Since your partner has almost certainly made a fourth-highest lead, you use the RULE OF ELEVEN.

> When your partner makes a fourth-highest lead in some suit, subtract the size of the card led from eleven. The result is the number of cards in that suit in the other three hands which are larger than the card led.

Automatically you subtract seven from eleven and learn that there are four cards higher than the seven outside of your partner's hand. You can see all four of these cards, two in the dummy and two in your own hand. Thus you learn that the declarer has no card higher than the seven. There is no need to play your ace or even your ten. You can play your two and let your partner's seven win the trick. If you had played your ten, you would then be on lead and you could not continue spades without giving the dummy a trick with his king.

The rule of eleven is useful in a limited number of cases, but it gives you the edge when one of those cases comes up.

Special Indications for the Opening Lead

Occasionally the bidding gives you a special indication as to the best opening lead. You need to recognize these cases.

Lightner Slam Double. If your partner doubles a slam contract when you will have the opening lead, he is asking you to make an unusual lead, not the one you would have made without the double. That means that you should not lead trump or any suit which your side has bid. Usually the Lightner double is used against a slam in a suit and your partner may well have a void somewhere if you can only figure out where. Whatever the case, your partner is convinced that the slam will be defeated only if you find the unusual lead which his hand requires.

3 Notrump Doubled. Most good players use the double of a 3 NOTRUMP contract as a lead-directional bid when their partner will be on lead. If your partnership is on this wavelength, and your partner doubles the opponents' notrump game contract, he wants you to be sure and lead the suit which your side has been bid and not be frightened off by the opponents who apparently have a stopper in your suit. If your side has not bid, then he wants you to lead the first suit bid by the dummy. If the dummy hasn't bid, then lead your shortest suit and hope that your partner has a very large number of cards in that suit.

Takeout Double Converted to Penalty. If you make a takeout double, your left-hand opponent passes, and then your partner passes, his only excuse for such an action (other than temporary insanity) is a long strong holding in the opponents' proposed trump suit. If the opponents leave the contract there, you must unconditionally lead a trump. Once the opponents' trumps are drawn with the help of your partner's strong holding, your side's other high cards can bring about the set without being trumped.

Artificial Bid Doubled. If your partner doubles an opponent's artificial bid, such as a Stayman club bid or a Blackwood response, he is asking for the lead of that suit. Of course he must feel quite sure that the opponents cannot possibly play in that suit or his double may backfire.

Long Suit in the Dummy. When the dummy has bid what is apparently a long suit, but that suit does not become trump, you should go into emergency mode. The declarer will try to draw trump and then play the dummy's suit while discarding his losers in some other side suit. Your side must get to its winners as soon as possible before this can happen. If you have one or more high cards in a suit which the opponents have not bid, that is probably the suit to lead—even if you hold a tenace or a doubleton honor which you would not normally lead away from. Yes, you may give away a trick by this dangerous lead, but more often you will save the day.

The Opening Lead Against a Small Slam

The question of whether to lead an ace against a small slam arises frequently. While opinion is mixed, generally the answer is yes if you are playing duplicate for matchpoints and do not suspect that an opponent is void in that suit. The reason is that, if nothing else, it will prevent the opponents from making seven odd tricks, and the overtrick is very important in duplicate. Conversely, the answer generally is no at other forms of bridge where the number of points made is the score. Then preventing the overtrick is of little importance but setting the slam is of greatest importance. Leading your ace may help the declarer make his slam contract in the same way that it can help the declarer make other contracts.

If you hold two aces against good opponents, the chances are very great that they have a void in one of the suits, but against lesser opponents you may be able to cash both aces and destroy their morale. Holding an ace-king, the king is usually a good lead, but it may be difficult to know whether to continue with your ace—the declarer may have started with a singleton. Your partner's signal and the cards in the dummy may help your decide.

A lead from a king-queen or any 3-card sequence headed by an honor is a safe lead against any contract. When you also hold an ace in another suit, a lead from a good sequence may establish the second trick that you need to defeat a small slam. Against a notrump slam contract, a lead from a long suit is fruitless unless the suit is headed by a 3-card sequence. You have to count on high cards, not long cards, to defeat any slam.

When you don't have a good lead against a small slam, a safe lead is best, one which won't lose a trick that you wouldn't have lost in any case. A trump lead from small trumps is a favorite lead—it tends to be safe and may reduce needed ruffing power in the dummy. Leading top of nothing also is usually safe. But leading away from a single honor is unsafe—this kind of lead works only when your partner also has an honor in the same suit, and this is unlikely against a slam contract.

The Opening Lead Against a Grand Slam

Good opponents are cautious about going into a grand slam, so you are unlikely to win the first trick. If you don't have a strong sequence to lead from, play it very safe. A trump lead from small trumps may work. If you don't give away a trick, the opponents may make a mistake or simply find that they have to give you a trick. This is not the time for signals which will help the declarer decipher your hand, although occasionally a count signal will help your partner know what to discard. Attitude and suit preference signals are only useful if your partner gets on lead, but then the contract is already defeated.

Chapter 15 ////////////////////////////////////

SPECIAL
SITUATIONS
////////////////////////////////////

A
When There Is A Partscore

General Notions

In rubber bridge and Chicago bridge, the score for odd tricks bid
and made may be accumulated over several hands to make a game.
If in one deal you bid 2 SPADES and make three, the two tricks
which you contracted for count 60 points toward a game. You now
have a partscore (also called a PARTIAL) of 60. A total of 100 such
points, won over one or more deals, makes a game. Once a game is
made, any partscore held by either side can no longer be used
toward making the next game. A fuller explanation of rubber
bridge and Chicago bridge is contained in the appendix.

A partscore of 20 or 30 does not change your subsequent
bidding very much. To complete the game you must bid at least to
the 3-level, and when you are strong enough to do that, the
opponents won't be interfering very much unless they are able to
preempt. You will bid rather normally, but you will stop at the
lowest level where you have a fit and sufficient score for game.

There is no reason to go higher unless the opponents are outbidding you or you feel that you may have a slam.

In the same sense, when the opponents have a small partscore, your bidding will not change. But when one side or the other has an ADVANCED PARTSCORE of 40 or more, your tactics have to be modified.

YOU HAVE AN ADVANCED PARTSCORE (MAYBE THEY DO TOO)

When you have an advanced partscore, 40 or more, you can conceivably complete your game with a successful contract at the 1-level or 2-level. But if you can bid no higher than that, the opponents will certainly be bidding also—they will seldom let you play at the 2-level and almost never at the 1-level. When you have an advanced partscore, you can expect a competition unless it is evident that one side has the preponderance of points. Therefore, unless your hand is extra strong or extra weak, you must prepare for competition right from your first bid. This is particularly true if the opponents also have an advanced partscore.

With an advanced partscore, you will want to open the bidding aggressively and respond to your partner's opening bid aggressively. If you hold a good 5-card suit, you should open with as little as 11 points, much as if you were overcalling. When your partner opens the bidding and you can support his suit, do so even if you are a point or two below the usual 6 points. If you cannot make a raise, stretch a little bit to make some other bid. Of course if it turns out that you both have overbid, you may not fare so well, but the prospects for a game make the risk worthwhile. Besides, the opponents may bid their own suit rather than doubling you, rescuing you from your own problem.

In any competition, the side with the spades has the advantage—they can outbid any other suit without going up another level. The heart suit is somewhat less advantageous, but at least it is better than a minor. But if you hold both hearts and spades, you are in the best position of all. When you are well fixed to play in spades, you may open with a point or two below normal.

When your side has an advanced partscore, phase one of your bidding will go along as usual—the process of finding a fit remains the same. If your partner bids a suit at the 1-level and you have support, you will raise it to the 2-level even if it is not necessary to complete your game. The opponents will not let you play at the 1-level if they can help it, and by raising immediately you may keep them out of the bidding altogether. If your partner makes a 2-over-1 response which completes your game, you may consider passing with support for his suit. But even though you are already at the 2-level, you have to consider whether you are giving the opponents a chance to bid by passing instead of raising.

With an advanced partscore, you will stop at the end of phase one if you have already bid high enough to complete your game. If the opponents outbid you, then you have to consider whether to bid again, to pass or to double. But otherwise, if the captain proceeds into phase two after a constructive limit bid has been made by your side, and the bid was not necessary to complete a game, he must have a slam in mind. Such a bid is a slam invitation and is not forcing unless it is a jump bid. In the same sense, if phase one ends with a jump limit bid, and the same bid without the jump would have completed your game, the jump is a slam invitation.

A major problem, when the case arises, is stopping at game at a low level and thereby missing a slam. To help avoid this, several bids remain forcing even if they would complete your game. A jump shift is still forcing and an opening strong two bid is still forcing, both bids becoming forcing for *one round*. There is no standard procedure for an opening strong artificial 2 CLUBS because it has been used mostly for duplicate. It is sensible to allow the bidding to stop at 2 NOTRUMP or 3 in a major or 4 in a minor if game has been reached and neither partner has made a jump bid.

ONLY THE OPPONENTS HAVE AN ADVANCED PARTCORE

When the opponents have an advanced partscore and you do not, they have an advantage over you. If you make a sacrifice to prevent them from making a game, their partscore will still be there for the next hand and they will still have the same advantage over you. Therefore, when you are preempting in this situation, cut your overbid margin by one trick. You do not want to lose more than 300 points to stop their game, which means going down by one trick doubled and vulnerable, or two tricks doubled and not vulnerable.

The other side of the coin is your own lack of an advanced partscore. If you have the opportunity to make a game yourself, you will have to go all the way to the normal game level (or possibly one level less if you have a small partscore). You will need your normal bidding methods to get there. Thus, when it is the opponents who have the partscore, the only difference in your tactics is to be cautious not to over-sacrifice.

B

When Opening

Distributional Opening Hands

Sometimes you will have a hand which adds up to 13 points, but many of the points will be in distribution. It is always necessary to distinguish between hands which contain a fair share of HCP and those which are short of HCP but contain a lot of playing tricks or have a high total count. Therefore, when your hand contains a lot of distribution points, check to see that it contains at least 10 HCP before you make a constructive opening bid. You must not open without 10 HCP unless you can open with a preemptive bid.

♠ —
♡ K 9 8 6 5 4
◇ Q 7
♣ A 10 7 3 2

Here there are 13 points but only 9 HCP so an opening bid of 1 HEART would not be appropriate. A 2-suited hand does not lend itself to preempting, so this hand has to be passed until someone else opens.

Duplicate players know the advantage of having their side make the opening bid. Playing at matchpoints, they will open a 12-point hand if they hold a good 5-card suit. But this is less successful at other forms of scoring.

Opening Third Hand

When your partner is the dealer, he is the FIRST HAND and you are the THIRD HAND in the bidding. If the bidding starts with two passes, you are in a position to open as the third hand. If your hand is not too strong, you may stop to wonder where all the points are. Your partner has shown that he has less than 13 points and so has your right-hand opponent. Either everyone has a little and any bidding is going to be a competition for a partscore, or your left-hand opponent has a lot of points and your only chance to make a bid may be right now.

With as little as 11 points you can open the bidding as the third hand. Usually you will hold a good 5-card suit or will have 10 HCP when you are below the normal opening strength.

Opening Fourth Hand

When the bidding starts with three passes, you are the fourth hand. If you pass, the opponents will get no chance to bid. There is no reason for you to make a preemptive bid in this position since you can shut them out by passing. Neither do you want to make a constructive opening bid only to have the opponents outbid you.

When you open fourth hand, you should hold the normal strength for an opening hand or else you should hold spades. Holding spades, you can outbid the opponents at the same level as any overcall they may make. In that case you might consider opening the bidding a point or two under strength, especially at duplicate.

Choosing the Suit

When opening the bidding as the third hand or as the fourth hand, holding 11, 12 or even 13 points, many players will choose to bid a good 4-card major in preference to a 3-card minor or a poor 4-card minor. Their lack of strength suggests that a competition is about to begin and they do not want to get their partner off to a bad lead if the opponents take the contract. This will deceive their partner as to the length of the suit and so it must be done with caution.

When you are opening the bidding without a 5-card suit and have to choose between two 4-card minors (or between two 4-card majors, third or fourth hand), it is better to choose the higher ranking. You may very well want to bid both suits eventually. By starting with the higher ranking you will not have to reverse to bid the other one. This exception to the general guideline for picking suits occurs only on the opening bid.

C
When Responding

Highly Distributional Responding Hands

Here again you must distinguish between hands which hold their proper share of HCP and those which promise to take tricks without holding many HCP. Any constructive single-jump raise should be based on a hand which contains at least 10 HCP. With less you may be able to make a preemptive raise—a double or triple jump raise (but not above the level of game).

Once in a great while you may respond with a preemptive bid in a new suit. Suppose you hold a hand which could open 3 SPADES but your partner beats you out by opening 1 CLUB. You can still respond 3 SPADES, because this is a double jump and therefore shows a preemptive type of hand. (However, sophisticated players sometimes make another use of these bids.)

Hearts Over Spades

If your partner opens 1 SPADE, almost any hand on which you would want to bid 2 HEARTS will contain at least 5 hearts. With only four hearts, you will normally also have four clubs or four diamonds which you would bid first. Your partner will be counting on you for five hearts when he hears you bid hearts. Therefore, if that rare hand occurs where you are tempted to bid 2 HEARTS over 1 SPADE with only four hearts, bid a 3-card minor if necessary to avoid deceiving your partner. If he has four hearts also, he will bid them next so you will not lose the heart fit.

If you are the opener at 1 SPADE and hear your partner reply 2 HEARTS, you can raise hearts with only three of them. This is an important inference since a major suit is involved.

Bidding as a Passed Responder

When you have passed before your partner opens the bidding, you will necessarily hold something less than 13 points. If he opens in a suit, none of your bids will be forcing. Any jump bid you make will be based on a hand close to opening strength—11 or 12 points. Any 2-over-1 response you make will be based on a 5-card suit because your partner may need to pass rather than go any higher in view of your limited hand. If a fit with your partner brings your hand up to 13 points or more, you must give a jump raise all the way to the 4-level.

If you pass and then your partner opens in notrump, your bidding will be the same as if you had not passed. You may easily have enough for game even though you passed originally.

Combating the Opponents' Takeout Double

Perhaps your partner has opened the bidding and your right-hand opponent makes a takeout double. For example:

PARTNER	RHO	YOU
1 HEART	DOUBLE	???

There is a simple guideline which will suffice until you become quite sophisticated:

> **When your right-hand opponent makes a takeout double, REDOUBLE with 10 HCP or more.** *Any* other bid shows less than 10 HCP and is nonforcing.

The redouble, although strong, is not forcing. With a balanced hand, the opener usually passes to see what the responder wants to do next. However, he will do better to bid if his hand is unbalanced.

When you have less than 10 HCP, the strength may very well be divided between the two sides, and a competition for a partscore is likely to develop. With a fit for your partner, you should raise his suit even if you are short a point or two from the usual raise. With no fit, you can escape into any promising long suit, even at the two level, without holding a lot of points and without forcing your partner to bid again. Your partner should be cautious about bidding again unless your first response was a redouble.

NOTE: Most sophisticated players make an exception to the guideline, treating a new suit at the *one* level as unlimited and forcing, the same as if the double had not been made. This practice has not yet filtered down to the social players.

If you are on the receiving side of a redouble—your partner made a takeout double and your right-hand opponent redoubled—your side needs an escape. If you have any preference as to the suit your side might play in, bid it. If not, pass and leave it up to your partner to pick a suit.

What would you bid in the following cases, neither side vulnerable?

YOU	PARTNER	RHO
	1 HEART	DOUBLE

???

♠ 3 2
♡ 8 6 4
◇ Q 8 5 3
♣ Q J 5 4

Bid 2 HEARTS. It may keep your left-hand opponent from bidding, preventing him and his partner from finding a fit (which probably exists in spades).

♠ A 8
♡ 9 8 4 2
◇ A 10 8 5 3 2
♣ 7

You have only 8 HCP so you can't redouble. But your total count is high—you count an extra point for the 9-card fit and an extra point for the singleton, giving you 12 points in all. Low HCP and good distribution are the hallmarks of a preempt. Jump to 4 HEARTS.

♠ A J 8 4
♡ 10 9
◇ K Q 4 3
♣ K 4 3

Now a REDOUBLE is right. You do not have a fit for your partner unless he bids his hearts a second time or offers a second suit such as diamonds. You might end up bidding 3 NOTRUMP. Or you might double the opponents for penalty when they bid to keep you from playing in 1 HEART RE-DOUBLED.

♠ K Q 10 8 5
♡ J 8
◇ K 9
♣ 7 5 4 3

You have no fit and you hold only 9 HCP. Bid 1 SPADE. With another HCP you would REDOUBLE and plan to bid spades later (unless you have adopted the expert practice which allows you to bid your spades regardless of the extra HCP).

♠ 8 7
♡ 9
◇ 6 4 3 2
♣ A J 10 8 7 5

This distributional hand contains only 5 HCP. Your side will be in trouble if your LHO decides to pass for penalties instead of taking out the double. Bid 2 CLUBS. That will be at least as good a fit as you have in spades. Besides, it is better to play in the suit belonging to the weak hand.

The Negative Double

The NEGATIVE DOUBLE is a convention currently placed in Class B, but it is more important than some of those in Class A. Suppose your partner opens the bidding with 1 DIAMOND and you plan to respond with 1 HEART holding:

♠ 8 7
♡ K Q 7 5
◇ Q 3 2
♣ J 9 8 6

However, your right-hand opponent overcalls with 1 SPADE, leaving you frustrated. Since you seldom want to double a low-level overcall for penalties, the idea was born to use a double in this situation for takeout instead of for penalty. If you agree with your partner to use the negative double, the following applies.

If your partner's opening bid of 1 in a SUIT is immediately overcalled by a bid no higher than 2 SPADES, a DOUBLE by you is for takeout. You must hold:

- Four or more cards in each of the two unbid suits (if there is an unbid major and an unbid minor, you may have less than four cards in the unbid minor)
- 6 points if your partner can respond at the 1-level or 2-level
- 10 points if your partner can respond only at the 3-level

DEVALUATE YOUR HAND WHEN MAKING A NEGATIVE DOUBLE.

NOTE: Many partnerships make the negative double apply even if the overcall is as high as 3 SPADES. This is a good agreement if you are playing duplicate for matchpoints, but it is not as easy to handle.

The negative double asks your partner to take out the double into an unbid major suit if he holds four cards in that suit. If he cannot comply, he may take out in an unbid minor or otherwise bid as best he can. He may have to take out with only three cards in your suit and you may end up in a poor contract. That is why you must devaluate your hand, counting only HCP, when you figure your strength for a negative double.

After a negative double, both partners give up their forcing ability except that a cue bid in an opponent's suit remains forcing. Therefore all other bids after a negative double must be full-value bids. They must be as high as the perceived fit and partnership total permit.

YOU	PARTNER	RHO
	1 CLUB	1 SPADE

???

♠ 8 2
♡ K 9 8 5
♢ K 8 5 3
♣ 7 6 4

You have four hearts and want to find a fit in that suit. Make a negative DOUBLE. You can safely pass whatever your partner bids, so you can get by with a minimum 6 HCP. With poorer distribution you should have a little extra strength.

YOU	PARTNER	RHO
	1 CLUB	1 DIAMOND

???

♠ K Q 7 4
♡ A J 3 2
♢ K 9 7
♣ 8 4

DOUBLE for takeout. You have four hearts and four spades. You plan to jump to 4 in the major which your partner chooses, or to 3 NOTRUMP if he rebids his clubs.

YOU	PARTNER	RHO
	1 CLUB	1 HEART
???		

♠ A 8 7 3
♡ K 5 4 2
◇ 9 6 5
♣ Q 4

DOUBLE for takeout, then pass any minimum response by your partner. Your shortage in diamonds is more than made up by your extra HCP. If you had five spades, you should bid them rather than double.

YOU	PARTNER	RHO
	1 CLUB	1 SPADE
???		

♠ 9 7 5
♡ A J 8 5 2
◇ 7 5
♣ Q 5 3

Except for the overcall, you could have bid 1 HEART. You are not strong enough to bid 2 HEARTS but you can make a negative double. If your partner bids 2 CLUBS you can pass. If he bids 2 DIAMONDS you can escape with a nonforcing 2 HEARTS, but keep your fingers crossed. *Note:* Add a king to this hand and you should bid 2 HEARTS rather than double.

YOU	PARTNER	RHO
	1 HEART	2 SPADES (weak jump overcall)
???		

♠ 7 4 2
♡ J 3
◇ K J 7 4
♣ A J 5 3

There is no unbid major, but you hold four cards in each minor. DOUBLE, then PASS any response your partner chooses (except, of course, a cue bid of 3 SPADES).

D

When on the Defense

Balancing Over the Opening Bid

When a bid by your left-hand opponent is followed by two passes, you are in the PASSOUT SEAT—if you pass, the bidding will end. For example:

YOUR LHO	PARTNER	YOUR RHO	YOU
1 DIAMOND	PASS	PASS	???

Obviously your left-hand opponent has at least an opening hand and your right-hand opponent has next to nothing. You have some number of points, but where are the balance of the points? If your partner has a large share of them, your side may have a game in spite of the opening bid by the opponents. Even if he only has a moderate share of the balance of the strength, your side may be able to put up a fight for a partscore rather than give the contract to the opponents for a mere 1 DIAMOND.

When you make the first defensive bid for your side from the passout seat, you are making a BALANCING BID because it is based on certain assumptions as to where the balance of the points lie. In general, when making a balancing bid, you should bid as if you had 3 points more than you actually have.

	POINTS FOR NORMAL BID	POINTS FOR BALANCING BID
Overcall at 1-level	11 nominal	8 nominal
Overcall at 2-level	14 nominal	11 nominal
Takeout double	13	10
1 NOTRUMP overcall	16,17,18	13,14,15

This assumes that you have a knowledgeable partner who will subtract 3 points from his actual holding when deciding how to respond to your balancing bid.

NOTE: Experts balance with 1 NOTRUMP holding even fewer points. This is not for you. They may also balance with an offshape takeout double, perhaps with a 2-card minor. They accept some risk while hoping that their partner may be able to pass for penalties. (Their partner may have passed because his best holding was in the opponents' suit.)

Balancing after a Fit

When the opponents have found a fit but they have stopped bidding at the *2-level,* you can tell even more about the balance of the points.

YOUR LHO	PARTNER	YOUR RHO	YOU
		1 DIAMOND	PASS
2 DIAMONDS	PASS	PASS	???

If the opponents have stopped bidding at the 2-level in spite of having a fit, they must have only a limited amount of strength between them. In fact, your side will have about as much strength as their side has—about 19 to 22 partnership points including distribution. Don't worry if you are short of points because your partner will surely have the balance of the points to bring your side up to that total. But don't be over-optimistic if you have a lot of points because that only leaves a few for your partner. Your side should be safe at the 2-level with this total, but the 3-level will be out of reach unless you find a long (at least 9-card) trump fit.

When the opponents have found a fit, the chances are excellent that your side will also have a fit somewhere. If you have a good 5-card suit and you can overcall at the 2-level, do so. In these favorable circumstances you can stretch the nominal points for a balancing overcall considerably (7 or 8 will do) and you can overbid your playing tricks by four instead of by three.

For a takeout double the points are not nominal and you should not go below the 10 points needed for a balancing takeout double. But if you have the points and the right shape, and your partner has room to respond at the 2-level in at least one suit, make the takeout double.

When the opponents' fit is at 2 SPADES, it is difficult to make either an overcall or a takeout double with any safety—there is no room left at the 2-level. You should almost never try to balance over 2 SPADES when vulnerable. But you might occasionally give it a go, not vulnerable, with a shapely hand—perhaps overcalling on a 6-card suit or making a takeout double on perfect 4-4-4-1 distribution.

If you make a balancing bid and then the opponents bid on, don't chase after them unless you have found a long trump fit. They may well have gone too high. You will need rather good distribution to be bidding at the 3-level. If the opponents make a series of bids and still do not seem to have found a fit, this is not the time for you to balance. Theory says that if one side does not have a fit, the other side probably does not either.

E

When Using Conventions

Advanced Features of Blackwood

You may want to pass over this section, which describes some features of Blackwood that are seldom needed. Besides, most social players are not familiar with them. Therefore, before you use any of these features, be sure that your partner understands them.

Replying to Blackwood with a Void. When you hold a *useful* void (not in a suit your partner has bid), you may reply to a Blackwood 4 NOTRUMP in the suit dictated by the number of aces which you hold, but at the 6-level instead of at the 5-level. You may suppress the showing of a void and show only your aces when you judge that to be best.

Replying to Blackwood After Interference. If the opponents interject a bid immediately after your partner bids a Blackwood 4 NOTRUMP, you may reply using a convention called DOPI (pronounced "dopey"). The two parts of the name, DO and PI, suggest the bid to make:

When replying to Blackwood after interference, use DOPI:

- Double with O (zero) aces (DO),
- Pass with I (one) ace (PI),
- Bid the next available denomination (even notrump) with 2 aces,
- Bid up one more denomination with 3 aces,
- And still one more with 4 aces.

DOPI can also be used with the Gerber convention.

Getting into 5 Notrump After Blackwood. On rare occasions, after you have bid a Blackwood 4 NOTRUMP and received your partner's reply, you may decide that you need to be in 5 NOTRUMP. If you now bid 5 NOTRUMP yourself, you would be asking for kings, but if you bid a suit which your side has not bid before, you are asking your partner to bid 5 NOTRUMP which you will then pass. The main use for this comes when your suit is clubs or diamonds and you find that your partner does not have enough aces to go on to a small slam. If your partner's reply precludes stopping at 5 CLUBS or 5 DIAMONDS, then 5 NOTRUMP may be the only hopeful contract.

NOTE: This practice is not used with Gerber since it is not necessary. 4 NOTRUMP and 5 NOTRUMP bids are natural when using Gerber.

Advanced Considerations with Stayman

If you respond to your partner's 1 NOTRUMP with a Stayman 2 CLUBS and then bid a minor at your next turn, you are showing a strong hand which will make at least a game in your minor. For this reason, many partnerships agree that an immediate response of 3 CLUBS or 3 DIAMONDS is a "drop dead" bid based on minimum values and at least a 6-card suit. With a strong hand they will start with Stayman with or without a 4-card major and then bid their minor. This agreement is a small departure from the guidelines given previously, but is valuable for the rare occasions when it is applicable.

Sometimes, after your partner opens or overcalls with 1 NOTRUMP, the next opponent interferes by putting in a bid. Generally you will not want to play in notrump when this happens, but there are exceptions when you have the opponent's suit stopped.

With an invitational hand, you may find it profitable to double the opponents. You might bid 2 NOTRUMP instead, but the payoff is usually greater with a double. And lastly, you might bid a 5-card suit. "Drop dead" bids no longer apply. There is no need to rescue your side from a bad notrump since the opponents have already done that. When you hold less than invitational values you will merely pass.

With game-going values you may double the interfering bid or jump in a 5-card major or perhaps bid 3 NOTRUMP if that looks better than doubling. If this is a hand on which you would have used Stayman if the interference had not made it impossible, a cue bid in the opponents' suit (the interfering suit) may be used as a substitute for Stayman. This artifice asks your partner to bid a 4-card major if possible or otherwise to bid 3 NOTRUMP. As with other advanced devices, be sure your partner understands this one before you use it.

When your partner opens or overcalls with 1 NOTRUMP and the next opponent interferes with a DOUBLE, it is still possible to bid 2 CLUBS. For the sake of simplicity, you may wish to use this bid as Stayman, but sophisticated partnerships declare Stayman to be OFF (not in effect) after a penalty double while "drop dead" bids remain ON. This allows 2 CLUBS to be used as a natural bid, like a 2-bid in any other suit, to escape from an unhealthy notrump.

F

When Depressed About Your Bridge

Your Mistakes Loom Large

So you think you are unique? Every bridge player at every level makes mistakes. But the more you play, the more you recognize where you are going wrong and the more you see how to avoid it. Study and reading about bridge will accelerate this process. Everybody gets depressed at times. There is a story about a famous expert player who seemed quite moody after a tournament session. Suddenly, in the middle of dinner he cried out, "I could have made that last contract!" Even though it took quite a time before he could even identify what his mistake was, he had the depressed feeling that he had made one and couldn't get it off his mind.

To play bridge and enjoy it, you have to be comfortable about making mistakes. But not all things which go wrong are mistakes. None of us can foresee exactly how the cards will lie, so we have to accept some poor results, even from our most brilliant efforts.

Some people like rubber bridge because it tends to conceal their mistakes. A poor result for a session of rubber can just as easily stem from a run of poor cards coming their way. Duplicate may seem more stern, in that you have an immediate comparison of your own results with those of others. But you will often be surprised to find out that others also made that same 4 SPADE bid that you did and that they also went down two. And perhaps someone went down three.

A lot of bridge is skillful guesswork. Concentrate on building up your skill. Look at why the mistake was made without bewailing it. Then enjoy the game and leave the past behind.

YOU'VE BEEN DOUBLED!
We all have. Erase the exclamation mark.

Once that you have decided not to panic, you can handle it. You may go down, but that's bridge. Just don't rush out to bid another suit unless you feel the situation won't be any worse. An SOS redouble may help, if your partnership uses that gadget. But most of the time it is better to stay with the present contract rather than to seek out a nonexistent better contract—the opponents have already considered that you might run out to another contract and are waiting to double you there too.

YOU DOUBLED THEM AND THEY MADE IT
Not all of your doubles will result in a set, but most of them should. If you only double a sure thing, you are much too timid. This is normal at first, because your defense may not be very strong. But if the opponents are at your level, their declarer play won't be any stronger than your defense. On the other hand, it is sensible to be just a little conservative in doubling stronger opponents. Test the water with some doubles and you will learn how far you can go.

YOU HAVE TO PLAY THE SLAM
Slams are usually easier to play because you have all the big cards. In any case, they are no more difficult than any other hand. It is true that at rubber bridge a lot of points are riding on the result. But that is what makes rubber bridge exciting and fun. At duplicate, a slam contract is just another hand where you will either do better or worse than the competition—the others who play the same hand. That takes the tension off of a slam hand, which is often harder to bid than to play.

YOU HAVE BIG-NAME OPPONENTS

Most opponents are friendly, no matter how big their reputation is. Not only that, they are tolerant of your mistakes and may even give you some pointers on the hand if you ask after the play is over. No truly good player is scornful of your ignorance, since he or she was once in just the same position you are in now.

The myth that runs through the mind of the average player is that the super players will make one big score after another, defeat all his contracts, and generally make him look foolish. Nonsense! No player can make a two into an ace. Expert players make whatever they can out of the cards which are dealt to them. It is true that they seldom make mistakes and give you an undeserved trick, but whatever you can make without the help of a mistake is probably what you will make against any opposition.

YOU'RE HOOKED

Welcome to the club!

APPENDIX

APPENDIX

A
Rubber Bridge

The Rubber

In rubber bridge, the opposing sides play to win two games out of three. This match is called a RUBBER. Bonus points are scored for winning the rubber, no bonus points being given on each deal or after each game. A game may be stretched over more than one deal, so a rubber requires a variable number of deals to complete.

The first side to accumulate 100 points for odd tricks that were contracted for and made wins the current game. Bidding and making 3 NOTRUMP would score 100 points, 4 HEARTS or 4 SPADES would score 120 points, 5 CLUBS or 5 DIAMONDS would score 100 points, so any of these would win a game. However you could also win a game by bidding and making 2 SPADES (60 points) in one deal and then bidding and making 3 HEARTS (90 points) in the next deal. The two together would be more than enough to win a game.

Scoring Rubber Bridge

The score pad for rubber bridge is arranged to keep track of the progress of the game and the rubber. It has a printed line across it, which is simply called THE LINE.

WE	THEY
40	

If you are keeping the score, you put the score for your side in the WE column and the score for the opponents in the THEY column.

Suppose on the first deal of the rubber, your side bid and made 2 DIAMONDS. You write 40 points below the line. Since 40 points makes only part of a game, it is called a PARTSCORE.

WE	THEY
20	
40	
80	

Perhaps on the next deal your side bids 4 CLUBS, but makes five. The four that you bid gives you 80 points toward a game and you write this below the line. The overtrick gives you 20 points but this is written just above the line to keep it separate from the points which count toward game.

Now you have 120 points below the line, so you have completed a game. You draw a line below the 80 to mark the end of the game. You now start anew to build up points for your next game.

In rubber bridge, you become vulnerable when you have won a game. You are now vulnerable but the opponents are not.

WE	THEY
20	100
40	
80	
90	

Now you bid 3 HEARTS which you just make. You get 90 points below the line toward your next game.

On the next deal you try to complete your game, but the opponents manage to set you by 1 trick. They score 100 points because you are vulnerable. This goes above the line on their side.

WE	THEY
500	
50	
20	100
40	
80	
90	120
140	
920	220

On the next deal the opponents bid 4 SPADES and make their contract. They score 120 points below the line. Now you both have won a game, you both are vulnerable, and your 90 points no longer count toward the next game.

Fortunately you now bid and make 2 NOTRUMP DOUBLED. The 70 points for your two odd tricks is doubled, giving you 140 points below the line for a second game. You draw a double line to indicate the end of the rubber and you give yourself 50 points above the line for making a doubled contract and 500 points above the line for winning the rubber, two games out of three.

Now you can total the points for the rubber. You have won 920 points to their 220. (If you had won the first two games, that would have ended the rubber and you would have received 700 points instead of 500.) For the next rubber you can change partners or opponents or continue as before.

There are a few special things to note about rubber bridge. If you decide to stop playing before a rubber is finished, any one side which has won a game receives 300 points and any one side which has won a partscore toward the next game receives 50 points. In all forms of bridge except duplicate, if either side holds four of the five honors in the trump suit, that side gets 100 points above the line. For holding all five trump honors or for holding the four aces when the contract is notrump, that side receives 150 points. At rubber bridge, if a deal is passed out, no score is awarded and the deal passes to the next player.

Rubber Bridge Scoring Summary

TRICK SCORE awarded *below* the line:

To declarer's side for odd tricks BID AND MADE when the contract is in . . .	NOTRUMP	NOTRUMP	♠ or ♡	◇ or ♣
	FIRST TRICK	ADDITIONAL TRICKS	EACH TRICK	EACH TRICK
Undoubled	40	30	30	20
Doubled	80	60	60	40
Redoubled	160	120	120	80

PREMIUM SCORE awarded *above* the line:

To the declarer's side for making the contract when the declarer is . . .	Not Vulnerable	Vulnerable
For a small slam	500	750
For a grand slam	1000	1500
For each overtrick		
Undoubled in ♠, ♡, NOTRUMP	30	30
Undoubled in ♣ or ◇	20	20
Doubled	100	200
Redoubled	200	400
For making any doubled or redoubled contract	50	50

To the defenders' side for setting the contract when the declarer is . . .	Not Vulnerable		Vulnerable	
	FIRST UNDERTRICK	ADDITIONAL UNDERTRICKS	FIRST UNDERTRICK	ADDITIONAL UNDERTRICKS
Undoubled	50	50	100	100
Doubled	100	200	200	300
Redoubled	200	400	400	600

To either side for:

Winning a rubber two games to none	700
Winning a rubber, two games to one	500
Winning the only game in an UNFINISHED rubber	300
Winning the only partscore in an UNFINISHED game	50
Holding four of the five trump honors	100
Holding all five trump honors	150
Holding all four aces at a notrump contract	150

B
Chicago Bridge

The Chukker

Chicago bridge has been popular mainly as a money game, but it can also serve as a purely social game. Chicago is a form of progressive bridge where four deals make a round, or a CHUK- KER as it is commonly called. As in rubber bridge, a partscore carries over to the next deal within the chukker, but not from one chukker to the next. A total of 100 points accumulated for odd tricks bid and made complete a game.

NOTE: First read about rubber bridge in order to understand Chicago bridge.

As in all progressive bridge, on the first deal neither side is vulnerable, on the second and third deals only the dealer's side is vulnerable, and on the last deal both sides are vulnerable. If a deal is passed out, it does not count as one of the four deals and the same player deals again.

NOTE: For Chicago bridge, some players prefer to have only the nondealer's side vulnerable on the second and third deals.

When a game is completed, a game bonus is awarded immediately according to the vulnerability of the side on the deal which completed the game. This is instead of a rubber bonus since there is no rubber in Chicago bridge. The scoring is otherwise the same as for rubber bridge except for a partscore bonus on the fourth hand, as noted below.

Scoring Chicago Bridge

The score pad for Chicago bridge is identical to that for rubber bridge except that it has a large X at the top. You can use a score pad for rubber bridge and draw the X yourself.

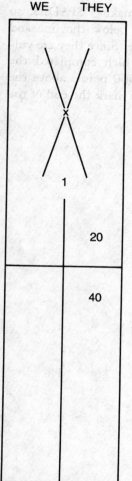

As the first deal of the chukker begins, a 1 is written in the section of the X which faces the dealer. Here we assume that you are keeping score and that you are the dealer.

Suppose their side bids 2 CLUBS and makes three. You give them 40 points below the line for the two tricks that they contracted for and 20 points above the line for the overtrick.

WE   THEY

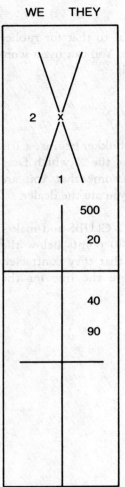

2

X

1

500

20

40

90

Now you write a 2 in the next section of the X and proceed with the second deal.

They bid and exactly make 3 SPADES, so they receive 90 points below the line and that completes the game. Since they are vulnerable on the deal which completed the game, you give them 500 points above the line. You draw a line to mark the end of the game.

WE   THEY

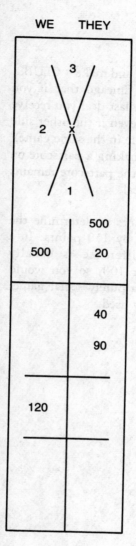

	500
500	20
	40
	90
120	

On the third deal, you bid 4 SPADES, which you make. You receive 120 points below the line and 500 above (since you are now vulnerable).

WE   THEY

```
        3   /
        X   4
    2  / \
       /   \
        1  \
```

WE	THEY
100	500
500	20
	40
	90
120	
80	
800	650

On the last deal you bid and make 4 CLUBS. It is a special rule of Chicago that if you make a partscore on the last deal you receive a bonus of 100 points (even if the other side previously got a partscore in the same game). There is no bonus for making a partscore on any other deal, even if the partscore remains at the end of the last deal.

Now you total the points to determine the winner. You have won by 150 points. In a money game, the difference is usually rounded to the nearest 100, so you would have won by 200. In a purely social game, rounding is not usually used.

If you are keeping a running score over several chukkers, each person on the winning side is credited with a plus score equal to the difference between the scores for the two sides. Each person on the losing side receives a minus score based on the same difference.

C

Duplicate Bridge

Duplicate bridge has become the most popular form of bridge whenever there is more than one table in play. Each deal is played two or more times by different players. Your success depends on your doing better on each hand than others who play the identical hand.

Duplicate bridge is not more difficult, so you should not avoid it for that reason. However, the skill levels of the players stand out more clearly at duplicate and you must learn not to let your ego be bruised. Duplicate is a fine game for competition and for building up your skill. It also eliminates the boredom of a run of bad cards. Some other player must play with the same bad cards, and you are challenged to do better with them than he does.

The best way to get familiar with duplicate bridge is to play in one of the clubs which is franchised by the American Contract Bridge League. There are many clubs throughout the country holding duplicate games in the evening and in the daytime. The cost is about the same as for a movie. Membership is not a requirement to play in one of these clubs, but you may join the ACBL for a nominal fee and receive their monthly bulletin full of bridge news and tips on playing bridge. For a list of clubs in your area, or for membership information, write or call:

American Contract Bridge League
P.O. Box 161192
Memphis, TN 38186
901-332-5586

You do not have to make a reservation to play unless it says so on the listing. But if you plan to go without a partner, first call the director of the club as given in the listing. An "open" game is open to all players, expert or novice. An "invitational" game is limited to invited players. A "novice" game is limited to players who have not yet earned many masterpoints, but the level of skill is usually at least that of the average social game.

The Duplicate Board

Since the same hand is played by several players, it must be kept intact. A plastic or metal BOARD holds the four hands of a deal in four pockets built into the board. The cards must not be mixed during the play, so the cards for each trick are not thrown into the center of the table for the winner of the trick to pick up. Instead, each person plays his card immediately in front of himself, and at the end of the trick he turns the card over in front of himself, pointing the card toward the side which won the trick. Your played cards might look like this:

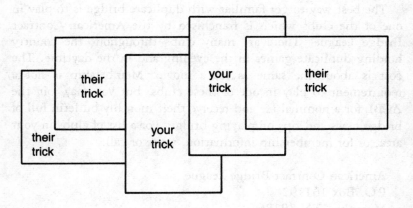

If you are the declarer, you do not play the cards from the dummy yourself. Instead, you call out the card which you wish to have played and the dummy then plays it as you instructed, keeping it in front of himself. At the end of the deal, each person picks up his cards and puts them back in the board for play by others.

NOTE: The duplicate style of handling the cards is also useful at other forms of bridge without boards, when you want to be able to hold a POST-MORTEM (discussion after the deal is over). The duplicate style of play keeps the hands together for everyone's review later, after which they can be reshuffled for the next deal.

In duplicate, markings on the board tell which side or sides are vulnerable for that deal. The dealer is also indicated on the board for the purposes of showing who has the first chance to bid. It does not matter who actually deals the cards and puts them in the pockets.

Scoring for duplicate and for game-in-hand is the same, except that the person keeping the score for duplicate writes it on a TRAVELER, a special score sheet which stays with the board. After the first score is recorded, the scorer folds the traveler twice to conceal the writing and tucks it in among his cards in the board. After the same board has been played again, the traveler is opened and the score from the repeat playing is added to the traveler.

When the board is to be played no more, the traveler is MATCHPOINTED. You are given one matchpoint for beating another player who played the same hand as you, and you are given half a matchpoint if you tied. The final winner is the player who has accumulated the most matchpoints over all the boards played.

Duplicate at Home

For a home duplicate game of two or three tables, you will need four boards and should also have a pad of the smallest size travelers and a pad of the smallest size RECAP (recapitulation) sheet on which to record the matchpoints. You can obtain bridge equipment (and books also) from either of these two mail-order supply houses. Write and ask for their catalog.

Barclay Bridge Supplies   Baron Bridge Supplies
8 Bush Avenue, Box 909   151 Thierman Lane
Port Chester, NY 10573   Louisville, KY 40207

Take a piece of cardboard (or paper) 8½″ x 11″ for each table. Mark one of the short edges NORTH and then mark the other edges EAST, SOUTH and WEST.

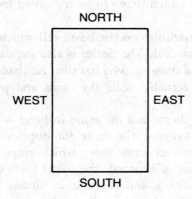

Put one of these GUIDECARDS on each table with the North sides all pointing in the same direction (not necessarily toward the geographical North).

For each board, shuffle and deal a pack of cards, then place the hands in the pockets of the board. Put one board on each table with its North end pointing in the same direction as is marked on the guidecard. Put the remaining boards on a side table.

For PAIR play (partners stay the same) give each pair of partners a number, and have them sit according to one of the following diagrams.

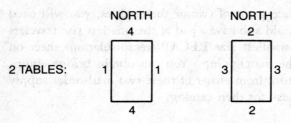

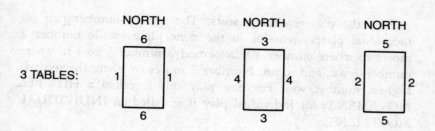

3 TABLES:

For INDIVIDUAL play (partners change after each round) give each player a number and seat them as follows.

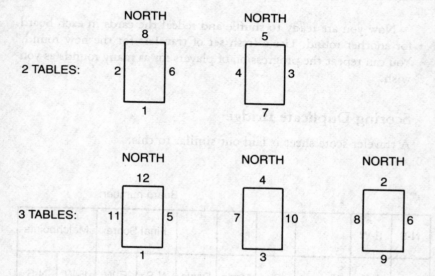

At each table the players will play and score the board on the table. If the deal is passed out, everyone scores zero—the board is not redealt at this time. The North player is now responsible for exchanging the board just completed with another from the side table. He is also responsible for pointing the North end of the new board in the same direction as the North end of the guidecard.

After everyone has played all four boards, they can be match-pointed, or this task can be deferred until later.

Now the players change seats. The highest-number pair (or individual player) remains in the same place, while number 2 moves to where number 1 was formerly, number 3 goes to where number 2 was and so on. Number 1 moves to where the second-highest number was. For pair play this is called a HOWELL MOVEMENT; for individual play it is called an INDIVIDUAL MOVEMENT.

NOTE: If you wish, you can purchase Howell and individual guidecards instead of using homemade ones. The commercial cards have printed directions to help the players move to their next seat.

Now you are ready to shuffle and redeal the cards in each board for another round. Use a fresh set of travelers for the new round. You can repeat the progression of players for as many rounds as you wish.

Scoring Duplicate Bridge

A traveler score sheet is laid out similar to this:

Board number:

N-S	E-W					Final Score		Matchpoints	
Pair	Pair	Contract	By	Made	Down	N-S	E-W	E-W	N-S
1									
2									

The score is always entered by NORTH (the player sitting in the North position). *Important:* He must enter the score on the line which is preprinted with his number in the first column. For example, after board 1 has been played at both tables in a two-table game, it might look like this, North being a member of pair 2:

Board number: 1

N-S	E-W					Final Score		Matchpoints	
Pair	Pair	Contract	By	Made	Down	N-S	E-W	E-W	N-S
1									
2	3	2S	N	2		110		1	0
3									
4	1	2H	S	3		140		0	1

On this board, pair 2 played North-South against pair 3 playing East-West. The contract was 2 SPADES by North (the declarer). He made two spades and thus scored 110 points including the partscore bonus. At another time, the board was played by pair 4, North-South, against pair 1. The contract was 2 HEARTS by South, making three, and giving a score of 140 for North-South.

NOTE: A contract of 2 SPADES DOUBLED is written as 2S^x, or if REDOUBLED, as 2S^xx.

Later, when the board was matchpointed, pair 2 and pair 4 were compared against each other since they both played the North-South hands on this board. Pair 4 got a better score than pair 2. In the matchpoint area, in the N-S column, pair 4 received 1 matchpoint for beating one other pair and pair 1 received a 0. Pairs 1 and 3 played the East-West hands and so they are matchpointed against each other. Pair 3 only let North-South win 110 points as compared to the 140 points which pair 1 gave up. Thus pair 3 beat pair 1 and receives 1 matchpoint while pair 1 gets 0. If there had been a tie, the two pairs being compared would each have received a half of a matchpoint.

The matchpoints are then entered on the recap sheet, which will be totaled up after all play is finished.

Name	Pr	Total	Bd 1	Bd 2	Bd 3
John and Mary	1		0		
Helen and Joe	2		0		
Sue and Tom	3		1		
Si and Miriam	4		1		

Here is an example from a three-table game.

Board number: 1

N-S	E-W					Final Score		Matchpoints	
Pair	Pair	Contract	By	Made	Down	N-S	E-W	E-W	N-S
1									
2									
3	4	1NT	E		1	50		0	2
4									
5	2	1NT	E	1			90	1x	x
6	1	1NT	E	1			90	1x	x

It is simpler to matchpoint a board if you realize that the best matchpoint score which anyone can receive is 1 less than the number of times the board has been played. Thus in this case, a top North-South pair would receive 2 matchpoints, the next best pair 1 matchpoint, and the bottom pair 0 matchpoints.

Actually, North-South pair 3 scored 50 points for setting the 1 NOTRUMP contract and thus beat the other North-South pairs. They received 2 matchpoints. If the other two North-South pairs had not tied, one would have received 1 matchpoint and the other 0. Because of the tie, they are matchpointed between 1 and 0, each getting ½. (We usually write an "x" instead of "½" on the traveler.)

The East-West pairs 1 and 2 tied for the top matchpoint score, so they split the 2 and the 1 which they would otherwise have received. Each was given 1½ matchpoints.

NOTE: Notice that on any one line the East-West matchpoints plus the North-South matchpoints are always equal to the highest possible matchpoint score—2 in this case. For boards which have been played three times, the total matchpoints awarded to all North-South pairs is always 3 (2 + 1 + 0) and likewise for the East-West pairs. If the board had only been played only twice, as in the previous case, these totals would be only 1.

When playing an individual game, the North player has a different number from the South player. The score is placed on the traveler line corresponding to North's number, and South's number is written beside North's. In the next column, the numbers for both East and West are entered. The matchpoints scored for North-South are recorded on the recap sheet for North and for South separately, and a similar recording is made for East and West.

Duplicate Bridge Scoring Summary

SCORE awarded:

To declarer's side for odd tricks BID AND MADE when the contract is in . . .

	NOTRUMP FIRST TRICK	NOTRUMP ADDITIONAL TRICKS	♠ or ♡ EACH TRICK	◇ or ♣ EACH TRICK
Undoubled	40	30	30	20
Doubled	80	60	60	40
Redoubled	160	120	120	80

To the declarer's side for making the contract when the declarer is . . .

	Not Vulnerable	Vulnerable
For a partscore	50	50
For a game	300	500
For a small slam (in addition to game bonus)	500	750
For a grand slam (in addition to game bonus)	1000	1500
For each overtrick		
Undoubled in ♠, ♡, NOTRUMP	30	30
Undoubled in ♣ or ◇	20	20
Doubled	100	200
Redoubled	200	400
For making a doubled or redoubled contract	50	50

To the defenders' side for setting the contract when the declarer is . . .

	Not Vulnerable FIRST UNDERTRICK	Not Vulnerable ADDITIONAL UNDERTRICKS	Vulnerable FIRST UNDERTRICK	Vulnerable ADDITIONAL UNDERTRICKS
Undoubled	50	50	100	100
Doubled	100	200	200	300
Redoubled	200	400	400	600

D
Game-in-Hand

The Round

Game-in-hand, sometimes called PARTY BRIDGE, is an older form of progressive bridge, but it is still popular for social games. Four deals make up a round. When several tables are playing at once, they will all finish at about the same time since they all will play the same number of deals. This makes it convenient to change opponents or partners at the end of the round. The progression described for duplicate bridge may be used. As an alternate method the winning pairs, at each table except the first, move to the next lower numbered table. The losing pairs, at each table except the last, move to the next higher numbered table.

As in all progressive bridge, on the first deal neither side is vulnerable, on the second and third deals only the dealer's side is vulnerable, and on the last deal both sides are vulnerable. If a deal is passed out, it does not count as one of the four deals and the same player deals again.

Scoring Game-in-Hand Bridge

The scoring is the same as for duplicate bridge except that scoring for honors is allowed as in rubber bridge. A rubber-bridge score pad may be used, but all scores are placed below the line. Part-scores do not carry over to the next deal. Thus each deal is scored separately, and it is conventional to draw a line across the two columns just below the scoring for each deal. This makes it clear how many deals have already been played.

E
The Laws

The official laws of bridge are published in two small books. For duplicate bridge you use *Laws of Duplicate Contract Bridge,* and for the other forms of bridge you consult *Laws of Contract Bridge.* The differences are small except where the nature of the game demands it.

In a formal duplicate game, there is an experienced director who *must* be called when any irregularity occurs, such as a lead or a bid out of turn. The director will then inform the players of the correct way to proceed. In other games, unless they are sponsored by a club which has specific rules, it is up to the players to decide what to do in case of an irregularity. For a serious game, the official laws are used. But for a purely social game, players often overlook an irregularity or make some simple adjustment for it unless someone knows the official way to proceed.

The laws of bridge also tell how to play when no irregularity is involved. Here are some of the correct procedures which you should know.

Review of the Bidding. If you do not hear a bid, you may ask immediately to have it repeated. But if you need a REVIEW (need to have all of the bids repeated) you may ask an opponent to do this when it is your turn to bid or when it is your turn to make your *first* play. After that, at your turn to play, you may only ask what the final contract is. At any time when it is your turn to bid or to play, you may ask for an explanation of an opponent's bid or play. Only the partner of the player making the bid should answer your request.

Change of Bid. If, by a slip of the tongue, you make an unintended bid, you may immediately change it if you do so without pause for thought. You might say "one heart, I mean one spade" but you should only do so if "one spade" is what you intended all along.

Dummy's Rights. As dummy you must not participate in the play or make any comment. You cannot point out any irregularity after it occurs until the play is over. At duplicate, you must not voluntarily look at anyone else's hand, including your partner's. At all forms of bridge, if you have not voluntarily looked at someone else's hand, you may:

- Ask any player who did not follow suit whether he could have done so—this can be a boon to your partner if he has made a mistake.
- Tell your partner where the lead is (in his hand or in the dummy hand) for the next trick so that he won't make a mistake.
- At duplicate, you may tell any player that he has a trick turned the wrong way.

Inspecting a Played Trick. Any player except the dummy may ask to have the cards from the last trick turned faceup so that he can look at them. At duplicate bridge you may ask to see the last trick up to the time when you turn your own card over and put it on the table. At other forms of bridge you may ask the person who picked up the entire trick to display it again, providing that you ask before you or your partner play to the next trick.

Unfortunately, the laws are not written as understandably as they might be. Nevertheless, you may want to have a copy of them on hand so that you can learn about them.

F

Alternate Point Count

It seems that there are as many ways of counting points as there are authors. They all give approximately the same result, with a difference of a point or two in some cases. The method popularized by Charles Goren, based on counting short suits, is the one most commonly used. However, a statistical analysis of some 250 hands has shown that it is not the most accurate. Methods which count both short suits and long suits, as recommended by other experts, came out statistically better. The best of these were used to produce the method recommended in this book. It came out best of all in the analysis, and it is also easy to use. You are strongly urged to adopt it, even if you have to shift from some other method which you previously used. However, the following describes an acceptable but more complicated alternative based on the traditional method.

HIGH-CARD POINTS
High cards are counted 4-3-2-1 for ace-king-queen-jack. (Every method is identical in this respect.)

DISTRIBUTION POINTS FOR NOTRUMP BIDDING
Add 1 point if you hold a 5-card suit.

DISTRIBUTION POINTS FOR TRUMP SUIT BIDDING
Add 1 point for each doubleton, 2 points for each singleton, 3 points for each void.

EXCEPTIONS: Count only 1 distribution point for a singleton king, queen or jack. Do not count any distribution points for a doubleton headed by a queen or which contains a jack. In such cases, an excessive count would arise if the full value were given to both the high cards and the short suit. But for notrump bidding, the high cards retain their full value even in such cases.

DEVALUATION/REVALUATION

When only a 7-card trump fit has been found, or when it is necessary to play in notrump with a hand containing a singleton or void, discard all distribution points.

When at least an 8-card trump fit has been found, the dummy hand is revaluated for the trump contract, providing the dummy holds at least three trumps, by adding 1 additional point for each singleton and 2 additional points for each void. This revaluated count is reduced by 1 point for an 8-card fit and increased by 1 point for a 10-card fit.

When at least an 8-card trump fit has been found, the declarer hand is revaluated for the trump contract, providing it contains at least six trumps, by adding 1 additional point for each singleton and 2 additional points for each void.